THE
CANADIAN
DESK
COMPANION

THE
CANADIAN
DESK
COMPANION

STRATHEARN

This edition published by
STRATHEARN BOOKS LIMITED,
Toronto, Canada

© 2003 Geddes & Grosset, David Dale House,
New Lanark, ML11 9DJ
Maps on pages 33,35,37,39,41,44,46,48,50,52,54,59 and 61
supplied by GEOATLAS® © 2000 Graphi-Ogre - All rights reserved

ISBN 1 84205 369 8

Printed and bound in Poland

Contents

Contents

The Nation of Canada

Geography and Climate

Physical description

The world's second largest country in area after Russia, Canada has a surface area of 9,984,670 square kilometres (3,848,900 square miles), of which 91% is land and the remainder fresh water. It occupies the full sweep of the North American continent from longitude 52° west on the Atlantic coast of Newfoundland to longitude 88° west at the Pacific islands of British Columbia, a distance exceeding 5,000 kilometres (3,100 miles). Northwards it extends between latitudes 42° and 83° for 4,600 kilometres (2,800 miles) beyond the Arctic Circle into the islands of the frozen seas between Baffin Bay and the Beaufort Sea. In the northwest it is bounded by the U.S. state of Alaska. The southern boundary is with the U.S.A. It follows the 49th parallel from the Pacific coast to the eastern border of Manitoba, then a more irregular line through Lakes Superior and Ontario and to the right of the St. Lawrence River, turning south between New Brunswick and the U.S. state of Maine to reach the Atlantic coast.

The topography of the northeast is dominated by the ancient pre-Cambrian rocks of the Canadian Shield, one of the oldest rock surfaces in the world, bordering the east side of Hudson Bay, and with the Laurentian Mountains to the south. To the east are the hills and valleys of the Appalachian areas of the Atlantic provinces and southern Québec. A lowland region stretches west from the St. Lawrence through southern Québec and Ontario, meeting the vast expanse of the interior plains which stretch across the Prairie Provinces of Alberta, Saskatchewan, and Manitoba. These end abruptly in the Western Cordillera, formed out of several mountain ranges and plateau-lands, including the Rocky, Cassiar, and Mackenzie Mountains. Mt. Logan, Canada's highest peak (5,959 meters, 19,550 feet), rises in the St. Elias Mountains of the Coastal range. The continent breaks up into islands towards the North Pole, some of them very large and mountainous.

Lakes and rivers

Canada is estimated to hold about a quarter of the world's fresh water supply, and there are very many lakes and a number of major river systems. Ontario alone is estimated to have about a quarter of a million lakes. Lake

Superior is the world's largest body of fresh water. It and three of the other Great Lakes, Huron, Erie, and Ontario, are shared with the U.S.A. The largest lake wholly within Canada, the Great Bear Lake (31,328 square kilometres, 12,092 square miles), is in the Northwest Territories, as is the next in size, the Great Slave Lake (28,568 square kilometres, 11,027 square miles). Another vast lake is Lake Winnipeg in Manitoba (24,387 square kilometres, 9,413 square miles). Saskatchewan's largest lake is Lake Athabasca at 7,935 square kilometres (3,063 square miles). Some very large lakes are artificial or enhanced in size by dams, such as the Smallwood Reservoir in Newfoundland (6,527 square kilometres, 2,519 square miles) and the Williston Lake in British Columbia (1,761 square kilometres, 680 square miles).

Among rivers, the Mackenzie is Canada's longest at 4,241 kilometres (2,480 miles); its system drains northwards from the Great Slave Lake and Great Bear Lake. The Peace River (1,923 kilometres, 1,195 miles) and its tributaries drain much of Alberta. Other great rivers include the Nelson (2,575 kilometres, 1,600 miles), the Saskatchewan (1,939 kilometres, 1,205 miles), flowing eastward into Hudson Bay, the Fraser (1,370 kilometres, 851 miles), and the Yukon (3,184 kilometres, 1,978 miles), flowing into the Pacific Ocean, though much of the Yukon is in Alaska. On the Atlantic side, the St. Lawrence flows eastwards for 3,058 kilometres (1,900 miles), and its greatest tributary is the Ottawa River (1,271 kilometres, 788 miles), flowing south from the inland wilderness of Québec province. Many Canadian rivers are navigable by motor vessels and barges, and form important transport routes.

Islands

Among the vast number of islands within Canadian territory are some of the world's largest. Baffin Island, the fifth largest in the world, has an area of 507,451 square kilometres (186,742 square miles) while another 37 islands exceed 1,000 square kilometres (386 square miles), including Victoria Island (217,291 square kilometres, 83,874 square miles). Many of these islands lie north of the Arctic Circle, and are scantily populated, or have no regular inhabitants. On the west coast, Vancouver Island is the largest island in western North America (31,285 square kilometres, 12,076 square miles). The largest island on the east side is Newfoundland (108,860 square kilometres, 42,020 square miles).

Climate

Canada forms a number of distinct climatic regions from west to east and from south to north. With a northerly global location and a land surface stretching almost to the North Pole, the general climatic picture is one of long winters and warm summers, with brief spring and autumn seasons. In the coastal areas to the east and west, the sea exerts a mildening influence, with more rain, snow, and fog but a narrower range of temperature extremes. East of the Rockies, a drier, 'continental' climate prevails. Calgary in Alberta has an average 399 millimetres (15.7 inches) of annual precipitation compared to Vancouver on the coast with 1,167 millimetres (45.9 inches). Summers are hotter, winters are colder. This pattern extends across the Prairie Provinces to Ontario, where the Great Lakes exert an oceanic-type influence on the populated southern strip. In northern Ontario, Québec, and into the Northwest Territories and Nunavut, arctic influences increasingly come into play, though summers can be surprisingly warm, and there are wide variations in temperature between different places on the same latitude.

Average maximum and minimum temperatures (Celsius) in capital and major cities

City	Coldest month	Warmest month
Calgary	January (-15.7)	July (23.2)
Charlottetown	January (-12.2)	July (23.1)
Edmonton	January (-17)	July (23)
Fredericton	January (-15.4)	July (25.6)
Halifax	February (-10.6)	July (23.4)
Montréal	January (-14.9)	July (26.2)
Ottawa	January (-15.5)	July (26.4)
Québec City	January (-17.3)	July (24.9)
Regina	January (-22.1)	July (26.3)
St. John's	February (-8.7)	July (20.2)
Toronto	January (-7.9)	July (26.5)
Vancouver	January (-0.1)	August (21.7)
Victoria	January (-0.3)	July (21.8)
Whitehorse	January (-23.2)	July (20.3)
Yellowknife	January (-32.2)	July (20.8)

Environmental issues

Clean air and clean water are both rallying cries for Canada's environmentalists and a major problem for Environment Canada, the government ministry responsible. Acid rain is a serious threat to natural life, and over 14,000 Canadian lakes are estimated to have lost their fish stocks as a result. It is also a major threat to forest growth. In the past twenty years, Canada has reduced its sulphur dioxide emissions by half, but much of Canada's acid rain is generated in the U.S.A., which has been slower to respond to the problem. Canadian meteorologists have also been closely involved in monitoring the increase in global warming and in estimating its effects on the environment.

Government and Political Structure

Canada is an independent state, organized as a constitutional monarchy, on a federal basis. The head of state is the British monarch, who is represented by a Governor General. In modern practice, the Governor General is an eminent Canadian citizen, appointed by the Prime Minister. The three elements in the

9

Canadian legislature are the House of Commons, the Senate or Upper House, and the Governor General. The constitution, confirmed in its present form on 17 April 1982, includes a charter of rights and freedoms as well as provisions to recognize the country's multicultural heritage, to affirm the existing rights of native peoples, to confirm the principle of equalization of benefits among the provinces, and to strengthen provincial ownership of national resources. The Canadian Parliament, which meets in Ottawa, is a bicameral legislature. The House of Commons has 295 elected members and the Senate has 104 members, appointed by the Governor General on the recommendation of the Prime Minister. The maximum life of a parliament is five years. The Senate may introduce Bills, except financial Bills, and has a little-exercised right to block legislation. Its prime purpose is to give Bills a second reading and to clarify their content.

National symbols

Canada has the following national symbols:

- The arms of Canada – combining the royal arms of Great Britain with a triple maple leaf, and the motto *Mari Usque Ad Mare*, 'From Sea to Sea'.
- The flag of Canada – composed of two red rectangles separated by a white square on which is represented a single red maple leaf (inaugurated 15 February 1965).
- The official symbols of Canada – the maple tree and maple leaf. The beaver (*Castor canadiensis*) is also an official symbol of Canada.
- Official tartans – the following provinces and territories have each designated an official tartan: Alberta, British Columbia, Manitoba, New Brunswick, Nova Scotia, Northwest Territories, Prince Edward Island, Saskatchewan, Yukon.

The Canadian Cabinet (December 2002)

The Rt. Hon. Jean Chrétien	Prime Minister
The Hon. David Collenette	Minister of Transport
The Hon. Ralph Goodale	Minister of Public Works
The Hon. Sheila Copps	Minister of Canadian Heritage
The Hon. John Manley	Deputy Prime Minister, Minister of Finance
The Hon. Anne McLellan	Minister of Health
The Hon. Robert Thibault	Minister of Fisheries and Oceans
The Hon. Rey Pagtakhan	Minister of Veterans' Affairs
The Hon. Bill Graham	Minister of Foreign Affairs
The Hon. Sheila Whelan	Minister for International Cooperation
The Hon. Allan Rock	Minister of Industry
The Hon. Lucien Robillard	President of the Treasury Board
The Hon. Martin Cauchon	Minister of Justice and Attorney General
The Hon. John McCallum	Minister of National Defence
The Hon. Wayne Easter	Solicitor General
The Hon. Jane Stewart	Minister of Human Resources Development

The Hon. Stéphane Dion — Minister of Inter-governmental Affairs
The Hon. Pierre Pettigrew — Minister for International Trade
The Hon. Dion Boudria — Leader of the Government in the House of Commons

The Hon. Lyle Vanclief — Minister of Agriculture and Agri-food
The Hon. Herb Dhaliwal — Minister of Natural Resources
The Hon. Claudette Bradshaw — Minister of Labour
The Hon. Robert Nault — Minister of Indian Affairs and Northern Development

The Hon. Elinor Caplan — Minister of National Revenue
The Hon. Denis Coderre — Minister of Citizenship and Immigration

Prime Ministers of Canada since Confederation

(Parties: Con – Conservative; Lib – Liberal; PC – Progressive Conservative)

J. A. Macdonald (Con)	1857–73
Alexander Mackenzie (Lib)	1873–78
J. A. Macdonald (Con)	1891–92
John Sparrow/David Thompson (Con)	1892–94
Mackenzie Bowell (Con)	1894–96
Charles Tupper (Con)	1896
Wilfrid Laurier (Lib)	1896–1911
Robert L. Burden (Con)	1911–17
Arthur Meighen (Con)	1917–20
William Lyon Mackenzie King (Lib)	1921–26
Arthur Meighen (Con)	1926
William Lyon Mackenzie King (Lib)	1926–30
Richard B. Bennett (Con)	1930–35
William Lyon Mackenzie King (Lib)	1935–48
Louis St. Laurent (Lib)	1948–57
John G. Diefenbaker (PC)	1957–63
Lester Pearson (Lib)	1963–68
Pierre Elliott Trudeau (Lib)	1968–79
Charles Joseph Clark (PC)	1979–80
Pierre Elliott Trudeau (Lib)	1980–84
Brian Mulroney (PC)	1984–93
A. Kim Campbell (PC)	1993
Jean Chrétien (Lib)	1993–

Accredited political parties in Canada (2002)

(* indicates seats in House of Commons)
*Bloc Québecois**
Canadian Action Party
Canadian Reform Conservative Alliance
Christian Heritage Party of Canada

Communist Party of Canada
Green Party of Canada
Liberal Party of Canada*
Marijuana Party
Marxist-Leninist Party of Canada
Natural Law Party of Canada
New Democratic Party*
Progressive Conservative Party of Canada*

The Order of Canada

This system of national awards to honour distinguished citizens was introduced in 1967, replacing the previous 'imperial' British awards. It has three classes, rising from Member to Officer then Companion. Approximately 4,000 persons hold the award. The Governor General is its chancellor, and its motto is *Desiderantes meliorem patriam*, 'They desire a better country'. In addition, certain provinces also have their own internal honours and awards.

The provinces and territories

Provinces
Alberta
British Columbia
Manitoba
New Brunswick
Newfoundland and Labrador
Nova Scotia
Ontario
Prince Edward Island
Québec
Saskatchewan

Territories
Northwest Territories
Nunavut
Yukon Territory

A series of constitutional amendments made between 1867 and 1982 defined the role and powers of the provincial administrations. The provinces exist in their own right, as part of the constitution. Territories are created by federal law and though territorial administrations have broadly similar powers to those of the provinces, they are somewhat more restricted and the federal government has a greater degree of involvement.

In each of the ten provinces, the sovereign is represented by a lieutenant governor. Provincial assemblies consist of a single house of elected members. They make laws on most internal matters including direct taxation within the province, the management of public lands and resources, education, welfare, health, policing, justice, prisons, and transport.

The relationship of provincial governments to the federal government, and the status of individual provinces within the Confederation, remain important issues.

An Outline of Canadian History

(*See also* A Chronology of Events in Canadian History)
Human occupancy of Canada goes back perhaps 20,000 years, when the North American and Asian land masses were joined where the Bering Straits now are. Both animals and humans travelled from Asia into North America and in this way the 'native peoples' arrived, their tenure of the land so ancient that they can well claim to be aboriginal.

Over many centuries, in the various climatic and landscape regions, shared ways of life evolved, though the tribes who shared them were often at war with one another. In the north, Inuit and Aleut peoples perfected a way of life that both suited and drew on an apparently hostile environment. Hunters of whales, seals, fish, and caribou on land, they drew not only their food but tools and clothing from their prey. They followed its seasonal movements, being as adept on water as on land.

In the forested zones, liberally provided with rivers and lakes, the Woodland Indian tribes used their birch-bark canoes for mobility. In the north and west, nomadic hunter-gatherers spoke the various Athapascan and Algonquian languages. The tribes of the southeast began to establish permanent settlements, and to practice agriculture on the fertile soil. These were the tribes who later formed the Iroquois League, and they evolved formal systems of diplomacy, trade, and warfare. On the great plains, the inhabitants relied primarily on the apparently numberless bison for food, hides, bone implements, and glue. The wooded Pacific coast region, rich in fish as well as land and wildlife, and with ample supplies of large timber, sustained elaborate Indian cultures.

The first Europeans to come were eleventh-century Vikings, but their knowledge was lost for centuries. A new 'discovery' took place when fishermen from Portugal, Spain, France, and then England ventured further and further out into the Atlantic. The teeming cod banks off Newfoundland were well known by the fourteenth century, and it is more than likely that some of the fishers landed, or were swept ashore. But it was men searching for the westward sea route to China who definitively found the American land mass blocking their way and inadvertently 'discovered' Canada. It seems that the very first colonists were Portuguese, but John Cabot, sailing from Bristol in 1497, and Jacques Cartier, sailing from St. Malo in 1534, launched the English-French rivalry that was to haunt Canadian history and politics into the twenty-first century.

The country's name was bestowed by Cartier, who, hearing the Indians on the St. Lawrence refer to their villages as *kanata*, took it to be the name of their country. Interest in exploring the interior was slow to arise, until the demand in Europe for fur, especially beaver fur, drove explorers back to Canada. In 1605 the French Samuel de Champlain founded a fort at Port Royal in the Annapolis Basin, Nova Scotia, but three years later he established a more permanent habitation at Québec. *La Nouvelle France* was on the way to being established, and meanwhile the English had claimed Newfoundland in 1583. They were also strongly established in New England to the south. English claims on the mainland were intensified with the founding of the Hudson's Bay Company, given a royal monopoly to trade in natural resources, in 1670. Throughout the seventeenth century, both colonial powers made allies with, and war on, the Indian peoples at different times, and the Iroquois struggled to maintain their own position. In 1690 the English adventurer, Sir William Phips, was repulsed with some disdain from an attack on Québec, governed then by the Comte de Frontenac; and another more official expedition came to grief under Admiral Walker in 1711, when it was wrecked on Anticosti Island in the St. Lawrence Gulf.

By the Treaty of Utrecht, 1713, France formally ceded Nova Scotia to Great Britain and gave up claims to the Hudson Bay area. Its other Canadian possessions were retained, and soon a fort-building race was under way. War erupted again in 1744, and again in 1756. Amid the many captures and counter-captures, the British succeeded in forcing out large numbers of the French-speaking inhabitants of Cape Breton Island and Nova Scotia. Immigrants from New England reaped most of the benefits. The Seven Years' War (1756–63) was fought between imperial powers on a semi-global scale in Europe and North America and on the high seas. British troops and their Indian allies cut off Québec from French settlements further west. By 1759 the French forts on the Great Lakes were in British hands. On 12 September of that year the British, under General James Wolfe, captured Québec in a battle that saw the deaths of both Wolfe and the French commander, the Marquis de Montcalm. The French regrouped at Montréal and remained strong enough to besiege Québec. Fortune turned on which fleet would come up the St. Lawrence first when the ice melted. But Britain by then had an iron command of the sea. A British fleet and three land armies converged on the French position, and the French Governor General, Vaudreuil, surrendered on 9 September 1760. All of Canada was confirmed as a British possession, now with some 80,000 additional citizens who had been faithful subjects of King Louis of France.

The British administrators speedily found that necessary reassurances and concessions to the French, enshrined in the Québec Act of 1774, were hotly resented by their own settler population and the adjacent, fiercely Protestant New Englanders. But the British and French Canadians did not rise with the American colonists in 1775. Local militias joined with imperial troops to fight back invasion by the Americans, and though Montréal was occupied for several months, the insurgent Americans were eventually thrust back. Many British Loyalists left the new United States once its independence was established, and sought new land in Nova Scotia to the north, the Eastern Townships of Québec, and in areas to the west. Canada gained around 50,000 immigrants in just a few years. Up to 1791, most of southeast Canada was known as Québec; in this year the land was divided into Upper Canada (now in Ontario) and Lower Canada (present-day Québec). Then, as now, English speakers predominated to the west, French speakers to the east.

On the western coast, although European explorers had been visiting since the sixteenth century, there had been no attempt at colonization, and the Coastal Indians had only one another to disturb their peace, unlike the Indian inhabitants of the east. Now, however, with the era of empire-building in full swing, and with rising British anxieties about the expansion of the U.S.A., British attention was also focused on the west coast. Under Captain George Vancouver, the Royal Navy surveyed the complex coastline, and, for the first time, Europeans crossed the Rocky Mountains and reached the coast from the interior. They were Scots, employed by the North West Company. At this time, the agricultural potential of the great plains was not apparent, but the riches of wildlife, fish, and timber in the far west were obvious. British colonies were established, first on Vancouver Island, and later on the mainland.

In 1812 hostilities broke out again between Britain and America and there was heavy fighting in Canada. American forces were defeated at Queenstown Heights, above Niagara, though York (now Toronto) was captured and burned. Cessation of hostilities left 'British North America' intact.

Government of the colony was corrupt and kept in the hands of a few ruling families, a situation which inevitably produced adverse reactions. In Upper Canada, opposition was led by William Lyon Mackenzie, in Lower Canada by Louis-Joseph Papineau. There were other grievances. The large Métis element in the population, of mixed Indian, Inuit and European (largely French and Scottish) descent, was adversely affected by the amalgamation of the Hudson's Bay and North West Companies. A liberal-minded Governor General, 'Radical Jack', the Earl of Durham, attempted to improve government in 1841 with his concept of 'responsible government' with a wider electorate. This wider electorate did not include the native peoples, whose woodland and prairie territories were being increasingly occupied by pioneering settlers from east and south, and also straight from Europe. Scots were prominent but Scandinavians, Swedes, Ukrainians, Germans, and Irish were also coming in increasingly large numbers, driven by poverty or oppression, and lured by opportunity.

Opportunity shone most brightly in the form of gold. The first Canadian gold rush was in 1858. But these stampedes were temporary things, while the steady process of occupying the interior had permanent effects. Population was moving faster than government, and bison-hunting Métis and cow-rearing farmers were at odds with each other. Although the border remained secure, the carnage of the U.S. Civil War impressed Canadians with the need for unity, and a conference in Charlottetown, Prince Edward Island, to discuss the possible union of the Maritime Provinces, a group of provinces comprising New Brunswick, Newfoundland, Nova Scotia, and Prince Edward Island, was unexpectedly expanded by representatives from the two Canadas. From this came the proposal for the Canadian Confederation, confirmed by the British North America Act of 1867. A federal government was to rule, from Ottawa, but the provinces were to retain substantial internal autonomy. Even so, the completion of the Confederation would be a piecemeal affair. In a sense, it is still happening. British Columbia joined in 1871, Prince Edward Island did not join until 1873, and Newfoundland stayed out until 1949.

Most trouble came from the prairie area. The federal government had purchased a huge tract of former Hudson's Bay Company land in 1868, and was confronted by the Red River Rebellion of the Métis under Louis Riel. With nothing to lose, the Métis rose again in 1885, the year the transcontinental railway was completed. Their way of life was doomed. They had virtually wiped out the bison, and new farming techniques were turning the prairies into wheatlands. Police organization, local government, and, finally the formation of the provinces of Alberta and Saskatchewan in 1905, set the seal on the new order of things.

In the twentieth and twenty-first centuries, the main themes of Canadian history have been the breaking of the ties of imperial control, the re-emergence of Québec separatism, the accommodation and acknowledgement of the place of native peoples within the Confederation, and the country's peaceful but not always harmonious relationship with the U.S.A. During World War I, Canada was 'automatically' included in the British Empire's declaration of war on Germany; in World War II, Canada made its own decision to declare war in September 1939. Although the Queen is still sovereign as a constitutional monarch, the Governor General, her representative, is now appointed by the Prime Minister. There are Canadian republicans, but also Canadian monarchists. More detail on the Québec situation will be found in the section on that province. Although native peoples constitute a very small percentage of Canada's population, there has been increasing recognition through the years of both the exploitation and oppression suffered by them during the centuries of colonization, and of their long history within the country. The recent creation of the territory of Nunavut in 1999 is a sign of the new acceptance of partnership and common goals between modern Canada and the descendants of its early inhabitants.

Apart from some residual frontier disputes, such as the one over the British Columbia–Alaska oceanic boundary, the main focus of Canada–U.S. relations has been on trade, particularly in relation to 'reciprocity' (as it was known early in the twentieth century) or 'free trade'. With a smaller internal market, Canadian manufacturers have always been afraid of the country being swamped by goods produced in the U.S. Despite much opposition, free trade has been sustained, and Canada has joined in moves towards a wider American Free Trade Area. Suspicions on both sides about subsidies and produce-dumping frequently cause short-term tariff hikes and counter-hikes.

The heritage industry

In modern countries, where change happens so quickly, a heritage industry can achieves two things. One is to help validate the recent past for those who might feel that its disappearance has made their lives meaningless, as in a town that has lost its mine or steelworks. The other is to interpret the country's past to visitors and travellers, and in the course of doing so, to foster the tourist industry. In Canada, both aspects are important, but with so many new citizens, the country's many heritage centres are also used to explain Canada's history and character, and to help support its ethos. There are 188 national parks and historic sites across the country, and many hundreds more set up on a provincial or local basis. The national parks, of course, also preserve and protect some of the planet's most beautiful and remarkable landscapes together with their flora and fauna.

The People of Canada

Population

The population of Canada in 2002 was 31,414,000. This represents a rate of growth of 3% from 1998. All provinces and territories have shared in this growth, with the exceptions of the Yukon Territory, whose small population has diminished slightly, and Saskatchewan, which has also recorded a small net decrease; the least growth generally has been in the Prairie Provinces. More than 80% of Canada's inhabitants live in the south of the country, within 160 kilometres of the U.S. border. The majority of Canadians are of European origin. Native American peoples, Indian and Inuit, account for about 1.4% of the inhabitants.

Language

The two official languages are English and French, and all official announcements are made in both languages. In 1996, 16,890,615 Canadians noted English as their mother tongue; 6,636,660 noted French, and 107,945 noted both English and French. Many other language groups were identified, the largest being Chinese, with 715,640 noting it as their mother tongue; Italian, with 484,500; German, with 450,140; Spanish, with 213,410; Portuguese, with 211,290; and Punjabi, with 201,785. The largest native language group was Cree, with 76,840 noting it as their mother tongue. Modern Canada is an ethnically diverse country, with the majority of recent immigrants coming from Asia.

Citizenship

Modern Canada is a relatively new nation and, with its many ethnic and language groups, takes the matter of citizenship very seriously. Canadian citizenship is automatic to those born in Canada and to those born elsewhere with a Canadian parent. Citizenship is also granted to immigrants, normally after a specified residence period. New citizens must have a knowledge of English or French, and be able to display knowledge of Canada's law, politics, history, and geography by answering test questions. An oath of citizenship is formally administered, and there are regular re-affirmation ceremonies in the annual Citizenship Week which has nationwide events to promote a sense of Canadian unity. The oath taken by all new citizens runs as follows:

'I swear that I will be faithful and bear true witness to Her Majesty Queen Elizabeth the Second, Queen of Canada, her heirs and successors, and that I will faithfully observe the laws of Canada and fulfil my duties as a citizen.'

Native Peoples

In one sense, the far northwest is the cradle of all American peoples. It was across the land link from Asia that the first settlers of the continent came, around 20,000 years ago. Successive groups came over a very lengthy period of time. The most recent was the Eskimo–Aleut group, whose arrival is estimated as having occurred more than 8,000 years ago. Before them, the speakers of a language group known as Na-Dene had spread through the continent. They were originally hunter-gatherers. Family and kin groups spread apart and began to define their own territories, and the origins of the later tribes lie in this. Over the centuries, great changes occurred in the cultures and ways of life of the tribes, even before the arrival of Europeans in the east, north, and west brought major disruption. The modern history of the tribal peoples, except to some extent for those in the arctic north, is of loss of territory, overwhelming cultural invasion, and a low place in a political and economic framework which they have had no part in devising. During the twentieth century there gradually arose a new appreciation of the native peoples' values, traditions, skills, and potential contribution to a new and inclusive nationhood. But great gulfs remain between the 'consumerist' culture of European Canadians and the more self-contained and environmentally conscious traditions of the Indians and Inuit, between an essentially urban way of life and an essentially rural one.

Although the location of the many different Indian tribes has always been quite fluid, native peoples can be grouped, mainly by language, in several different regions. (The distribution of the tribes in the north, as described below, is more or less as they can be found today. But in the other regions, because of white settlement and land exploitation, the distribution refers rather to how things were in the nineteenth century.)

The north

Here the population forms three groups, distinguished by their languages: the Aleut, the Yup'ik, and the Inuit–Inupiaq. In general the Aleut and Yup'ik are found in the western areas of arctic and subarctic Canada, and the Inuit in the eastern areas, including Baffin Island. As with all tribal groups, their distribution has little to do with modern frontiers, and Inuit territory extends into Greenland. This is the only area where native peoples form a majority of the population.

The east

A number of large tribes lived in the area round the Great Lakes and along the St. Lawrence. The Chippewa (Ojibwa) were to be found north of Lake Superior, with the Algonquin and Nipissing to the east. On the lake peninsula were the Neutral and Huron. The Iroquois were on both sides of the St. Lawrence, with Algonquin to their north and the Maliseet-Passamaquoddy and Micmac living in what are now the Maritime Provinces. From the eighteenth century, the French and British recognized the existence of the Five Nations of the Iroquois Confederacy, namely the Mohawk, Oneida, Onondaga, Cayuga and Seneca, with the Tuscarora making a sixth nation in the course of the century.

The centre

The vast area encompassed by the Prairie Provinces and westwards into the Yukon was populated by over thirty tribes, some very small in number, and with a population of hardly more than sixty thousand all told. The main division was between Athapaskan language speakers to the west, and the Algonquian language group to the east.

The mountains

The valleys and plateau lands were occupied on the western side by Salish-speaking tribes, Lillooet, Shuswap, Thompson, Nicola, Okanagan, and Lakes; to the east of them lived the Kutenai, speaking a language distantly related to Algonquian.

The west coast

A complex and varying pattern of tribes occupied the islands and the coast, with a range of cultural characteristics and language groups. Vancouver Island was the land of the Nootkans; on the facing mainland were the Salish, with a succession of other tribes occupying the territory to the north – Kwakiutl, Oowekeeno, Bella Coola, Bella Bella, Haihais, Haisla, Tsimshian, Gitksan, Nishga, Haida, and Tlingit. The west coast of Canada is an area where tribal traditions and customs are still very much part of life and local politics.

The Capital

Ottawa, in Ontario but right on the border with Québec, was selected in 1858 as the capital of the province of Canada, combining the two provinces then known as Upper and Lower Canada. This role continued when the

Dominion of Canada was formed in 1867. Originally Ottawa was a village at the northern end of a canal constructed to link the Ottawa River to Lake Ontario, via the Rideau River. Known then as Bytown, after Colonel John By, who commanded the troops who dug the canal, its Indian name *Ottawa* was adopted in 1854. It is now a major city, whose population (combined with Hull across the Ottawa River) exceeds 1,000,000 people. Apart from Parliament and government offices, a number of national institutions are located here, including the National Gallery, the National Library, and several other national museums.

Canada in the World

Canada is a country that takes its responsibilities to the rest of the world seriously. It is the third largest contributor to the budget of the United Nations. Its world role is sustained by various agencies. Chief among these is the diplomatic service of the government, but Canadian multinational companies also play a large part. Members of Canadian businesses, universities, institutes, and national organizations participate actively in a wide range of international bodies and forums. Other international links are maintained by cultural organizations and by individual arts groups and practitioners.

A number of key aspects help to define Canada's place on the world stage:

1. *Canada's vast physical extent, and its proximity to the polar regions.* This gives the country a powerful voice, as well as responsibility, in the increasingly serious issues regarding global climate and global pollution.
2. *Canada's immediate proximity to the United States of America, the country's prime trading partner and ally.* The Canadian–U.S. border is by far the longest open and undefended frontier in the world, although since the 'war on terrorism' began in 2001, 43 key crossing-points are monitored. Canada is not a neutral state, but its independent stance on many issues – notably on the Vietnam War between 1965 and 1974, when many young Americans took refuge from the draft in Canada – and its strong commitment to the United Nations, has enabled Canadian troops to play peacekeeping roles in various world hot spots.
3. *Canada's contribution to world trade.* Canada is a major producing and consuming nation.
4. *Canada's membership of the British Commonwealth of Nations.* This has given Canada an interest in the problems of post-colonial African and Asian Commonwealth states. Canadian aid and diplomacy have often been deployed in Commonwealth causes.

A fifth aspect might be Canada's position with involvement in both the English and French-language cultures, but this contributes more prominently to the country's international cultural life.

Defence

The Canadian armed forces are organized as a single national defence force, with army, navy and air force components. In August 2001, armed forces personnel numbered 56,800: 18,600 in the army; 9,000 in the navy; 13,500 in the air force; and 15,700 in undefined service. In addition there were 34,500 reservists. The federal defence budget in 2000 was $10,800 million. Canada's defence forces are highly technologized and a high proportion of the budget is spent on the maintenance and development of equipment. Apart from a commitment to NATO, and the necessary roles of patrolling two coastlines and the northern frontiers, Canadian forces are often used in UN-sponsored peacekeeping missions. Their last engagement in warfare was in the Gulf War of 1991.

Society

Canada is regularly cited as the best country in the world in which to live. Judged on standards of income, opportunity, freedom, social services, health care, education, and crime level, Canada occupies an enviable position among the nations. But no large and complex modern society is without problems and worries.

Health and welfare

In a United Nations index on health and welfare, Canada ranks third among the countries of the world. All of the population have access to fresh water and effective sewage management. Mortality among under-5s is 6 per 1,000 live births, and the proportion of population affected by HIV/AIDS is 0.3% (both 1999 statistics). Health services are provided free to Canadian citizens, and there is a physician for every 450 people. The standards of health care are among the highest in the world.

Housing

In the second half of the twentieth century there was a marked trend away from rented housing and towards home ownership, and this continues. In 2000, 66.7% of Canadians owned their own homes, mostly mortgaged. There is also a continuing trend towards individual family homes, with the proportion of people living in apartment blocks diminishing year by year.

Education

Elementary and secondary school education is administered by the provinces. For children from 6 to 15 or 16 years old (depending on the province) education is compulsory and free. Province-run schools are normally co-educational. Some provinces allow schools to be run by religious groups. In 1999 the total school enrolment was 5,368,185, or approximately 18% of the population. The vast majority of students attend public schools; in 1999 the number was 4,999,348. Private schools were attended by 297,798 students; federal schools accounted for 71,039.

After school, some 75 universities and 275 other tertiary education institutes offer higher education and vocational courses. Students must pay their own way, though some institutions have private endowments and state grants. Most students take out an assisted loan, for repayment after graduation, and vacation work is common. University enrolment of full-time students in 1999 was 560,376. For 2000–2001, the federal education budget was $4.832 million, or 2.6% of federal spending. The provinces and territories spent $40,555 million, or 20.1% of their total spending, on education.

Justice, law and order

Crime and violence are relatively low in Canada, certainly by comparison with the U.S.A., and Canadian cities are among the world's safest. The federal police force is the Royal Canadian Mounted Police; this also provides basic policing of all provinces except Ontario and Québec, which have their own police forces. At the top of the justice system is the Supreme Court of Canada, which is the highest court and ultimate court of appeal. Next is the Federal Court, which deals with all claims by or against the Crown (i.e. the federal government), and the Court of Appeal. Each province has its own provincial court system, headed by a chief justice.

Religion

The Canadian state is secular and there is freedom of worship. About 75% of the population have at least nominal attachment to one of the major Christian churches, Anglican, United, and Roman Catholic. In Québec province, Catholics are in a substantial majority. Virtually all other world faiths are represented. The number of Muslims in Canada is estimated at around 260,000 (1991); the number of Jews at around 320,000 (1991); and there are also large Sikh and Buddhist groups.

Media

Each Canadian city has its own daily newspaper, but two can claim to be nationally available, the *National Post* and the Toronto *Globe and Mail*. There were 101 daily newspapers in 2001, and around 1,100 weekly or twice-weekly community papers. A wide range of special-interest journals and magazines is also published, in addition to imported English- and French-language publications.

The Canadian Broadcasting Corporation (CBC), a nationally funded broadcaster, covers the country with TV and radio broadcasting in English and French. It is estimated to reach 99.5% of the population. It also operates Radio Canada International, on short wave, which broadcasts to a worldwide audience in eleven languages. Commercial stations such as Global, CTV, and Baton Broadcasting Systems are widely watched. With access to major

U.S. channels, and a vast range of options via satellite and cable TV, Canadians have one of the widest ranges of station choices in the world. In March 2001, Canada had 476 outlets for AM radio and 1,357 for FM. The regulation of radio, TV and telecommunications is exercised by the Canadian Radio-TV and Telecommunications Commission.

Book publishing is a vibrant industry in Canada, though globalization of major publishers has reduced the number of larger Canadian-owned companies. Canadians have access to the entire output of the American, British, and French publishing industries.

The nationwide availability of new technology, including the extension of broadband access, has made Canada an important user of email and the Internet.

Economy

The national currency is the Canadian dollar, divided into 100 cents. Broadly based as it is upon primary products, agriculture, manufacture, and services, the Canadian economy is a strong one. The principal adverse effects on it come either from economic downturn in the adjacent U.S.A., reducing Canadian exports, or from falls in world prices of metal ores. The general picture in Canada over recent decades has been of economic expansion and diversification.

Gross national product (GNP)

World Bank figures for 2000 put the Canadian GNP at U.S.$647,126 million, working out at U.S.$21,050 per head of the population.

Banking

The central bank is the Bank of Canada, and it is responsible among other things for conducting monetary policy, issuing and controlling the currency, and regulating credit and currency 'in the best interests of the economic life of the nation.' Eight major commercial banks deal with personal and corporate finances through chains of offices. In addition there are numerous more specialized banks, many of them Canadian branches of institutions established elsewhere.

Stock exchanges

The country's largest stock exchange is in Toronto and there are also stock exchanges in Montréal and Vancouver, where shares in Canadian companies are traded.

Labour

In 2001, the Canadian labour force – persons aged over 15 and under 65 – numbered 16,246,300. Of these, 15,078,800 were in employment, and 1,169,600 were unemployed or between jobs.

Federal budget

In 2000-2001, the federal budget was $190,409 million. The main sources of federal revenue in the same period were as follows (in millions of dollars):

Personal income taxes: 88,156
Corporation income taxes: 27,619
General sales taxes: 38,773
Gasoline and fuel taxes: 4,788
Alcohol and tobacco taxes: 3,227
Customs duty: 2,791
Other taxes: 542
Contributions to social security plans: 19,086
Sale of goods and services: 4,255
Investment income: 6,533

The main areas of 2000-2001 federal expenditure were as follows (in millions of dollars):

Total expenditure on all items: 181,340
General services: 8,429
Protection of persons and property: 19,248
Transport and communications: 1,974
Health (including hospital care): 3,920
Social services: 51,574
Social assistance: 49,006
Education: 4,832
Resource conservation and industrial development: 5,716
Foreign affairs and international assistance: 4,606
General transfers to other levels of government: 25,822
Debt charges: 44,984

Trade and Industry

Agriculture

The typical image of agricultural Canada is of the prairie wheat crop, with its miles of rippling grain. But this belies the diversity of Canadian agriculture, which has evolved to suit its many terrains and climatic variations, as well as market needs. Wheat, though still the largest field crop, is reducing in quantity. In 1996, just under 10 million hectares (24,710,000 acres) were given over to wheat; by 2001 this was down 16.7% to 8,310,787 hectares (20,535,954 acres). Barley production is also falling, down 10.4% from its 1996 level of 5,241,923 hectares (12,952,791 acres) to 4,696,911 hectares (11,606,067 acres) in 2001. Cultivation of alfalfa and other forms of maize is increasing, with 4,504,042 hectares (11,129,487 acres) under cultivation in 2001 compared with 3,598,461 hectares (8,891,717 acres) in 1996. This reflects an increased demand for animal feedstuffs.

The farm animal population grows steadily. Farmers' returns showed a cattle population of 15,551,449 cattle in 2001, an increase of 4.4% on 1996's figure of 14,893,034. In the same period, other species had increased by a greater degree. Pigs in 2001 numbered 13,958,772, an increase of 26.5% on the 1996 figure of 11,040,462. The number of farms rearing pigs grew in the same period by over 26%. The poultry population of hens, ducks, geese, and turkeys totalled 126,159,520 in 2001, an increase of 23.4% against the 1996 figure of 102,255,149.

Changes in the pattern of agriculture are reflected by the steady decrease in the number of farms. In 1996, Canada had 276,548 farms of all sizes. By 2001 the number was down to 246,923, a drop of around 2% each year. This reflects a continuing drift from the land to the cities that has been going on for many decades, a growth in the size of farms, and the ever-increasing mechanization and semi-industrialization of agriculture.

Changes in consumer eating habits, and the demands of the supply chain, have influenced farmers' activities. Blueberries as a crop have risen from 36,222 hectares (89,504 acres) in 1996 to 43,982 hectares (108,679 acres) in 2001, a rise of 21.4%. Vine cultivation in the same period has risen from 7,515 hectares (18,569 acres) to 10,589 hectares (26,165 acres), an increase of 40.9%, incidentally revealing the renaissance of Canada's wine industry. Apple cultivation, on the other hand, a traditional practice of many farms in the Maritime Provinces, is falling, from 31,592 hectares (78,064 acres) in 1996 to 25,825 hectares (63,813 acres) in 2001, a drop of 18.3%. These selected statistics show a growing trend in Canadian farming towards the supply of food for packaging and processing. It is underlined by the rapid and continuing development of greenhouse and tunnel cultivation. In 1996 this covered 12,913,404 square metres (15,444,431 square yards); by 2001 it had risen by 42.1% to 18,352,645 square metres (21,949,763 square yards), and this trend will no doubt continue.

With a relatively short growing season over most of the country, the high level of investment required in modern-day farming, and the demands of a supermarket and chain store industry that looks for uniform size, colour and appearance, the issue of genetically modified seed use, and the potential in the future of animal cloning, are much-debated issues in Canada as elsewhere. Although 'green' politics has yet to break through at a provincial and national level, there is a strong latent sense of environmental responsibility among Canadians.

Fisheries

International controversy relating to oceanic fishing rights, zonal boundaries, and diminishing fish stocks continue to affect this industry. The sea fishing fleets of Newfoundland and Nova Scotia have been greatly reduced in recent years. In 2000, 967,900 metric tonnes of fish of all kinds (live weight) were landed, a 4% drop on the previous year. With an economic value in 1999 of $19,878,940, the future of fishing is a major economic issue. The principal species caught are Atlantic cod, herring, and salmon, and Pacific salmon and herring. The shellfish industry is important on both coasts. Canada does not practice whaling, but around 250,000 seals are caught annually.

Furs

One of Canada's oldest pursuits, the fur industry, remains significant today: 2,130,515 pelts were traded in 1999. The modern fur industry consists of pelts from farmed animals, such as beaver, muskrat, fox, chinchilla and marten. Of the traded pelts, the largest proportion (613,000) came from Ontario, with 426,000 from Newfoundland–Labrador, 270,000 each from Québec and British Columbia, and 125,000 from Manitoba.

Industry

Canadian industry represents around 75% of the country's gross national product and is thus of crucial importance in maintaining the nation's wealth and living standards. The industrial base is both diverse and modern, centred on transportation, food products, electrical equipment, paper and chemicals. The value of shipments from Canadian industry in 1999 was $490,343,200. The ten largest contributors were as follows (in dollars):

Transportation equipment: 125,034,300
Food industries: 52,352,800
Electrical and electronic products: 36,760,600
Paper and allied products: 33,150,300
Chemicals and chemical products: 32,351,300
Wood industries: 30,600,600
Primary metal industries: 27,528,000
Fabricated metal industries: 26,883,900
Machinery: 16,890,500
Printing and publishing: 16,526,300

Electronics and transportation equipment are among the fastest-growing industries.

Trade

Canada is a major trading nation, and one that normally enjoys a surplus of export revenue over import costs. In 2001, exports totalled $414,638.2 million, and imports were $350,622.7 million. The U.S.A. is by far the country's major trading partner, absorbing more than three-quarters of all Canadian exports and supplying more than two-thirds of all Canadian imports.

Canada's Main Trading Partners

Exports in 1996 and 2001 in $ millions

Country	1996	2001
U.S.A.	222,416.3	350,908.1
Japan	12,423.4	9,481.5
United Kingdom	4,608.5	6,573.5
Other EU countries	12,796.3	15,726.7
Total exports	280,079.3	414,638.2

Imports in 1996 and 2001 in $ millions

Country	1996	2001
U.S.A.	180,010.1	225,028.2
Japan	7,227.4	585.2
United Kingdom	5,581.1	11,863.4
Other EU countries	14,994.7	23,225.1
Total imports	237,688.6	350,622.7

The very substantial positive trade balance between Canada and the U.S.A. more than compensates for the adverse balance with other major industrial economies. Canada has little need to import primary products of any kind. Imported goods consist of the following: manufactured articles (such as industrial equipment, automobiles, trucks, and consumer goods); electronic equipment, defence equipment, textiles (such as cotton and silk), foodstuffs, and other natural products from hotter regions, including rice, fruit, tea, coffee, hardwoods, and mineral products not found in Canada (such as bauxite and industrial diamonds); specialist products from the international drinks and foods industries; books and other media items; and luxury goods.

Many items in some of these categories are also exported from Canada. The prime export items are cereal crops, lumber and lumber products, meat, fish and poultry products, electric power, and a range of minerals including petroleum, coal, natural gas, copper, nickel, lead, zinc, molybdenum, silver, gold, platinum, and uranium. As in most countries, Canada also has a hidden but substantial 'unofficial' economy that is nowadays chiefly founded on the drug trade and other forms of organized crime.

Transport

Highways, railways, canals, and aircraft all play a part in Canadian transport. *Transport by road*: there are over 1,427,000 kilometres (886,000 miles) of highway, of which around 15,000 kilometres (9,321 miles) form federal roads and highways. The longest of these is the Trans-Canada Highway, which runs 7,800 kilometres (4,847 miles) from St. John's to Victoria. Most passenger transport is by road, and few Canadian families do not own, or have access to, a car. Automobiles are by the most frequently used means of personal transport.

27

Transport by rail: Canada's national rail company, VIA Rail, crosses the country, and also links with the U.S. network, which is on the same standard gauge. Much long-distance freight is still sent by rail. New rail lines have been built to facilitate mineral extraction from remote mining areas in the north. Transcontinental passenger trains still operate, although most passenger travel by rail is on rapid-transit systems in the larger cities. In 1998 the railways' freight revenue amounted to $6,786,685 million, the passenger revenue to only $207,557 million.

Transport by river, lake, canal: the prime inland navigation route is the St. Lawrence Seaway, established to bring ocean-going ships into the heart of the continent by linking the Great Lakes with the Atlantic Ocean, and completed in 1959. Its main limitation, apart from the subsequent development of super-size vessels, is that it is blocked by ice between mid-December and mid-April. The Great Lakes themselves form an important transport route. There are thousands of kilometres of navigable rivers and lakes across the country, though much of their use nowadays is for leisure. The lumber industry still uses rivers for floating and rafting logs downstream.

Transport by air: air transport began in a small way in the 1920s but is now a very important element in the transport pattern. Shuttle services link Montréal and Toronto, and frequent flights serve to link other major cities. From the east coast to the west coast remains a relatively long-haul flight, taking from five to seven hours. International air connections are made at Montréal, Toronto, Winnipeg, and Vancouver.

Transport in winter: another form of winter land transport, independent of the road network, is the snow tractor, which is widely used in the Prairie Provinces and in northern areas for cross-country transport, using frozen lake surfaces as well as the snow-surfaced landscape. Seaplane, ski-plane and helicopter services reach out to distant communities which might be cut off by land transport in winter.

Tourism

The number of visitors to Canada in 2000 was 19.6 million. Of these, 15.2 million came from the U.S.A. The remaining quarter came chiefly from Europe and Japan. The income from tourists was reckoned at $18,000 million. Although travel facilities, accommodation, and length of season reduce rural Canada's potential for increasing tourist traffic, especially in the northern areas, the same factors act as a spur to visitors who wish to see a landscape which is still 'unspoiled' and a scene which does not consist of other visitors.

Culture

In Canada, the keyword to reflect the country's national diversity is not 'melting pot', as in the U.S.A., but 'mosaic'. The country has a rich and vibrant cultural life which has spread from the twin pillars of English and French traditions into something much more varied and unashamedly modern, and the aboriginal peoples' traditions are no longer excluded as 'folklore' or 'craft'.

While the introduction of a wide-ranging multiculturalism has been successful, the essential duality of Canadian cultural life has remained a central government concern since the days of Pierre Trudeau's premiership. Then, for the first time, there was a major effort to make English-speaking Canadians more bilingual, and to promote, as part of Canadian identity, bilingualism and the sharing of the two cultures.

The Canada Council, founded in 1957, is the national agency for the arts, with a brief to foster what is best and also what is specifically Canadian in origin or inspiration.

Literature

In literature, Canadian writing forms a distinctive region of English and French, and is by no means a 'provincial' school. On the short list of ten writers nominated for Britain's most prestigious literary prize in 2001, four of the nominated authors were Canadian or resident in Canada. The works of Canadian novelists such as Robertson Davies and Margaret Atwood are available throughout the world. Other international successes include Mordecai Richler, Carol Shields, Michael Ondaatje, and, in French, Anne Hébert. Earlier twentieth-century figures with a worldwide reputation include the humorist Stephen Leacock and the economic historian J. K. Galbraith.

Theatre

The first recorded theatrical show in Canada took place at Port Royal in 1606, and other theatrical performances took place in Montréal and Québec during the seventeenth century. Theatres opened in the larger cities during the later nineteenth century, and the famous theatre at Stratford, Ontario, opened in 1957. Nowadays, established and touring companies bring a wide range of classical and modern drama to Canadians in cities and towns across the land, although the prime centres are Toronto and Montréal.

Music, opera and ballet

Professional symphony orchestras exist in Calgary, Edmonton, Hamilton, Kitchener-Waterloo, Montréal, Ottawa, New Brunswick, Nova Scotia, Saskatoon, Thunder Bay, Toronto, Victoria, Vancouver, and Winnipeg. There are many smaller orchestras and musical groups, as well as a vibrant pop, jazz, and folk music industry. Music festivals are frequent. Opera is regularly performed by the Canadian Opera Company in Toronto (and on tour), and by Montréal Opera, Edmonton Opera, Québec Opera, Opera Hamilton, Pacific Opera Victoria, and Vancouver Opera. Apart from the National Ballet of Canada, there are ballet companies in Winnipeg and Montréal, and provincial companies in Alberta and British Columbia.

Art and sculpture

The Toronto-based 'Group of Seven' in the 1920s was the first self-proclaimed national school of artists 'imbued with the idea that an Art must grow and flower in the land before the country will be a real home for its people'. Their paintings of the Canadian landscape did much to support this idea. The group's leading figure was the Montréal painter, A.Y. Jackson. Inevitably their work became something to surpass or depart from, and Canadian painters were very much alive to what was happening elsewhere. Québec artists had strong connections with France, where the cubist and surrealist revolutions were happening.

Modern Canadian artists have been strongly influenced by abstract expressionism. In recent years, there has also been increasing recognition of the art practiced by Inuit and First Peoples artists. Canada has a range of great art galleries, including the National Gallery, the Art Gallery of Ontario, with its superb Henry Moore collection, and the Vancouver Art Gallery with its totem paintings by the British Columbian artist, Emily Carr.

Architecture and townscape

An unusually perceptive early traveller remarked that the Inuit igloo was comparable in its combination of form and function to the Greek temple. The same might be said of the tepee of the Plains Indians, while the wooden architecture of the tribes of the Pacific coast is on a monumental scale. The first European buildings, other than rude cabins, were the *habitations* – fortified settlements begun by Champlain in the early seventeenth century. Fortress architecture loomed large for over 200 years, culminating in the great stone citadels of Louisbourg, Halifax and Québec.

Some of the oldest towns, such as Montréal and Québec City, preserve an irregular central street pattern based on original pathways, but the typical Canadian urban layout, as exemplified by Toronto and most other cities, is the rectangular grid, with two intersecting main streets. Two towns, Québec City and the old Nova Scotian port of Lunenburg, are classed by the United Nations Educational, Scientific and Cultural Organization (UNESCO) as world heritage sites.

The earliest public buildings were churches, often placed in commanding sites. The early colonial wooden churches were gradually supplanted by more permanent and grander buildings in classic, Romanesque, or gothic styles. Similar styles were employed for the provincial and national parliament buildings, and for the major railroad stations. But perhaps the most recognizably Canadian architecture is the form of French Renaissance style deployed in the vast chateau-hotels erected in the late nineteenth century by the Canadian Pacific Railway at Québec City, Banff, and Vancouver, among other places. Modern Canadian architecture is eclectic and cannot be said to express a particularly national spirit or style. Contemporary town planners' response both to street congestion and to long winters has been the development in the larger cities of extensive pedestrian areas, either underground or at upper-story levels. The Underground City in Montréal and the PATH system of Toronto are the most extensive.

Sport and Leisure

Just about every sport and pastime imaginable finds practitioners in Canada. The major professional sports, Canadian football, baseball, and ice hockey, have teams in every city and the leagues and provincial conferences are followed avidly by spectators, TV viewers, and readers of the press. The Toronto Bluejays participate in the U.S. Major League.

At an amateur level, all the main sports are organized on a national and provincial basis. Around one third of the population participates regularly in some form of sport. The main national forum for athletics and field sports is the Canada Games, which take place every second year, alternately as Winter and Summer Games. Each Games is held at a different 'mid-sized' city venue and their progress round the country has led to the building of many excellent stadiums and sports complexes.

At the Sydney Olympics of 2000, Canadians won the following medals:

- gold in the triathlon, tennis, and wrestling
- silver in canoeing, synchronized diving, and judo
- bronze in canoeing, trampoline, rowing, swimming, diving, and synchronized swimming

The most popular sports among Canadian men are golf, hockey, baseball, and swimming. Among women, swimming comes top, followed by golf, baseball, and volleyball. Canadians are particularly keen on winter sports, and figure and speed skating, skiing, and curling are all very popular.

Natural Resources

Water

With around a quarter of the world's fresh water reserves, and with political control over a large part of the subarctic ice, Canada's water usage and management are likely to become important issues in the twenty-first century. Water power is also the prime source of electricity generation, with huge potential still unused. Canada currently produces around 550,000 million kWh annually.

Minerals

Canada has vast reserves of minerals and fossil fuels, many of them located in remote and sparsely inhabited regions, though mineral exploitation in the more populous southern strip has been going on for more than 200 years. Ores being mined in 1999 were bismuth, cadmium, cobalt, copper, gold, iron, lead, molybdenum, nickel, platinum, selenium, silver, uranium, and zinc. Non-metallic resources being mined or extracted include asbestos, coal, gypsum, natural gas, nepheline, syenite, petroleum, potash, salt, and sulphur. In addition, vast amounts of sand and gravel are extracted every year for use in the construction industry, and stone is quarried, both for building and for road stone.

Prospecting for minerals continues, and though it is likely that most significant deposits have now been identified, new discoveries have meant that reserves of certain minerals, such as crude oil, have increased over recent years despite extensive extraction. Known reserves (1999) are as follows:

Crude petroleum: 1,448,000,000 cubic metres
Natural gas: 1,809,000,000 cubic metres
Crude bitumen: 229,800,000 cubic metres
Coal: 8,623,000,000 tonnes
Copper: 8,402,000 tonnes
Nickel: 5,683,000 tonnes
Lead: 1,845,000 tonnes
Zinc: 10,159,000 tonnes
Molybdenum: 121,000 tonnes
Silver: 15,738 tonnes
Gold: 1,415 tonnes
Uranium: 312,000 tonnes

Canada is also the world's main source of potash, and a major source of asbestos. There are extensive deposits of iron ore. Production of rare metals such as selenium and tellurium is also carried on.

Forest

In 1991, 4,175,800 square kilometres (1,611,859 square miles) were under forest. Of this, 2,447,700 square kilometres (944,812 square miles) were classed as 'productive', i.e. commercially useful timber. Of the latter, almost a half was contained in the two provinces of Québec and British Columbia. Most of the commercial timber is softwood produced to feed the demands of the newsprint, paper, and packaging industries, but hardwoods are also produced. In 1999, roundwood removals from Canada's forests yielded 158,763 cubic metres of softwood and 34,402 cubic metres of hardwood.

The Provinces and Territories

Alberta

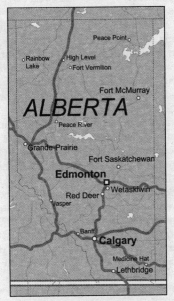

Name: the name is in honour of Queen Victoria's daughter, Princess Louise Alberta, wife of the Marquis of Lorne, Governor General. Alberta, along with Manitoba and Saskatchewan is one of the so-called Prairie Provinces.

Emblems: the wild rose, the lodgepole pine, the great horned owl.

Motto: Fortis et Liber, 'Strong and free'.

Population (2002): 3,113,600.

Capital: Edmonton, Canada's fifth largest city. The 36 municipalities forming Greater Edmonton are home to over 900,000 people. Focally placed on transcontinental routes running east, west, north, south, and northwest, the city is a major communications hub.

Physical description: with a land area of 661,848 square kilometres (243,560 square miles), it is the sixth largest of the provinces and territories. Southwestern Alberta is a mountainous region that includes the Monashee and Cariboo ranges of the Western Cordillera, rising to high peaks and with glaciers in the upper valleys. Alberta's highest point is Mt. Columbia (3,747 metres, 12,293 feet). Towards the central south, the foothills gradually give way to flat prairie country. The central area of the province is rich farming land, with woods, hills, and lakes. South of the 55th parallel the rivers flow east into Saskatchewan. To the north of the 55th parallel is a vast region of woods and grassland, still thinly populated, and with large extents of marsh known as muskeg. In it two great river systems flow northwards: the Peace River flows to the Great Slave Lake; the Athabasca to the lake of the same name.

Climate: Alberta has a continental-type climate, with long, cold winters, a brief, brilliant spring, and hot summers. On the west, the rain shadow of the mountains can produce long periods of drought.

Agriculture: in the eastern prairie area, wheat and other cereal crops are grown. To the west, stock rearing is more common. In the country between Calgary and Edmonton, mixed farming is practiced, with dairy herds and market gardens.

Minerals: southwest and central-south Alberta have large deposits of coal and natural gas, and the latter is a prime source of energy, along with hydroelectricity generated in the mountain valleys. Oil is extracted from a major field centred on the city of Drumheller. In the north of the province there are further oil and gas deposits, and rock salt is mined.

Industry: much of Alberta's mineral wealth is transported elsewhere by train and pipeline, but manufacturing industry related to mining, transport, and farming is important in the cities.

History: long a wilderness inhabited by nomadic tribes, the region was part of the Hudson's Bay grant of 1670. For another 200 years, little changed, though trading stations were established here and there, and pioneer families and communities began to establish farms. The completion of the Canadian Pacific Railway in 1885 opened up the area, and towns like Calgary and Edmonton began to grow. In the early twentieth century there was a rush of settlement, as not only the farmlands but also the mineral resources of the south began to be exploited. Alberta was constituted a province in 1905.

British Columbia

Name: the name of Canada's westernmost province ultimately honours Christopher Columbus and also recalls its original status as part of the British Empire.

Emblem: the dogwood.

Motto: *Splendor sine occasu*, 'Splendour undiminished'.

Population (2002): 4,141,300.

Capital: Victoria, on Vancouver Island, a pleasant city on a fine natural harbour, with tourism, service industries, and administration its main occupations.

Physical description: with a land area of 944,735 square kilometres (364,668 square miles), it is the fifth in size among the territories and provinces. Mountains, deep valleys, and a heavily indented and islanded coastline largely define the landscape of British Columbia: geologically it is a continuation of the Western Cordillera, which covers most of the province, dividing between the Rocky Mountains on the border with Alberta, and the Coast Range, with a wide central area of mountains and plateaus separating the two main ranges. The highest peaks extend far above the tree line into regions of perpetual snow and ice with large glaciers. The highest point is Mt. Fairweather (4,663 metres, 15,298 feet). Rivers drain

35

to east and west from the watersheds, with the Fraser system dominating in the south of the province and leading to the Pacific; and the Peace River flowing from the vast man-made Williston Lake to the east and north. The lower slopes, valleys, and islands are heavily forested, with cedar, spruce, and Douglas fir among the most common trees.

Climate: on the coastal side, the sea promotes a mild, moist climate, without great extremes. In the south of the province, there is an almost Mediterranean-type climate. Inland of the coastal range, it can be very dry, and temperatures vary from summer maxima of around 37° to winter lows of -32° or lower. On the eastern slopes of the mountains, the warm Chinook wind has an alleviating effect, though it also promotes a dry climate and dry soil. In the north, the climate becomes subarctic both on the coast and inland.

Agriculture: forestry is by far the most important form of cultivation. Forest parks now preserve the remaining specimens of the giant firs and cedars which once grew in vast numbers. Softwood trees are grown in huge plantations and the logs are usually floated down to the sea. In valleys and on grassy plateau areas, cattle and sheep are raised, and wheat and other cereals are grown in the Peace River valley. On the coastal side, fruit trees are also cultivated. Fisheries are important in the sea and the rivers, especially salmon.

Minerals: falling water is an important resource in British Columbia and virtually all its electricity is hydrogenerated. The province also has deposits of lead, zinc, gold, copper, asbestos, and silver. Coal is mined around Fernie, in the Rocky Mountains, and there are also coal deposits on Vancouver Island.

Industry: cheap power has encouraged the growth of power-intensive industry such as aluminium smelting. Lumber-related industry is widespread, with sawmills and pulp mills. In the Vancouver–Victoria area there is a diversity of industry including chemicals and electronics. Tourism is also a major contributor to the province's economy.

History: occupied by coastal Indian tribes from prehistoric times, British Columbia's first European visitors came by sea up the Pacific coast. The Spanish explorer, Juan Pérez, came in 1774, and the British Captain Cook in 1778. The coast was surveyed between 1792–94 by Captain George Vancouver of the Royal Navy, and was at that time claimed for Great Britain. In 1793, Alexander Mackenzie, a Scottish fur trader, crossed the Rockies to Cascade Inlet. The North West Company was established to trade in furs and other natural products of the region; in 1821 it merged with the Hudson's Bay Company. In 1843, Fort Victoria, site of the present provincial capital, was established by Sir James Douglas on behalf of the Hudson's Bay Company. Vancouver Island later became a Crown colony, with Douglas as its governor. In 1858, shortly after gold was found in the Fraser River valley, the mainland was also designated as a colony and named British Columbia. Vancouver Island was incorporated with it as a single colony in 1866. Five years later, British Columbia agreed to join as one of the provinces of the newly formed Dominion of Canada, so long as a railway connection was provided to link it to the eastern provinces. The first transcontinental line was completed in 1885. Despite this, the western province naturally has many north–south links with the U.S. states on either side, as well as a 'Pacific rim' presence.

Vancouver: though not the provincial capital, Vancouver is by far the largest city of British Columbia, and third largest in Canada, with a population of 545,674 in 2001, and with almost 2,000,000 people living in the metropolitan area. It is the chief port, and manufacturing and business centre of the province. A city of many ethnic groups, it has one of the largest and oldest 'Chinatowns' in North America. Vancouver's location, its parks, botanical gardens, and museums, make it a popular tourist venue, and it is the country's main film production centre.

Manitoba

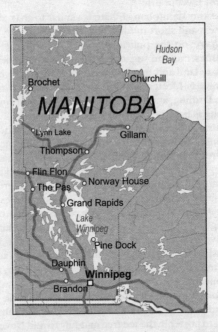

Name: the name is said to come from an Indian phrase, meaning 'God that speaks'. It is the easternmost of the Prairie Provinces.

Emblems: the great grey owl, the crocus, the white spruce.

Motto: *Gloriosus et liber*, 'Glorious and free'.

Population (2002): 1,150,800.

Capital: the city of Winnipeg, whose name comes from the Cree Indian phrase *win nipee* ('muddy water'), referring to the great lake of the same name. It is a spacious city of 640,000 people, spread over 462.1 square kilometres (178.4 square miles), and it is home to almost half the province's population.

Physical description: with an area of 647,797 square kilometres (250,050 square miles), it is eighth in size among the provinces and territories, and only very slightly smaller than Saskatchewan. Much of the area was once submerged under a huge lake, and it remains a lowland region still dominated by water features. Lake Winnipeg is the largest of many thousands of lakes, and north of it lies an extraordinary complex of inland waters, reaching to and beyond the province's northern boundary at the 60th parallel. On the northeast, Manitoba is bounded by Hudson Bay. On the west side, reaching into Saskatchewan, is a more hilly region, rising to summits mostly of around 750 metres (2,250 feet). The highest point is Mt. Baldy (832 metres, 2,729 feet). In the south there are great extents of almost level prairie.

Climate: the Manitoban climate is similar to that of Alberta, with long, cold winters and short but hot summers.

Agriculture: on the prairie, wheat is the prime crop, though oats, barley, potatoes, rye, and sugar beet are also grown. There are also large areas of pasture land and, apart from stock rearing, much of Canada's honey production is located here. In the northern part of the province there is little farming, and the prime form of cultivation is forestry. Commercial fishing is based chiefly on Lake Winnipeg.

Minerals: Flin Flon, in the northwest of the province, is the main centre for a mining industry that extracts copper, zinc, gold, silver, cadmium, and tellurium. Other gold-producing areas are at Bissett, Herb Lake, and Snow Lake, and nickel is extracted at Mystery Lake and Moak Lake, near Thompson. In the southwest, near Virden, there are oil deposits. Sands and gravels are also extracted in large quantities.

Industry: most manufacturing industry is concentrated in and around Winnipeg and the industrial base is quite diverse. Parts are made for the automotive and aircraft industries. There is textile weaving and a clothing industry based on this plus locally available furs and leather. Mineral smelting and processing is carried out at Flin Flon, and nickel is refined at Thompson.

Transport: Winnipeg's international airport is the central hub of internal Canadian air services. The port of Churchill on Hudson Bay is a major grain exporter in the ice-free mid-July to mid-November period, as it stands at the end of the shortest sea route from the prairies to Europe. A branch of the transcontinental railroad links it to the main system.

History: the first recorded European explorer was Pierre de la Vérendrye in 1739, but the first serious attempt at settling was made from Scotland in 1812, when a pioneering community established the township of Selkirk. The population remained very small through most of the nineteenth century. Up until 1867, Manitoba was the property of the Hudson's Bay Company, but in that year the new Dominion government purchased a large part of the territory lying on both sides of the Red River. At that time there was a rebellion among the Métis who lived and hunted in the region. This ended peacefully in 1870, but its leader Louis Riel had incurred deep hostility in Ontario. He was unable to take up his parliamentary seat and lived in exile in the U.S.A. In 1870 Manitoba was established as a province (albeit a much smaller province than today's Manitoba). By 1878 the railway had come, and this led to a substantial increase in population from the 12,000 or so of 1870. Land speculation led to further unrest among the Métis in 1885, and Riel returned to lead a second rebellion. This was put down by force, and Riel was captured, tried, and hanged at Regina. Manitoba joined the Confederation in 1905.

New Brunswick

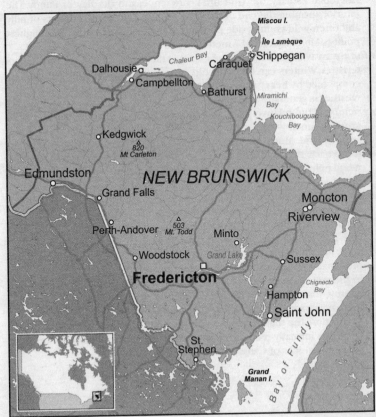

Name: named after the German state of Braunschweig, a possession of the royal British Hanoverians, New Brunswick, along with Newfoundland, Nova Scotia, and Prince Edward Island, is one of the Maritime Provinces.

Emblems: the purple violet, the black-capped chickadee.

Motto: *Spem reduxit*, 'Hope was restored'.

Population (2002): 756,700. Most people live around the coast and in the main river valleys (the St. John and Matapedia), which also form important lines of road and rail communication. The interior of the province is very sparsely populated.

Capital: Fredericton, population 46,500, an attractive town with many nineteenth-century buildings. The cultural centre of the province, it has two universities and the famous Beaverbrook Art Gallery.

Physical description: with a land area of 72,908 square kilometres (28,142 square miles), it is eleventh in size among the provinces and territories. The province occupies the end of the 'peninsula' formed between the St. Lawrence Estuary, the Gulf of St. Lawrence, and the Bay of Fundy. The interior, forming the end of the long Appalachian range, consists of hilly and often wild countryside penetrated by long river valleys. The highest point is Mt. Carleton (817 metres, 2,610 feet).

Climate: away from the coast, the climate takes on more continental characteristics. Winters can be very cold, especially in the uplands, and are accompanied by heavy snowfalls. On the coast and in sheltered valleys, the weather is generally milder.

Agriculture: the relatively dry and cool climate has encouraged vegetable growing, notably of seed potatoes. Mixed farming prevails, with much pasture land. Much of the province remains covered in forest, with extensive hardwood forests as well as quick-growing softwood to feed the wood pulp and paper industries. Shellfish are an important resource along the coast.

Minerals: zinc, potash, silver, lead, copper, and coal are all found. There are also extensive peat deposits, cut for horticultural use.

Trade and industry: New Brunswick employment is divided 72% to services, 22% to industry, and 6% to agriculture.

History: until the seventeenth century, the region was the hunting ground of nomadic Indian tribes. The first European settlers were French, but as in the rest of eastern Canada, the French and the British were soon in a contest for ownership. British possession was confirmed in 1713, and there was a steady increase in settlement during the eighteenth century. At this time the region was included in Nova Scotia. In 1784, New Brunswick was formally recognized as a separate province and it became one of the provinces of Canada in 1867.

Newfoundland and Labrador

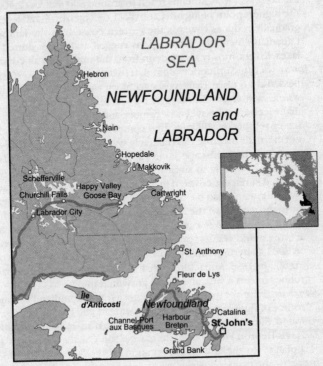

Name: its name bestowed by the explorer, John Cabot, in 1497, Canada's easternmost and most recent province is formed by this large island and the adjacent coastal region of Labrador. It is one of the four Maritime Provinces.

Emblems: the caribou, the pitcher plant. Other provincial emblems are the Newfoundland dog and pony, the black spruce, and the gemstone, labradorite.

Motto: *Quaerite prime regnum dei*, 'Seek first the kingdom of God'.

Population (2002): 531,600.

Capital: St. John's with a population of 102,000. With an average annual precipitation of 1,482 millimetres (58 inches), and 217 wet days a year, St. John's is Canada's wettest provincial capital.

Physical description: with a land area of 405,212 square kilometres (156,412 square miles), it is tenth in size among the provinces and territories. Lying across the entry to the Gulf of St. Lawrence, Newfoundland is shaped rather like an irregular triangle, with many peninsulas, and sides slightly less than 500 kilometres (310 miles) long. It is formed of the same rocks as the continent. These are at their highest on the western side, where the Long Range Mountains reach to around 800 metres (2,400 feet), with the highest point being Mt. Caubvik (1,652 metres, 5,420 feet); the height gradually reduces towards the eastern coast. Like the landscape of the Canadian Shield, the landscape is rugged and rocky, dotted with many lakes. Rivers, mostly short, drain from the interior to all coasts.

Climate: oceanic influences dominate, with a prevailing moistness and coolness and no great extremes, except on the northern Long Range coast where winter conditions can be severe. The Strait of Belle Isle is normally icebound between December and June. The Atlantic coasts are often enveloped in thick fog that comes in from the sea, a product of cold northern air meeting the relatively warm waters of the Gulf Stream.

Agriculture: the landscape is on the whole poorly suited to farming and farms exist mostly to supply local communities, but some two-fifths of the land surface is covered in forest, and lumber is an important industry. Newfoundland also has a large fishing industry, though over-exploitation by many nations of the once cod-rich Newfoundland Banks has brought about a reduction in catches and a shift of emphasis to crab and shrimp. It is the world's largest producer of cold-water cooked and peeled shrimp. In 2001, fisheries employed 14,600 people in the province, compared to 20,800 in 1991. Aquaculture (fish farming) now produces around 8,000 tonnes of fish a year and is still growing rapidly.

Minerals: there are many mineral deposits. Newfoundland is Canada's main source of fluorspar, while zinc, copper, lead, and gold are among the metals found. Substantial oil reserves are known to exist in the offshore Ben Nevis-Hebron Field, but in 2002 Chevron Canada Resources abandoned a plan to go ahead with exploitation.

Industry: the main industries are wood and fish-related: pulp and newsprint mills, and fish processing.

Transport: the highway between Port aux Basques and St. John's is a continuation of the trans-Canada highway, but the topography is such that it more than doubles the direct distance between these cities. Land travel is often compelled to take devious routes around the mountains. In the days of sea travel, and early transatlantic air travel, the island was strategically placed in global terms, on the routes between New York, the St. Lawrence, and the ports of northwest Europe, with Gander an important refuelling point.

History: in 1583 the Elizabethan adventurer, Sir Humphrey Gilbert, claimed Newfoundland on behalf of the English Queen Elizabeth I. The first colonial settlement was made in 1610, but English possession was challenged by the French, who established a colony at Placentia. It was not until 1713 that, under the Treaty of Utrecht, Newfoundland was formally accepted as a British colony. Unusually, the founding of settlements was resisted by the British government. This had much to do with the control of fishing rights. The wealthy few who controlled the Newfoundland fishing did not want to see colonists taking a share of their lucrative business. Settlers were refused permission to build houses or cut wood within six miles of the shore. These laws, very hard to enforce, were gradually relaxed. By 1832 the island had its own Parliament and in 1855 it became a self-governing British colony. The inhabitants voted against joining in the formation of Canada in 1867, and Newfoundland remained a self-governing colony. But in the slump year of 1933, with the island's economy in a state of collapse, elective government was suspended and a 'commission of government' controlled affairs through the 1930s, and the years of World War II. During 1939–45, the strategic position of Newfoundland again worked in its favour, and a strong war economy brought renewed prosperity. In a referendum in 1948, the islanders voted in favour of union with Canada, and Newfoundland, together with Labrador, became the country's tenth province on 1 April 1949.

Labrador: the name comes from the Portuguese explorer of 1530, João Fernandes, who was a *lavrador*, or landholder, in the Azores. The easternmost territory of Canada, administratively part of Newfoundland province, Labrador is very thinly populated. Stretching from the Hudson Bay coast to the Strait of Belle Isle, it has never been settled and was little explored before the twentieth century. The cold arctic current that sweeps past its coast means that the prevailing climate is chilly, and the landscape is usually snowbound except for the summer months. The south of the territory is thickly forested, mostly with black spruce; the ground cover of the north consists mostly of mosses and lichens. A varied wildlife is supported, including bear, beaver, muskrat, lynx, wolverine, red squirrel, and caribou among the animals, and ptarmigan, geese, grouse, and partridge among the birds. Fur trapping is Labrador's oldest human pursuit, but by far the most important nowadays is iron mining from the ore beds found between the headwaters of the Hamilton and Kaniapiskau Rivers, with Labrador City as the centre. Another centre of activity is Schefferville, just over the border in Québec province. A railway runs south through Labrador linking it to the St. Lawrence at Sept Îles. Copper and nickel are also mined, and prospecting for other minerals continues. Labrador's main settlements are Battle Harbour, the capital, Labrador City, Nain, and Goose Bay.

Northwest Territories

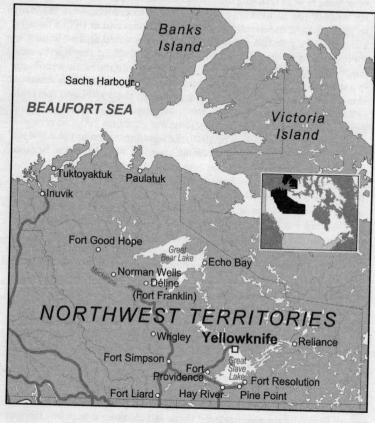

A vast semi-autonomous region lying north of the 60th parallel, east of the Yukon and bordering the Prairie Provinces to the south.

Emblem: the mountain avens.

Population (2002): 41,400. The population is very small and scattered in a number of mining communities.

Capital: Yellowknife. With a population of just under 18,000, it is said to be Canada's fastest-growing city. It provides administration, medical, and college facilities as well as being the region's main market centre.

Physical description: with a land area of 1,346,106 square kilometres (519,597 square miles), it is third in size among the territories and provinces. Lakes cover more than 10% of the surface. The western area is mountainous, with the Mackenzie Mountains rising to meet the Selwyn and Cassiar ranges. The highest point is Unnamed Peak (2,773 metres, 9,098 feet). The land falls away eastwards towards the long valley of the Mackenzie River, Canada's longest, which flows from the Great Slave Lake to the Arctic Ocean. East of the Mackenzie, a bare and rocky landscape reaches to the shore of Hudson Bay. To the north there is subarctic tundra. Beyond the north coast is the Arctic Archipelago, composed of many islands, some of them of great size, merging into the frozen sea towards the North Pole.

Climate: its far northern situation and proximity to the polar icecap ensure long, dark winters with deep snow and very low temperatures. During its brief summer, temperatures can rise as high as 27°C (80°F) around the Great Slave Lake.

Agriculture: virtually all of the foodstuffs consumed by the population are imported from elsewhere, as the soil and climate are not conducive to farming. There are extensive stands of forest in the Mackenzie Plains. Fur trapping remains an important activity.

Minerals: the region is rich in minerals. Gold, silver, uranium, copper, and nickel have all been identified in significant quantities. In addition there are oil and natural gas deposits. Canada's first diamond deposits have also been found here.

Industry: the only industries are those associated with the extraction and primary processing of metals and other mineral reserves.

Transport: the territory is very much dependent on air transport and every community has its airstrip. Hay River, on the south shore of the Great Slave Lake, is the terminus of a rail link to the national system, and there are road connections to other towns in the same region. Lack of suitable transport is a serious problem for the mining industries.

Wildlife: muskrats, foxes, beavers, lynxes, wolves, and martens live in the woods and marshes. Migratory birds, including vast numbers of wild geese and duck, flock to the Arctic coast springtime nesting sites

History: from 1670 the southern part of the region was part of what was known as Rupert's Land, and was administered by the Hudson's Bay Company. The northern part was under nominal British suzerainty. In 1870 both parts were integrated into the Dominion of Canada. The formation of the Prairie Provinces and northern extensions of Ontario and Québec reduced the size of Northwest Territories somewhat. The greatest reduction came with the formation of the separate territory of Nunavut in 1999, though even in its reduced form Northwest Territories is far bigger than many nation states.

Nova Scotia

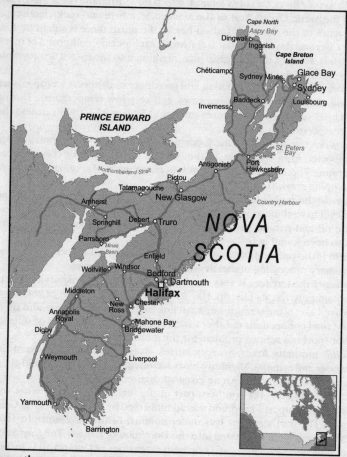

Name: the name means 'New Scotland'. Nova Scotia is one of the smallest but longest-established provinces. Nova Scotians have a keen sense of their own identity. Cape Breton Island, in particular, maintains the tradition of Gaelic speech and has many links with Celtic Scotland and Ireland. It is one of Canada's so-called Maritime Provinces.

Emblems: the red spruce, the mayflower, the osprey.

Motto: *Munit haec et altera vincit*, 'This defends, the other conquers'.

Population (2002): 944,800.

Capital: Halifax, with some 340,000 people in its metropolitan area, is the largest town and main port as well as the provincial capital. Its large and ice-free harbour is a major container port as well as Canada's prime Atlantic naval base. Founded in 1749, it is also one of Canada's oldest cities.

Physical description: with a land area of 55,284 square kilometres (21,340 square miles), Nova Scotia is twelfth in size among the provinces and territories. The province consists of the peninsula of Nova Scotia, joined to the continent by a narrow neck of land, and Cape Breton Island to the north, which is linked to Nova Scotia by a causeway across the Strait of Canso. Many small islands, mostly uninhabited, surround the coasts. The terrain is similar to that of New Brunswick, across the Bay of Fundy: hilly, wooded country with many valleys, the highest point being 532 metres (1,745 feet) above sea level. The watershed runs along the spinal ridge, with short, swift rivers reaching the sea on both sides. Cape Breton Island has a lower-lying area round the large Bras d'Or saltwater lake, but rises in the north to the Cape Breton Highlands. The Bay of Fundy has the world's largest tides, with a difference of 15 metres (45 feet) between high and low water at the head of the bay.

Climate: summers are pleasant, but winters are severe with heavy snowfalls, though without the extreme temperature lows found in the Prairie Provinces. Generally the influence of the sea makes for a milder, if wetter and windier, climatic regime.

Agriculture: the main agricultural area lies in and around the Annapolis Valley on the Fundy coast, where there is good soil and the mountain ridge provides shelter from northeasterly cold winds. There are many apple orchards. Mixed farming is the staple of the province and there is extensive breeding of stock and poultry. Although remote from the main centres of Canadian population, Nova Scotia has access to the New England region of the U.S.A. As elsewhere in Canada, forestry is of great importance, and the slopes of the province's low mountain ranges are clothed in spruce, fir, birch, maple, and pine. Fishing was an important industry for many coastal communities but, with dwindled stocks, its significance has receded in recent years. Fish farming has to a degree replaced sea fishing.

Minerals: coal is the main mineral resource, with mining districts around Sydney in Cape Breton Island and Pictou in northern Nova Scotia. Nova Scotia is an important source of gypsum, and rock salt is also produced.

Industry: steelworks at Sydney and New Glasgow use local coal and Newfoundland iron ore. Some lumber is exported but the province also has lumber mills.

History: originally populated by Indian tribes, the region's first European settlers were from France in 1604. They called the land Acadia. Possession was contested by the British. King James I granted the territory to the Scottish entrepreneur, Sir William Alexander, in 1621, under the name Nova Scotia. A large French element remained and the colony remained in dispute until 1713, when the Treaty of Utrecht confirmed British possession. In 1755 many French residents were expelled. After the American War of Independence, many American colonists who remained loyal to Britain sailed or travelled to set up new lives in Nova Scotia. The 'Highland Clearances' in Scotland during the late eighteenth and early nineteenth centuries resulted in the arrival of many Gaelic-speaking colonists who settled around Pictou and in Cape Breton Island – areas that still retain a Gaelic tradition. The province was the first to be established as self-governing from 1848. It also had Canada's first university, printing-press and newspaper. In 1867 it was one of the founding provinces of the new Dominion of Canada.

Nunavut

Name: the name means 'our land' in the Inuktitut language.

Emblems: the purple saxifrage, the rock ptarmigan.

Motto: *Nunavut Sanginivut*, 'Nunavut our strength'.

Population (2002): 28,700. About 85% of the people are Inuit, and 56% of the population is under 25.

Capital: Iqaluit. Formerly Frobisher Bay, on Baffin Island, Iqaluit has a population of 3,600. It is also a trading and educational centre, and home to the Arctic College, whose courses focus on Nunavut's cultures and environment.

Physical description: with a land area of 2,093,190 square kilometres (807,971 square miles), Nunavut is by far the largest of the territories and provinces, occupying almost a quarter of the entire country. The highest point is Barbeau Peak on Ellesmere Island (2,626 metres, 8,615 feet). Most of the landscape is bare and bleak, and covered in snow all or most of the year, but its austere beauty attracts more visitors each year.

Climate: the brief summers can be warm, but the territory lies mostly north of the Arctic Circle, and long, dark, very cold winters are the dominant aspect of the climate.

Minerals: the bleak landscape contains a variety of mineral deposits, with more still being prospected. The Polaris lead-zinc mine on Little Cornwallis Island is the most northerly mine in the world, producing 1,000,000 tonnes of refinable ores annually.

Economy and industry: though extreme climatic conditions mean that mining is expensive, and only high grade and valuable ores are exploited, minerals are one of the three main bases of the economy. The others are fur trading and tourism. Government salaries and subsidies are a further support.

History: human occupancy of the subarctic region goes back for many thousands of years. Under British rule it became part of the Northwest Territories. Its modern development began in 1965 when the Canadian government first unveiled plans to reorganize the administration of the arctic territories. Years of discussion and campaigning by the Inuit people followed. A plebiscite held in the Northwest Territories in 1982 resulted in a 90% majority vote among the Inuit for a separate eastern division. Another decade of wrangling ensued over the border between the Northwest Territories and Nunavut until a new plebiscite in 1992 brought agreement. In June 1993 the Canadian government passed the Nunavut Act, and in 1999 the territory and government of Nunavut finally came into being.

Ontario

Name: the province's name has been traced to the Iroquois for 'beautiful lake', and also to Seneca's *entohonorous*, 'the people'.

Emblems: the white trillium flower, the eastern white pine, the common loon.

Motto: *Ut incepit fidelis, sic permanet*, 'Loyal it began, loyal it remains'.

Population (2002): 12,068,300. More than a third of the country's population live in Ontario, making it Canada's most populous province.

Capital: Toronto, Canada's largest city, has 2.8 million inhabitants, and around 4 million in the metropolitan region. Toronto is the fifth largest municipal government region in North America. It is the main industrial and economic centre of Ontario and of all Canada. Ethnically it is highly diverse, with over 100 different ethnic and language groups represented. Over 50% of its citizens were born outside Canada. The name comes from an Indian word for 'meeting place', and it was an Indian centre before the first European settlement was made by the French in 1750. Under British control it was named York until its present name was given in 1834, when it became a city. Today, metropolitan Toronto covers 632 square kilometres (244 square miles). It was the first Canadian city to construct a subway, and its CN tower, at 533 metres (1,750 feet), is among the world's tallest buildings. Among other 'firsts', it claims the world's largest underground pedestrian area. Some 90% of foreign banks in Canada are established here, and electronics and telecommunications are important aspects of a very diverse industrial base. Toronto is also a major publishing and media centre, and is the largest centre of English-language theatre after London and New York.

Physical description: with a land area of 1,076,395 square kilometres (415,488 square miles), it is fourth largest among the provinces and territories. To the south, Ontario's shape is defined by the line of the Upper St. Lawrence River and the north coasts of Lakes Superior, Huron, and Ontario. The part of the province south of the Ottawa River, once a vast forested zone, is now a region of fertile rolling farmlands. To the north, the landscape is an enormous plateau region, scraped by ice sheets, and often lacking soil and vegetation. On glacial soils there are forests, but much of the ground is heath or bare rock, interspersed with a multitude of lakes. The highest point of land is Ishpatina Ridge (693 metres, 2,273 feet). In the north the rivers drain into Hudson Bay, in the west to Lake Winnipeg, in the south to the Great Lakes and the St. Lawrence.

Climate: the climate is essentially a continental one, of cold winters and hot summers, but in the south it is modified by the presence of the Great Lakes, making winters and summers a little moister and milder. Nevertheless it can become cold enough to freeze up Niagara Falls. In the scantily populated north, there is again a marine influence on the climate.

Agriculture: climate, fertile soil, and a densely packed population have influenced the development of mixed farming in the southern part of the province. In the Lake Peninsula between Toronto and Niagara, vines, tobacco and peaches can be grown. In the north, farming is much more localized, depending on the soil and the proximity of a market. Lumbering is much more important, with spruce and poplar grown for packaging and newsprint.

Minerals: north of Georgian Bay there is a region of rich mineral deposits, including uranium, nickel, and copper. The Creighton nickel-copper mine near Sudbury is the deepest in Canada at 2,200 metres (7,218 feet). Other minerals mined in Ontario include iron, platinum, gold, and zinc.

Trade and industry: Ontario is the most highly industrialized of the provinces. Employment is divided 64% to services, 34% to industry, and 2% to agriculture. Oil from the Alberta field comes across Canada by pipeline to be refined at Sarnia. A variety of manufacturing industry is located in the cities of Toronto, Hamilton, London, and smaller centres. Mineral processing is a major industry at Sudbury. Transport, trading, banking, and media are all important.

History: the region had been Indian territory since prehistoric times when the first European exploring party, under Samuel de Champlain, reached

Lake Huron in 1615. French trading posts and mission stations were established along the shores of the Great Lakes, but the inland regions remained Indian territory. The British took possession in 1763. At that time it was all part of Québec, or New France. Between 1783 and 1791 many British Loyalists removed from the U.S.A. to set up home in British North America; and in 1791 the eastern and western areas of Québec were separated politically and known as Lower and Upper Canada respectively. Upper Canada's first capital, at Niagara, was uncomfortably close to the U.S.A., and York (later renamed Toronto) replaced it. In 1812 invading American forces destroyed the town. The Act of Union of 1840 once again brought Upper and Lower Canada together in a single province. However, with the establishment of the Confederation in 1870, Upper Canada became the province of Ontario. By this time it was already well populated in the southern part and, with the development of railways and the discovery of mineral reserves, it quickly became Canada's most industrialized province.

Prince Edward Island (P.E.I.)

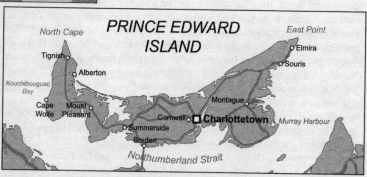

Name: the name was given in 1798, in honour of the Duke of Kent, father of Queen Victoria. This is Canada's smallest province, both in size and population, and is one of the four Maritime Provinces.

Emblems: lady's slipper flower, northern red oak, the blue jay.

Motto: *Parva sub ingenti*, 'The small protected by the great'.

Population (2002): 139,900. P.E.I. is the most densely populated province of the Confederation, with almost 25 persons to the square kilometre, compared to a national average of 3.

Capital: Charlottetown. With a population of 33,000, Charlottetown is the island's only urban centre. It has the highest average snowfall of the provincial capitals, with 338.7 centimetres (133 inches) a year.

Physical description: with a land area of 5,660 square kilometres (2,185 square miles), P.E.I. is the smallest of the provinces and territories, occupying 0.1% of Canada's total area. Lying in the south of the Gulf of St. Lawrence, it is separated from New Brunswick by the Northumberland Strait, some 30 kilometres (18 miles) wide. Much indented by the sea, it is almost divided in two at Hillsborough Bay. The island terrain is relatively low, nowhere rising over 150 metres (450 feet) and is intensively farmed, with most of the original forest cover long vanished.

Climate: the climate is much the same as Nova Scotia, with pleasant summers but heavy snowfalls in winter. The influence of the sea makes for a milder, if wetter and windier, climate.

Agriculture: a well-developed pattern of farmland covers most of the island. The red soil is fertile and produces crops of potatoes, wheat, and barley. Stock rearing is important, both for beef and dairy farming, and there are many pasture fields. Pigs and poultry are also farmed. On the coast, shellfish rearing is important, notably lobsters.

Industry: industry revolves around the needs and products of the farms. Food processing, freezing, and canning are important. There is also a substantial tourist industry, with coastal fishing and first-rate golf links among the attractions.

Transport: the Confederation Bridge, 12.9 kilometres (8 miles) long, joins the island to the mainland, between Borden and Carleton. Opened in 1997, this is the world's longest bridge over seasonally icebound waters. There is a good road network, and a railway links Charlottetown with Tignish in the north. Train ferries between Tormentine and Borden provide a connection with the mainland network. Car ferries also operate on this route and from Pictou in Nova Scotia. Icebreakers make it a year-round service. The main airport is at Charlottetown.

History: originally occupied by Indians of the Micmac and other tribes (who still occupy a reservation on the island) and called by them *Abegweit*, 'Home cradled in the waves', the island was identified by Jacques Cartier in 1534. Samuel de Champlain gave it the name Île de St. Jean. During the French-British war over possession of eastern Canada, the British landed in 1758 and drove out some of the French residents. It was confirmed as a British possession in 1763, and given colony status in 1769. Charlottetown was the venue of the inter-provincial conference of 1864 which led to the formation of the Dominion of Canada in 1867, but Prince Edward Island was not one of the founding provinces. It joined the federation soon after, in 1873.

Tradition: the island was the home of L. M. Montgomery, author of the *Anne of Green Gables* stories enjoyed by generations of children. Her house is now a museum.

Québec

Name: Québec is Canada's second largest province, three times the size of
  France. The name is from *kebek*, the Iroquois for 'narrowing of the waters', describing the St. Lawrence at Québec City.

Emblems: the Madonna lily, the snowy owl.

Motto: *Je me souviens*, 'I remember'.

Population (2002): 7,455,200.

Capital: Québec City. Canada's oldest city, Québec City has a population of
  180,000. Winding, narrow streets link its Upper and Lower Towns. There
  are many historic sites, including the Ursuline Convent (1639) and the

Basilica Notre Dame (1647) as well as the fortress. Its industries include shipbuilding and repair, wood pulp, textiles, food, and drinks.

Physical description: with a land area of 1,542,056 square kilometres (595,233 square miles), it is exceeded in size only by the vast area of Nunavut. Bounded on the east by Labrador, on the south by New Brunswick and the U.S. state of New York, and on the west by Ontario and Hudson Bay, the vast spread of Québec province reaches from the St. Lawrence to the Arctic. North of the St. Lawrence lie the rocky uplands of forest and wilderness known as the Canadian Shield, an ancient landscape formed by ice sheets and pocked with innumerable lakes. Its southern boundary is the Laurentian Mountains, a range stretching 1,600 kilometres (1,000 miles) and rising to heights of around 900 metres (2,700 feet) north of Québec City. The highest point in the province is Mt. D'Ilberville (1,652 metres, 5,124 feet). The St. Lawrence valley forms a wide lowland region between Montréal and Québec, and to the south the land rises into forested hills bordering on the U.S. states of Vermont and Maine. Rivers flow to all points of the compass, but the main systems are those of the Ottawa River in the west, the Saguenay in the east and the Caniapiscau in the north.

Climate: the southern part of the province has warm summers and cold, snowy winters. Autumn, though brief, is brilliant with the red and gold foliage of the maple and other deciduous trees. To the north the climate is increasingly subarctic.

Agriculture: the St. Lawrence lowlands are intensively farmed. Meat and dairy products, eggs and poultry, and market gardening reflect the needs of a substantial urban population. South of the St. Lawrence, farmland and deciduous forest share the valleys and hill slopes. In the north there are huge forest areas, chiefly of softwood trees. Québec supplies almost half the softwood used in Canada's vast lumber industry.

Minerals: iron ore is extracted at Schefferville, close to the Labrador border, and to the west of Ungava Bay in the far north of the province. In the south there are large deposits of the minerals that produce asbestos and have given the town of Asbestos its name. Gold, silver, and copper deposits are also worked. Québec has Canada's only titanium mine. There are mining centres at Abitibi, Temiscamingue, North Shore, Eastern Townships, and on the Gaspé peninsula.

Trade and industry: unlimited water power provides the province with cheap electricity and this is utilized in many forms of industry, including aluminium smelting, using imported bauxite, and other forms of metal processing. Automobiles, chemicals, textiles, and electronics also form part of a diverse industrial base. Apart from wood pulp and paper, many other timber products and by-products are manufactured and packaged. Employment in Québec is divided 68% to services, 29% to industry, and 3% to agriculture.

Political life: politics in Québec are quite different to those of any other province and impact heavily on federal politics. The reason for this lies in the fact that the great majority of the Québecois, over 6 million people, are of French descent and remain French-speaking, and in many ways form part of the French cultural universe. Although Canada is a secular state, with an increasingly secular outlook, the fact that the Québec population adheres overwhelmingly to the Roman Catholic Church serves to increase the sense of cultural difference. A separatist movement has become increasingly vocal and influential during the latter part of the twentieth century. Two provincial referendums on the issue have been held, in 1980 and 1995, and though both resulted in a vote in favour of continued union with the other provinces, the latter produced a majority of only 1%, and the issue of separatism remains very much an open one.

History: on his second voyage, in 1535, the French explorer Jacques Cartier sailed up the St. Lawrence and claimed the land he found on behalf of King François I of France. It was inhabited by numerous large Indian tribes, including Iroquois and Huron. The first French settlement was established by Samuel de Champlain in 1608 at Québec, head of navigation for seagoing ships, where he built a fort. The colony was known as La Nouvelle France, and run from 1627 by a monopoly business, the 'Company of One Hundred' (also known as the 'Company of New France'). But it attracted few settlers and there was little activity. From 1663 it was established as a royal province ruled by a Governor General, with an intendant as his head of administration.

Steady population growth now began, with towns forming round the forts at Québec, Montréal and Trois Rivières. As explorers pushed out further west, the area of the colony enlarged, but the bulk of the population was in the St. Lawrence Lowlands; by the middle of the eighteenth century it numbered around 65,000 people. Farming was the main occupation, though furs remained the chief source of wealth. Land was apportioned to a *seigneur*, who allocated it to tenants (the *habitants*) in long rectangular lots. From the earliest stage, however, the French domain was challenged by the English, who had settled in New England, and whose search for the Northwest Passage had introduced them to the northern wilderness. They used the voyages of John Cabot, Martin Frobisher, Henry Hudson, and others to claim possession of the regions north and west of New France. In 1629 they captured Québec City and held it for three years.

The original inhabitants, well organized in the Iroquois League, were alternately courted and attacked by the contending colonial powers. Caught in the middle, the Iroquois attempted to play off both sets of Europeans but their power was ultimately broken by the French. As a Catholic state, France included a missionary element in its colonial activity, and New France's first bishop arrived in 1659. By then, monks and nuns had already established convents and hospitals. Among the French governors were some very able men, but a fatal error was made in 1668 when two French explorers, Radisson and Des Groseilliers, failing to get backing from France, but receiving it in England, opened up the Hudson Bay fur trade for the new English Hudson's Bay Company.

From 1672, under one of its most energetic governors, the Comte de Frontenac, the colony's area and activities expanded, but from the late seventeenth and into the eighteenth centuries, as a result of warfare in Europe, decline began. Following the loss of Nova Scotia and Newfoundland in 1713, a great fort was begun in 1717 at Louisbourg, to guard access to the St. Lawrence. A fort-building race characterized the next thirty years, but, neglected by the French government, and with access to France made difficult by naval warfare, the colony was increasingly open to attack. Though at this time French explorers and settlers, such as the La Vérendrye family, were still establishing themselves in the west, the western forts, in the plains and on the Great Lakes, fell one by one to the British. The culmination came in the warfare that took place between 1754 and 1760; in 1759 the British captured the Québec fortress and in the following year the Governor General, the Marquis de Vaudreuil, was forced to surrender. In the Treaty of Paris, 1763, British possession of the French colony was confirmed.

Although large numbers of English-speaking settlers came to the province after 1760, Québec (characterized in 1791 as Lower Canada) has retained its French-speaking population, its language, religion, and traditions, at first under British rule and later as part of federal Canada. In the American invasions of 1775 and 1812, the Québecois fought with the other Canadian provincials for the defence of the British colony (though they had no cause to love the New Englanders). In 1841 the province was granted a degree of self-government and in 1849 the French language was given legal recognition. In 1867 Lower Canada was one of the founding provinces of the Confederation, and received the name of Québec province.

In the twentieth century the province shared in the economic growth of Canada, and the gradual shedding of colonial British links was welcomed. But Québec continued to be different, as shown by the resistance to conscription at the start of both world wars. Socially a conservative province, it was the last in Canada to give women the vote. In the 1960s the issue of separation became a dominant one and has remained so. Although the 'Quiet Revolution' initiated by the Liberal government of 1960 brought about progressive changes in federal attitudes to the province's unique status, it also saw the rise of political violence from the *Front pour la Libération de Québec* (FLQ), with bombs in Montréal in 1960, and the kidnap and murder of British diplomat James Cross and Québec government minister Pierre Laporte in 1970. In that year martial law was imposed for a time, and over 500 persons were arrested. In 1973 the *Parti Québecois* (PQ) emerged as a separatist party pledged to peaceful methods, and in 1976, under René Levesque, it won control of the provincial government. On a state visit that year, the French President, Charles de Gaulle, infuriated the Canadian government by expressing support for 'free Québec'. Many English speakers left the province in the wake of Bill 101, designed to preserve the supremacy of the French language in the province. A referendum in 1980 rejected independence for the province. Both federal and provincial governments have been preoccupied with the question of how to reconcile the Québecois desire for independence with the province's remaining part of Canada. The 'Meech Lake Accord' promoted by federal Premier Mulroney in 1987 fell in 1990 against opposition from other provinces, resulting in the formation of the *Bloc Québecois* by Québec politicians. A referendum on independence in 1995 rejected it by a majority of only 1%, resulting in controversy as some politicians accused immigrant voters of sabotaging the aspirations of the French-speaking Québecois. Discussions on the constitutional issue continue.

Montréal: though not the capital, this is by far Québec's largest city, the second largest in Canada, and the world's largest French-speaking city after Paris. The population is 2,800,000. Montréal is a major industrial, commercial and media centre, and an important port. Although it has always been an important city, its population doubled between 1941 and 1971. In 1976 it was the site of the Olympic Games. There are many modern buildings, and an underground pedestrian zone of 29 kilometres (18 miles). The city's four-line *Métro* runs on rubber tires. Montréal is ethnically diverse, with an Italian population of some 200,000 as the largest language group after French and English.

Saskatchewan

Name: the name comes from an Indian word, *kisikatchewin*, 'swift river'. It is one of the three Prairie Provinces.

Emblem: the prairie lily.

Motto: *Multis e gentibus vires*, 'Strength from many peoples'.

Population (2002): 1,011,800.

Capital: Regina, with a population of 187,500. The name was given in honour of Queen Victoria. Given city status in 1903, Regina is Canada's sunniest and driest capital city, with an average annual precipitation of 364 millimetres (14 inches), and 109 wet days a year. With potash mines and sodium sulphate extraction close by, the city has an industrial base as well as being an administrative and market centre. Steel, chemicals, and telecommunications are other important industries.

Physical description: with a land area of 651,036 square kilometres (251,300 square miles), it is seventh in size among the provinces and territories. The south of the province is prairie country, with wide level plains and gently rolling uplands. The Saskatchewan River, with its north and south branches, flows westward in deeply incised valleys. Farther north is 'parkland' country with groves of aspen and poplar trees. The north of the province is more rugged, with rocky and marshy terrain, and many lakes and rivers. The highest point is at Cypress Hills (1,468 metres, 4,816 feet).

The largest lake is Lake Athabasca (7,935 square kilometres, 3,063 square miles).

Climate: remote from the sea, the province has a continental climate, with hot summers and cold winters. Snow may lie on the ground for up to four months of the year.

Agriculture: more than 16,000,000 hectares (40 million acres) of arable land are under cultivation, and Saskatchewan produces about two thirds of Canada's wheat crop. Wheat is sown in spring, and grows and ripens rapidly during the hot summer months. Other crops include oats, barley, rye, rape, and flax. Mixed farming is practiced in the parkland regions, with beef and dairy cattle. Pigs and poultry are also farmed in large numbers.

Minerals: the southern part of the province has reserves of lignite (brown coal), oil, and natural gas. In the north there is extensive exploitation of metallic ores, notably around Uranium City, northeast of Lake Athabasca. Copper, zinc, gold, silver, and cadmium are also mined in addition to uranium. Canada is the world's main potash producer, and the province produces about 90% of the country's supply.

Industry: Saskatchewan is a primary producer region rather than a manufacturing one. Most industry is concerned with the preparation and packing of agricultural products, lumber, and metal processing.

History: once Plains Indian territory and very thinly populated (as much of it still is), this area formed part of the Hudson's Bay grant of 1670. The first white man to explore it was Henry Kelsey, a Hudson's Bay employee, during 1691 and 1692. French and British traders set up trading stations. During the nineteenth century it was thought unlikely that the vast plains could be used for anything other than grazing, with organized ranching replacing the huge herds of buffaloes. The arrival of the railroad, linking Regina with the east by 1882, increased the rate of settlement and also provided a means of bulk transport for farm produce. The development of new cereal strains such as quick-ripening wheat, and the mechanization of agriculture, followed. The old way of life made a last stand with the rising in 1885 of Indian and Métis nomadic peoples against the new order of things. Troops quelled the rising and its leader, Riel, was captured and hanged at Regina. From 1896 the pace of settlement increased further, with the population quadrupling in the first decade of the twentieth century, from around 100,000 to over 400,000. Many of the immigrants were from central and eastern Europe. In 1905 Saskatchewan province was formed and became part of the Confederation.

Yukon Territory

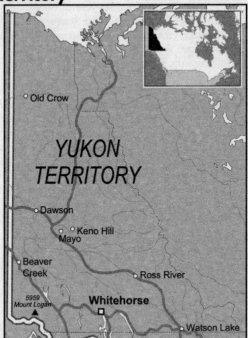

Name: consisting of the semi-autonomous far northwest of Canada, the Yukon Territory's name is taken from an Indian word, *yukoo*, 'clear water'.

Emblems: fireweed, the sub-alpine fir, the raven, and the gemstone, lazulite.

Population (2002): 29,900.

Capital: the capital, Whitehorse, is situated on the west bank of the Yukon River, and is the only city in the territory. It has a population of 23,000, and its main activities are administration, social and medical services, tourism, and mining support industries.

Physical description: with a land area of 482,443 square kilometres (186,223 square miles), it is ninth in size among the provinces and territories. The Yukon is a mountainous region, where the Western Cordillera spreads into the Selwyn and Ogilvie ranges. Here can be found Canada's highest point, Mt. Logan (5,959 metres, 19,550 feet). The main rivers drain eastwards into the Mackenzie system, apart from the Yukon River itself, which rises in the south of the territory and flows westwards through Alaska.

Climate: most of the territory is south of the Arctic Circle, but winters are long, dark, cold, and severe. Spring and summer are short seasons.

Minerals: gold, zinc, lead, and silver ores are mined, with a value to the territory of $97,000,000 in 2001. Of this, 92% was contributed by gold. There are also petroleum wells, while sands and gravels are excavated in vast quantities. In 1997, emeralds were discovered.

Transport: a railroad links Whitehorse with Skagway in Alaska, and the Fairbanks–Edmonton highway also passes through Whitehorse. The only other permanent routes are by river. Dirt roads extend into the country from various mining sites. Air transport is the main lifeline of the remote communities.

History: unexplored and uninhabited except by migratory Indians and wandering fur trappers until the nineteenth century, the name of the Yukon became synonymous with panning for gold in the mid-1890s. Fortune hunters flocked there and a new town, Dawson City, grew almost overnight to a population of 30,000. By 1899, when the surface gold was exhausted, the population had diminished with equal rapidity, though gold-mining by industrial methods continued at Dawson City until 1966. Dawson was superseded by Whitehorse as the capital in 1953.

A Chronology of Events in Canadian History

(BCE is an abbreviation for 'Before Christian or Common Era' – the years BC.)

*c.*12,000 BCE: incomers from Siberia leave traces in the Blue Fish Caves, Yukon.

*c.*9000 BCE: native peoples leave traces of habitation on the Eramosa River, near Guelph, Ontario.

*c.*4000 BCE: Eskimo and Aleut form separate groups in the Arctic.

*c.*500 CE: the bow and arrow are introduced among the Plains Indians.

*c.*1000: Leif Ericsson explores the coast of Labrador and Newfoundland. A Viking colony is established at L'Anse aux Meadows.

1450: around this time the Great League of Peace and Power is formed among the Five Nations of the Iroquois.

1492: Columbus sails to America.

1497: John Cabot explores the coast of Cape Breton Island, Newfoundland, and Labrador.

1498: Cabot is lost at sea, returning from his second visit.

1500: Gaspar de Corte-Real heads a Portuguese expedition to Newfoundland; he calls the latter, *Terra Verde*.

1504: first records of French fishers off Newfoundland.

1521: J. Alvares Fagundes establishes the first European (Portuguese) colony in North America on Cape Breton Island. It fails around 1526.

1527: John Rut is sent by King Henry VIII of England to find the Northwest Passage but he turns back at Hawke Bay, Labrador.

1534: King Francis I of France dispatches an expedition under Jacques Cartier. Cartier explores the coast of Newfoundland, Labrador, and the Gulf of St. Lawrence, encountering the Micmac and Huron peoples, and claims the land for France on 24 July.

1535: on his second voyage, Cartier sails up the St. Lawrence River to the Huron communities of Hochelega and Stadaconé, on the sites of present-day Montréal and Québec City.

1541: Cartier returns to North America and establishes the colony of Charlesbourg-Royal, the first French settlement in North America.

1542: the Sieur de Roberval arrives as the first lieutenant general of the new territories.

1576: the Company of Cathay is founded to exploit gold deposits on Kodlunan Island that turn out to be pyrites (false gold).

1577: Queen Elizabeth I of England commissions Martin Frobisher to seek the legendary Northwest Passage to Asia. He fails, but reaches the Hudson Strait.

1583: Sir Humphrey Gilbert explores the coast of Newfoundland.

1585: John Davis makes the first of three unsuccessful voyages to find the Northwest Passage to Asia.

1592: Juan de Luca lands on the coast of British Columbia.

1598: La Roche's colony is established on Sable Island.

1600: King Henry IV of France awards a fur trading monopoly to a group of French merchants.

1603: Samuel de Champlain makes his first voyage to Canada.

1605: Port Royal is established in Nova Scotia by the French under Champlain.

1606: Marc Lescarbot's masque *Le Théatre de Neptune en Nouvelle France* is performed at Port Royal.

1608: Champlain sails up the St. Lawrence and lays claim to Québec for France. Québec City founded.

1609: Champlain travels with the Algonquins to Lake Champlain. The French and Algonquins fight the Iroquois.

1610: Etienne Brulé becomes the first European to see Lakes Ontario, Huron, and Superior. Henry Hudson, seeking the Northwest Passage, explores Hudson Bay and is cast adrift by his mutinous crew.

1611: Etienne Brulé reaches Lake Nipissing.

1612: Samuel de Champlain is named as Governor of New France.

1613: Argall attacks St. Sauveur in Acadia. St. John's, Newfoundland, is founded.

1617: Louis Hébert, the first *habitant* (farmer), arrives in Québec; his wife, Marie, is Québec's first teacher.

1621: Sir William Alexander is awarded Nova Scotia by King James I of England.

1623: the founding of Avalon, Newfoundland.

1625: the Order of the Baronets of Nova Scotia founded. Jesuits arrive in Québec to begin missionary work among the Indians.

1627: the Company of One Hundred (also known as the Company of New France) is founded (29 April) by Cardinal Richelieu to exploit the resources of North America for France.

1629: David Kirke captures Québec for England (19 July).

1631: Thomas James sails into Hudson Bay and discovers James Bay. Searches for the Northwest Passage continue.

1632: The Treaty of Saint Germain en Laye returns Québec to France.

1634: the foundation of Giffard and Three Rivers.

1635: the founding of the Jesuit College at Québec.

1635:   Samuel de Champlain dies.

1637:   David Kirke is named as the first governor of Newfoundland.

1638:   Placentia, Newfoundland is founded.

1639:   one of numerous outbreaks of smallpox ravages the eastern Indian tribes. The Huron nation is reduced by half during the 1630s. Jesuits found Ste. Marie among the Huron. An Ursuline convent is set up in Québec.

1640:   discovery of Lake Erie.

1642:   Montréal is founded by the Sieur de Maisonneuve.

1644:   the founding of the Hotel-Dieu in Montréal.

1648:   the First Council of New France is held.

1649:   the Jesuit Father Jean de Brébeuf is martyred by the Iroquois at St.-Ignace (16 March). The Iroquois disperse the Huron nation.

1651:   Jean de Lauzon is appointed Governor of New France.

1654:   Robert Sedgwick seizes Port Royal; holds Acadia until 1670.

1657:   Pierre d'Argenson becomes Governor of New France. The Sulpician religious order is established in Canada.

1658:   François de Laval is made Apostolic Vicar of New France. The first girls' school in Montréal is established.

1660:   Adam Dollard des Ormeaux makes his last stand against the Iroquois at Long Sault (May).

1661:   D'Avaugour becomes Governor of New France. Radisson and Des Groseilliers explore as far as Hudson Bay.

1662:   Thomas Temple is appointed Governor of Nova Scotia.

1663:   Québec is declared a royal province, ending the rule of the Company of New France. The Sovereign Council is founded. The Québec Seminary is established.

1665:   the Carignan-Salières regiment under the Marquis de Tracy is sent from France to Québec as reinforcements against the Iroquois. Jean Talon becomes Québec's first Intendant. Courcelle becomes Governor of New France. Dutch pirates raid the Newfoundland ports.

1666:   Fort Temple is founded as an English stronghold in the struggle to control Acadia/Nova Scotia.

1667:   the Treaty of Breda returns Acadia to France.

1668:   the founding of Fort Charles (Fort Rupert) on Hudson Bay by the English. French explorers Radisson and Des Groseilliers are employed by English merchants to explore the Hudson Bay area. The Bishop of Québec founds Canada's first art school.

1671:   the English establish Fort Albany on Hudson Bay.

1672:   Louis, Comte de Frontenac, becomes the governor of French possessions in North America. Albanel completes an overland trip to Hudson Bay. The Hudson's Bay Company is granted a charter by King James II of England, with trade monopoly and notional control over vast territories.

1673: the foundation of Cataraqui (Kingston), Moose Factory, and Fort Monsoni.

1675: the founding of Fort Severn. Radisson returns to French allegiance.

1678: Louis Hennepin is the first European to see Niagara Falls.

1682: La Barre becomes Governor of Québec. The Company of the North is formed.

1683: Radisson again joins the English, working for the Hudson's Bay Company.

1685: the Marquis de Denonville becomes Governor of Québec. 'Card money' from cut-up playing cards is used instead of coin in Québec: not finally ended until 1763.

1686: Moose Factory and Rupert are taken by the French. John Abraham explores the Churchill River.

1689: Frontenac begins his second term as governor, and breaks the power of the Iroquois. Abenaki Indians seize Pemaquid. Massacre of Lachine (5 August). Henry Kelsey explores the north of Canada for the Hudson's Bay Company; he is probably the first European to see the prairies.

1690: the English capture Port Royal. Phips begins his siege of Québec. D'Ilberville sails into Hudson Bay. Dorchester, New Brunswick, is founded.

1693: the English retake Fort Albany from the French.

1694: D'Ilberville seizes York.

1696: D'Ilberville campaigns against the English in Newfoundland

1697: Callières becomes the administrator of Canada. First settlement at Moncton, New Brunswick.

1701: the Grand Settlement achieves treaties of peace signed between the Iroquois Confederacy and the French and English.

1702: the War of the Spanish Succession spreads from Europe to Acadia and New England. Leake ravages French Newfoundland.

1703: the Marquis de Vaudreuil becomes Governor General of New France and Beauharnois becomes Intendant.

1704: new flood of card money in Canada.

1705: J. Raudot becomes Intendant of Canada.

1706: the opening of Montréal's public marketplace.

1708: St. John's is taken by the French.

1710: Francis Nicholson captures Port Royal for England.

1711: an attempted invasion of New France by the English fails. Walker's fleet is wrecked on the Île-aux-Oeufs.

1713: the Treaty of Utrecht ends a long period of French-British warfare, confirming British possession of the Hudson Bay region, Newfoundland, and Acadia, except Cape Breton Island.

1717: the French begin construction of Fort Louisbourg on the Île Royal (Cape Breton Island) to deter the English from invading the St. Lawrence.

1720: Fort Rouille founded on the site of Toronto. Coal is first dug at Cow Bay, Cape Breton Island.

1721: Scroggs searches for the Northwest Passage, while Richard Norton explores the north by land.

1726: Beauharnois becomes Governor of New France, and Begon becomes Intendant.

1729: reorganization of Newfoundland by the English.

1730s: the Mississauga drive the Seneca Iroquois south of Lake Erie. Around now, the Blackfoot acquire horses.

1731–43: the La Vérendrye family organize expeditions beyond Lake Winnipeg and direct fur trade toward the east. They are the first recorded Europeans to sight the Canadian Rockies from the east.

1731: Gilles Hocquart becomes Intendant of New France.

1734: Pierre de la Vérendrye sets up Fort Maurepas.

1736: the Beauce country is opened for settlement.

1737: the opening of the North Shore road from Québec to Montreal. Establishment of the Grey Sisters order in Canada.

1738: the opening of the St. Maurice Ironworks. Founding of Fort La Reine (Portage la Prairie) and Fort Rouge (Winnipeg).

1741: the founding of Fort Dauphin (Dauphin, Manitoba) and Pas Koyac (The Pas, Manitoba).

1744: war between England and France spreads to North America (King George's War). In Nova Scotia, Duvivier takes Canso but fails to capture Annapolis.

1745: Massachusetts Governor, William Shirley, captures the French fortress of Louisbourg.

1746: the collapse of the revenge expedition of D'Anville.

1747: the Comte de La Galissonière becomes Governor of New France.

1748: cessation of hostilities: Louisbourg and the Île Royale are returned to France by the Treaty of Aix-La-Chapelle. Bigot becomes Intendant of New France

1749: Britain founds Halifax to counter the French presence at Louisbourg. La Jonquière becomes Governor of New France.

1750: French and British embark on a new round of fortification, including Fort Beauséjour (French) and Fort Lawrence (British) on the Chignecto Isthmus.

1751: a French expedition reaches the eastern edge of the Rocky Mountains.

1752: the first Canadian newspaper, the weekly *Halifax Gazette*, appears (23 March). The Marquis de Duquesne becomes Governor of New France.

1753: the Nova Scotia Militia is proclaimed.

1754: the beginning of the French and Indian War in America. Fort Duquesne is constructed.

1755: Britain disperses the French Acadians throughout other North American colonies. General Braddock takes command of British forces in North America.

1756: the Marquis de Montcalm assumes command of French troops in North America. The French, with Indian support, capture Fort Oswego.

1757: Fort William Henry is taken by the French.

1758: General Abercromby becomes British Commander-in-Chief. Generals Jeffery Amherst and James Wolfe capture Louisbourg; Forbes captures Fort Duquesne, and Bradstreet takes Fort Frontenac. Montcalm is victorious at Carillon. Nova Scotia's depleted population doubles with new settlers and the province is first to establish a House of Assembly.

1759: the British, with Indian support, take Fort Carillon and Fort Niagara, cutting off western French territory. Wolfe defeats Montcalm and takes Québec (13 September) but both generals are killed. Brigadier James Murray is appointed Governor of Québec.

1760: Lévis's French force to relieve Québec defeats the British at Ste. Foy, but fails to advance further. Governor General Vaudreuil (son of the Vaudreuil of 1703) surrenders at Montréal to General Amherst (9 September). Canada remains under British military rule until 1764.

1763: the Treaty of Paris is made: France cedes its North American possessions to Britain. A royal proclamation imposes British institutions on Québec.

1764: Murray becomes civil Governor of Québec, but his attempts to appease French Canadians are opposed by British merchants.

1768: Guy Carleton succeeds Murray as civil Governor of Québec.

1772: the Hudson's Bay Company opens Cumberland House on the Saskatchewan.

1774: the Carleton recommendations are instituted in the Québec Act, imposing British criminal law but retaining French civil law and providing guarantees of religious freedom for Roman Catholics.

1775: the American Revolution begins. Americans under Richard Montgomery capture Montréal (13 November) and are defeated at Québec (31 December).

1776: the siege of Québec is lifted with the arrival of a British naval squadron (6 May).

1778: on the last of three voyages to the west coast, Captain James Cook reaches as far north as the Bering Strait and claims Nootka Sound, Vancouver Island for Great Britain (29 March–26 April).

1781: the Great Slave Lake is named from the Awonak or Slave people (so named by the Cree).

1783: in Montréal and Grand Portage (in present-day Minnesota), the North West Company is formed by a group of trading partners. With the end of the American revolutionary war, the border between Canada and the United States is accepted from the Atlantic Ocean to Lake of the Woods. Large numbers of United Empire Loyalists leave the U.S.A. to settle in Canada, mostly in the Maritime Provinces. Pennsylvania Germans begin moving into Upper and Lower Canada (modern-day southwestern Ontario, and southwestern Québec).

1784: Nova Scotia is partitioned and the province of New Brunswick is formed. Thousands of Loyalists settle on land in Upper and Lower Canada, along the St. Lawrence River, the Bay of Quinte, and at Niagara.

1785: the city of Saint John, New Brunswick, is incorporated. Fredericton opens a Provincial Academy of Arts and Sciences, later the University of New Brunswick.

1789: Alexander Mackenzie makes a journey to the Beaufort Sea, on behalf of the North West Company, and 'discovers' Canada's longest river, later named the Mackenzie River. King's College, Halifax, is founded.

1791: the Constitutional Act divides Québec into Upper and Lower Canada (present-day provinces of Ontario and Québec) and provides for representative government.

1792: Captain George Vancouver begins a detailed survey of the Pacific coastline.

1793: Alexander Mackenzie crosses the Rockies to reach the Pacific at Dean Channel.

1794: an American diplomat, John Jay, oversees the signing of Jay's Treaty (19 November) between the U.S. and Britain. It promises British evacuation of the Ohio Valley forts and marks the beginning of international arbitration to settle boundary disputes.

1795: Fort Edmonton is founded.

1796: the township of York (later Toronto) becomes the capital of Upper Canada.

1798: the New North West Company is formed to compete with the North West Company.

1804: the New North West Company is absorbed by the North West Company. The earliest Fraktur paintings appear in Lincoln County, Ontario.

1805: Mennonites from Pennsylvania settle in the Huron-Erie Peninsula.

1806: *Le Canadien*, a Québec nationalist newspaper, is founded.

1807: slavery is abolished in all British colonies.

1812: the British–American War begins. Americans under General William Hull invade Canada from Detroit (11 July). Canadians are victorious at the Battle of Queenstown Heights (13 October). Scots begin the Red River settlement on lands granted to Lord Selkirk by the Hudson's Bay Company.

1813: American forces burn York (27 April). The Battles of Stoney Creek (5 June) and Beaver Dam (23 June) are Canadian victories. Americans win at Put-in-Bay, Lake Erie (10 September) and Moraviantown (5 October). At the latter, Shawnee Indian Chief Tecumseh, a British ally, is killed. The Battles of Chateauguay (25 October), with mostly French Canadian troops, and Crysler's Farm (11 November), with English Canadian troops, are Canadian victories over larger American forces.

1814: victories alternate between U.S. and British forces until the Treaty of Ghent ends the war (24 December).

1816: after several years of harassment by agents of the North West Company, Métis and Indians under Cuthbert Grant kill Robert Semple, Governor of Assiniboia, the Red River settlement, and twenty others at Seven Oaks (19 June).

1817: the Rush-Bagot Agreement limits the number of warships on the Great Lakes to a total of eight.

1818: Canada's border with the U.S.A. is defined as the 49th parallel from Lake of the Woods to the Rocky Mountains.

1819: the first steamship to go up the Ottawa River docks at Hull.

1821: the Hudson's Bay and North West Companies amalgamate, resulting in unemployment for a substantial proportion of their Métis workforce.

1822: Louis-Joseph Papineau, a member of the legislative assembly since 1814, travels from Montréal to England to oppose an Act of Union identifying the French Canadians as a minority without language rights. The act is not passed in the British Parliament.

1824: the Lachine Canal is completed, bypassing rapids on the St. Lawrence.

1829: the first Welland Canal is completed.

1830: the first shaft is sunk for deep coal mining at Sydney, Nova Scotia.

1832: Royal Engineer, Col. John By, completes building of the Rideau Canal.

1834: York is renamed Toronto. William Lyon Mackenzie becomes the city's first mayor.

1835: Joseph Howe, a Halifax publisher and editor since 1828 of the weekly *Nova Scotian*, is arrested for libel but successfully argues his own case for freedom of the press.

1836: opening of Canada's first railway line, the Champlain & St. Lawrence, from St. Johns, Québec, to La Prairie, Québec, with a locomotive, *Dorchester*, imported from England.

1837: a constitutional crisis erupts; after increasing protests against undemocratic government, and the failure of the executive committee to maintain the confidence of the elected officials, armed rebellions break out in Upper and Lower Canada, and are put down by force. The leaders, W. L. Mackenzie (Reformers) and Louis-Joseph Papineau (Patriotes) escape to the U.S.A.

1838: Lord Durham, as Governor General and High Commissioner of British North America, is sent to investigate the circumstances behind the rebellions of 1837.

1839: Durham's report recommends the establishment of responsible (i.e. non-oligarchic) government and the union of Upper and Lower Canada to speed the assimilation of French-speaking Canadians. Border disputes between lumbermen from Maine and New Brunswick lead to armed conflict in the Aroostook River valley (the Aroostook War).

1840: an Act of Union unites Upper and Lower Canada (10 February) as the Province of Canada. The Cunard Steamship Line is founded at Halifax.

1841: the union of Upper and Lower Canada is put into effect.

1842: the Webster-Ashburton Treaty ends the Aroostook War, with an agreed line for the Maine–New Brunswick border.

1843: Britain builds Fort Victoria on Vancouver Island.

1844: an amnesty in Montréal provides for Papineau's return.

1846: the establishment of 'responsible government' in Canada. The Oregon Treaty affirms the entire Canadian–U.S. border west from the Great Lakes along the 49th parallel to the Pacific coast.

1848–51: the 'Great Ministry' of Robert Baldwin and Louis H. Lafontaine establishes the principles of responsible government. Between now and 1850 *Le Répertoire Nationale*, a collection of earlier stories and legends, is published in Montréal by James Huston.

1849: an Act of Amnesty provides for W. L. Mackenzie's return from exile in the U.S.

1850: the site of By's headquarters during the construction of the Rideau Canal is incorporated as Bytown. Canada's first metal mine, for copper ore, is started at Bruce Mines, on the north shore of Lake Huron.

1851: Britain transfers control of the colonial postal system to Canada.

1852: Laval's Séminaire du Québec founds Université Laval, North America's oldest French language university.

1852-53: the Grand Trunk Railway receives its charter.

1854: Canada and the U.S. sign a Reciprocity Treaty, ensuring reduction of customs duties (6 June).

1855: Bytown is renamed Ottawa. The Militia Act provides for a permanent volunteer force. *La Capricieuse*, on a courtesy visit, is the first vessel to fly the French flag in Québec harbour since 1760.

1856: the Grand Trunk Railway opens its Toronto–Montréal line.

1857: Queen Victoria designates Ottawa as capital of the Province of Canada. Seventy people die when a bridge over the Desjardins Canal collapses under a train.

1858: Vancouver Island and British Columbia are designated as Crown Colonies. The Halifax-Truro line begins its rail service. Chinese immigrants from California arrive in British Columbia, attracted by the Fraser River gold rush. The first producing oil well in North America is opened, in Lambton County in Ontario.

1859: the University of New Brunswick is constituted. Blondin makes his first tightrope walk over Niagara Falls.

1860: the foundation stone of the parliament buildings is laid (1 September). The *Mouvement Littéraire de Québec* of romantic-rhetorical writers is founded.

1861: the Canadian Pacific Railway is founded. Joseph Howe becomes Premier of Nova Scotia.

1862: Mount Allison University accepts the first woman student in Sackville, New Brunswick. The 'Cariboo Road' (644 kilometres, 400 miles) is built along the Fraser valley in British Columbia by Royal Engineers and private contractors (to 1865).

1864: the Charlottetown Conference (1-9 September), originally intended to discuss the union of the Maritime Provinces, opens the way towards Confederation. The subsequent Québec Conference (10-27 October) identifies 72 resolutions setting out the basis for union. Ninety-nine immigrant passengers are killed in a train smash near Montréal.

1866: the Fenian Brotherhood, a group of radical Irish-Americans, mostly U.S. Civil War veterans, begins a series of raids on Canadian territory in the hopes of diverting British troops from the homeland. The most serious of these is the Battle of Ridgeway (2 June). The London Conference (4 December) passes resolutions that form the basis of the British North America (BNA) Act.

1867: the Confederation of Canada takes place. Britain's North American colonies are united by means of the BNA Act to become the Dominion of Canada (1 July). Sir John A. Macdonald, 'Father of Confederation', is Canada's first Prime Minister. Ottawa officially becomes capital of the Dominion.

1868: the 'Canada First' patriotic movement is founded. Thomas D'Arcy McGee, one of the fathers of Confederation, and a leading opponent of the Fenians, becomes Canada's first assassination victim, at the hands of a Fenian (7 April).

1869: Canada purchases Rupert's Land from the Hudson's Bay Company. Threatened by Canadian purchases of Hudson's Bay territories, and loss of livelihood, Louis Riel leads the Métis in occupying Fort Garry, on the site of Winnipeg

1870: the Red River Rebellion continues to resist Canadian authority in the northwest. The insurgents form a provisional government (January) but military action under General Wolseley ends this (August). When the Manitoba Act creates the province of Manitoba, the rebellion is finally ended.

1871: British Columbia and Vancouver Island join the Confederation (20 July).

1873: Prince Edward Island joins the Confederation. The 'Cypress Hills Massacre' of Indians by trappers, and general lawlessness in the mid-west, bring about the formation of the Northwest Mounted Police. Macdonald resigns over the Pacific Scandal (5 November), which brought attention to campaign contributions made by Sir Hugh Allan in exchange for a charter to build the Canadian Pacific Railway. The Liberal Party is formed; Alexander Mackenzie becomes Canada's second, and first Liberal, Prime Minister.

1874: Riel is elected to the House of Commons but opposition from Ontario prevents him from taking the seat (February). Anabaptists (Russian Mennonites) start to arrive in Manitoba from various Russian colonies.

1875: Riel is granted amnesty but with exile for five years. The Supreme Court of Canada is established. Jennie Trout becomes the first woman licensed to practice medicine in Canada, although Emily Stowe has been doing so without a license in Toronto since 1867. Grace Lockhart receives, from Mount Allison University, the first Bachelor of Arts degree awarded to a woman.

1876: the Intercolonial Railway, growing out of the Halifax-Truro

line, links central Canada and the Maritime Provinces (1 July).
The Toronto Women's Literary Club is founded as a front for
the women's suffrage movement.

1877: the provincial legislature creates the University of Manitoba,
the oldest university in western Canada.

1878: the Conservatives under Macdonald win the federal election.
Anti-Chinese sentiment in British Columbia reaches a high
point as the government bans immigrant Chinese workers
from public works. The first asbestos mine opens.

1879: Macdonald introduces his national policy, with protective
tariffs, a transcontinental railway, and opening up of the west
(12 March). Canada negotiates independent trade agreements
with France and Spain.

1880: Emily Stowe is finally granted a license to practice medicine
in Toronto.

1880–84: The Canadian Pacific Railway recruits thousands of low-paid
Chinese labourers for building the transcontinental line.

1883: Augusta Stowe, daughter of Emily, is the first woman to gradu-
ate from the Toronto Medical School. The Toronto Women's
Suffrage Association replaces the Literary Club of 1876.

1884: Joseph Tyrell discovers the skull of a dinosaur, named
Albertasaurus.

1885: Riel, who had returned to Canada in 1884, leads the aggrieved
and unemployed Métis in the Northwest Rebellion. The Métis
are defeated at Batoche (2–9 May); Riel is captured, and hanged
in Regina (16 November). The last spike of the transcontinental Canadian Pacific Railway is ceremonially hammered
in at the Eagle Pass, British Columbia (7 November).

1887: the Liberals choose Wilfred Laurier as leader. The first provincial Premiers' Conference takes place in Québec City.

1890: Manitoba Liberals under Thomas Greenway halt public funding of Catholic schools.

1893: the National Council of Women of Canada is founded.

1895: the Yukon is made into a provisional district, separate from
the Northwest Territories.

1896: the Liberals under Laurier (the first French Canadian Prime
Minister) win the federal election partly on the Manitoba
Schools Question, though his compromises are not instituted
until 1897. Gold is discovered in the Klondike (16 August).

1898: the Klondike Gold Rush is fully under way. The Yukon provisional district is officially confirmed as the Yukon Territory, a
territory separate from the Northwest Territories. Russian
Doukhobors, an anarchistic sect, are allowed to settle in Saskatchewan.

1899: the first Canadian troops to be sent overseas participate in the Boer War in South Africa (30 October). Canada's first woman lawyer is Clara Brett Martin.

1901: Marconi receives the first transatlantic radio message at St. John's, Newfoundland. First natural gas well drilled, near Medicine Hat.

1902: a train crash on the Grand Trunk Railway, near Hamilton, Ontario, results in 28 deaths.

1903: Canada loses the Alaska boundary dispute and the Alaska 'panhandle' is confirmed as U.S. territory (20 October). A landslip at Frank, Alberta, in the Crow's Nest Pass, kills 70 people. Silver is discovered in northern Ontario. Nude demonstrations by the extreme Doukhobor 'Sons of Freedom' take place near Yorkton, Saskatchewan, against government policy regarding individual ownership. Roald Amundsen makes the first transit of the Northwest Passage (1903–6).

1904: the Northwest Mounted Police is renamed the Royal Northwest Mounted Police (RNWMP), with headquarters at Regina.

1905: the Alberta and Saskatchewan provinces are formed, and the Northwest Territories created out of the former districts of Keewatin, Mackenzie, Franklin, and Ungava.

1906: Sir Adam Beck creates the Hydro-Electric Power Commission of Ontario (7 May), the largest such company in Canada.

1908: Peter Verigin, leader of the Doukhobors since his arrival in Canada in 1902, leads the extremist 'Sons of Freedom' to British Columbia.

1909: the Department of External Affairs is formed. The first Grey Cup is played. Canada's first powered air flight takes place at Baddeck, Nova Scotia.

1910: the Laurier government creates a Canadian navy with the Naval Service Bill. Forty-three die in a train crash near Sudbury, Ontario.

1911: Robert Borden and the Conservatives win the federal election, defeating Laurier on the reciprocity issue.

1912: a botanist, Carrie Derrick, is Canada's first woman professor, at McGill University.

1914: the Canadian Pacific ship *Empress of Ireland* sinks in the St. Lawrence within 15 minutes of a collision in dense fog – over a thousand lives are lost (29 May). The Hillcrest mine disaster at Turtle Mountain, Alberta, kills 189 miners. Political controversy is aroused on the issue of Sikh immigration with the arrival in Burrard Inlet, British Columbia, of the *Komagata Maru* with nearly 400 Sikh passengers from the Far East. Britain declares war on Germany (4 August), automatically drawing Canada into the conflict. The first Canadian troops leave for England (3 October). Parliament passes the War Measures

Act, allowing suspension of civil rights during periods of emergency. Oil is found in Alberta.

1915: in their first battle, the 1st Canadian Division face one of the first recorded chlorine gas attacks at Ypres, Belgium (22 April). The National Transcontinental, eastern division of the Grand Trunk Railway, completes a line from Moncton to Winnipeg.

1916: the parliament buildings are destroyed by fire (3 February). The 1st Canadian Division discovers that the Canadian-made Ross rifle (controversial since 1905) is unreliable in combat conditions. It is withdrawn from service and replaced by the British-made Lee-Enfield (August). The National Research Council is established to promote scientific and industrial research. Female suffrage is first granted in Canada in Manitoba.

1917: income tax is introduced as a temporary wartime measure. The Military Service Bill (11 June) sparks a conscription crisis dividing French and English Canada. A Union government (a coalition of Liberals and Tories) under Borden wins in a federal election in which all women of British origin are allowed to vote for the first time. The Canadians capture Vimy Ridge, France (9–12 April), and Passchendaele, Belgium (6 November), in two of the war's worst battles. The explosion of the munitions ship, *Mont Blanc*, in Halifax harbour wipes out two square miles of the city, killing almost 2000 people and injuring 9000 (6 December). The Québec railway bridge over the St. Lawrence is completed. In Alberta, Louise McKinney becomes the first woman elected to a legislature in the British Commonwealth.

1918: Canadians break through the German trenches at Amiens, France (8 August), beginning 'Canada's Hundred Days'. Armistice ends World War I (11 November). Imprisoned in South Dakota for pacifism, Hutterites flee northward into the Prairie Provinces.

1919: the Grand Trunk Pacific, western division of the Grand Trunk Railway, completes a line from Winnipeg to Prince Rupert. The Canadian National Railways is created as a Crown corporation to acquire and further consolidate smaller lines. The first successful transatlantic flight leaves St. John's, Newfoundland (14 June). During a general strike in Winnipeg (19 May–26 June), an armed charge by the police on 'Bloody Saturday' kills one and injures thirty (21 June). James S. Woodsworth and others are charged with seditious conspiracy. The federal government passes a Technical Education Act.

1920: Canada is a founder member of the League of Nations. The Progressive Party is formed by T.A. Crerar to obtain law tariffs for western farmers. The RNWMP is re-formed as the Royal Canadian Mounted Police (RCMP), with headquarters at Ottawa. The 'Group of Seven' artists is formed at Toronto.

1921: Mackenzie King and the Liberals win the federal election. Agnes Macphail becomes the first woman elected to Parliament (representing the Progressive Party). J. S. Woodsworth becomes the first socialist elected to the House of Commons. *Bluenose*, the famous racing schooner, is launched at Lunenburg, Nova Scotia (26 March). Insulin is discovered at the University of Toronto. Colonial Motors of Walkerville, Ontario, manufacture an automobile called the 'Canadian'.

1922: the Canadian Northern and Canadian Transcontinental Railways merge to form the publicly owned Canadian National Railways. Canada asserts its independence by not going to Britain's aid in the Chanak crisis in Turkey. Banting, Best, MacLeod, and Collip share the Nobel Prize for the discovery of insulin. Foster Hewitt makes the first hockey broadcast. A Provincial Franchise Committee is organized in Québec to work towards female suffrage in the province.

1923: Canada signs the Halibut Treaty with the U.S. without the traditional British signature. Mackenzie King leads the opposition to a common imperial policy at the Imperial Conference in London. The Grand Trunk Railway is taken over by the government. The federal government acts to prevent Chinese immigration on Dominion Day, called 'Humiliation Day' by Chinese Canadians.

1924: Major C. H. Douglas proposes the social credit monetary theory, which is taken up by A. B. Aberhart in Alberta. Doukhobor leader, Peter Verigin, is assassinated.

1925: Newfoundland women receive the right to vote. Only Québecois women remain outside the suffrage.

1926: the Balfour Report defines British dominions as autonomous and equal in status (18 November).

1927: Britain's Privy Council awards Labrador to Newfoundland rather than to Québec (1 March). The first coast-to-coast radio network broadcast celebrates the Diamond Jubilee of Confederation.

1928: the Supreme Court of Canada rules that the British North America Act does not define women as 'persons' and that they are therefore not eligible to hold public office.

1929: the British Privy Council reverses the Supreme Court decision of 1928. Women are legally declared 'persons' (18 October). The Wall Street Crash in the U.S.A. heralds years of economic slump. The Workers' Unity League is formed.

1930: the Conservatives under R. B. Bennett win the federal election. Jean de Brébeuf and other Jesuit martyrs are officially canonized. Cairine Wilson becomes Canada's first woman senator.

1931: the Statute of Westminster (11 December) implements the Balfour Report of 1926, granting Canada full legislative authority in both internal and external affairs. The Governor General becomes a representative of the Crown.

1932: the fourth Welland Canal completed, taking ships of up to 33,000 tons. Woodsworth joins in forming a democratic socialist political party, the Co-operative Commonwealth Federation (CCF), in Calgary. Bennett's government establishes repressive 'relief camps' to cope with the problem of unemployed single men.

1934: the Bank of Canada is formed. The birth of the Dionne quintuplets in Ontario attracts international media attention.

1935: about a thousand unemployed men from the western provinces begin the 'On-to-Ottawa' trek, to confront Bennett over the relief camps (3 June–1 July). In an attempt to remove a corrupt Liberal administration, Maurice Duplessis, a Québec Conservative, allies with a splinter group of Liberals under Paul Gouin to form the Union Nationale. In Alberta, the Social Credit Party gains power (until 1971). Novelist John Buchan (Lord Tweedsmuir) is made Governor General. Gold is discovered in the Northwest Territories, on the west coast of Yellowknife Bay.

1936: the Canadian Broadcasting Corporation (CBC) is founded, modelled on the BBC. Driven by the reformist Union Nationale, Duplessis ousts Gouin and becomes Premier of Québec. The Governor General's Literary Awards are instituted.

1937: the Rowell-Sirois Commission is appointed to investigate the financial relationship between the federal government and the provinces. Trans-Canada Air Lines begins regular flights (1 September). *Les Compagnons de St. Laurent* drama company founded in Québec.

1938: Franklin D. Roosevelt is the first U.S. president to make an official visit to Canada. The Workers' Unity League helps to organize the Vancouver Sit-ins, in which protesting relief camp workers and others occupy the Post Office and other public buildings. The demonstrators are forced out by police on 'Bloody Sunday' (19 June), with 35 people wounded.

1939: Canada declares war on Germany (10 September). Premier Duplessis opposes Québec's participation but is defeated by the Liberals on the issue (26 October).

1940: the Unemployment Insurance Commission is introduced.

Canada and the U.S.A. form a Permanent Joint Defence Board. Parliament passes the controversial National Resources Mobilization Act (June), which allows conscription for military service only within Canada. Idola Saint-Jean and other activists finally succeed in obtaining the vote for Québecois women. The RCMP vessel *St. Roch* makes the first west–east transit of the Northwest Passage.

1941: fluorspar is first mined, at Lake Ainslie, Nova Scotia.

1942: Canadians of Japanese descent (22,000) are stripped of non-portable possessions, evacuated, and interned as security risks (26 February). A national plebiscite approves amendment of the National Resources Mobilization Act to permit sending conscripts overseas (27 April), once again revealing deep divisions between Québec and English Canada. The Dieppe raid (19 August), Canada's first participation in the war in Europe, is a disaster, with 3,367 out of 4,963 Canadians dead or taken prisoner.

1943: Canadians participate in the invasion of Sicily (10 July), and win the Battle of Ortona, a German stronghold on the Adriatic (20–28 December).

1944: Canadian troops push further than other allied units on D-Day (6 June). Canadian forces fight as a separate army (23 July). The Family Allowance Act is passed (August). The CCF under Tommy Douglas wins the provincial election in Saskatchewan, forming the first socialist government in North America.

1945: European hostilities end (5 May). The first family allowance ('baby-bonus') payments are made (20 June). Canada becomes a founder member of the United Nations (26 June). Hostilities in the Pacific Basin end (2 September). Igor Gouzenko defects from the Soviet Embassy in Ottawa (5 September) and reveals the existence in Canada of a Soviet spy network. Canada's first nuclear reactor goes on stream in Chalk River, Ontario.

1948: Louis St. Laurent succeeds Mackenzie King as Prime Minister (15 November).

1949: Newfoundland ceases to be a separate British Dominion and joins the Confederation (31 March). Canada joins NATO. Canada's Supreme Court replaces Britain's Privy Council judicial committee as the country's final court of appeal.

1950: volunteers in the Canadian Army Special Force join the United Nations forces in the Korean War.

1951: census shows population as just over 14 million. The Massey Royal Commission reports that Canadian cultural life is dominated by American influences. Recommendations include improving grants to universities and the establishment of the Canada Council.

1952: Vincent Massey becomes the first Canadian-born Governor General. Canada's first television stations begin transmissions in Montréal and Toronto (September). A disaster is narrowly averted at the Chalk River nuclear plant.

1953: the National Library is established in Ottawa (1 January). The Stratford Shakespeare Festival opens (13 July).

1954: the first Canadian subway opens in Toronto (30 March). Viewers of the British Empire Games in Vancouver see two runners break the four-minute mile in the same race. Marilyn Bell is the first person to swim across Lake Ontario (9 September). Hurricane Hazel kills over 80 people in Toronto (15 October).

1955: the Canadian Labour Congress is formed. Riots in Montréal are caused by the suspension of hockey star Rocket Richard (17 March).

1956: the Liberals use a closure motion to curtail the 'pipeline debate', which begins with concern over the funding of the natural gas industry and ends in controversy over proper parliamentary procedure (8 May–6 June). The action contributes to their electoral defeat (after 22 years in power) the following year.

1957: John Diefenbaker and the Conservatives win a minority government (10 June). Ellen Fairclough becomes the first female federal cabinet minister. The Canada Council is formed to foster Canadian cultural uniqueness. Lester B. Pearson wins the Nobel Peace Prize for helping resolve the Suez Crisis (12 October).

1958: Diefenbaker's government gains the largest majority yet obtained in a federal election (31 March). A coalmine disaster at Springhill, Nova Scotia, kills 74 miners. The prototype Avro Arrow CF-105 interceptor aircraft is flown (25 March).

1959: the St. Lawrence Seaway opens (26 June). Diefenbaker cancels the Avro Arrow project, to public outcry.

1960: Liberals under Jean Lesage win the provincial election in Québec (22 June), inaugurating the 'Quiet Revolution', creating special status for the province within the Confederation. A Canadian Bill of Rights is approved. Native people win the right to vote in federal elections.

1961: the New Democratic Party (NDP) replaces the CCF.

1962: the Conservatives are returned to minority status in a federal election (18 June). Socialized medicine is introduced in Saskatchewan (1 July), leading to a doctors' strike. The Trans-Canada Highway opens (3 September). Canada becomes the third nation in space with the launch of the satellite *Alouette I* (29 September). Canada's last executions take place in Toronto (11 December).

1963: Liberals under Pearson win a minority government (8 April). The militant separatist *Front de Libération du Québec* (FLQ) sets off bombs in Montréal (April–May). A TCA flight crashes in Québec, killing 118 people (29 November). A replica of *Bluenose* is launched at Lunenburg, Nova Scotia.

1964: Canadians get social insurance cards (April). *Northern Dancer* is the first Canadian horse to win the Kentucky Derby.

1965: Canada and the U.S. sign the Auto Pact (January). The new national maple leaf flag is inaugurated (15 February). Roman Catholic churches begin to celebrate masses in French and English. The Hydro-Electric Power Commission of Ontario inadvertently causes a major power blackout in North America (9 November).

1966: the Munsinger affair (in which the Associate Minister of National Defence, Pierre Sévigny, had a liaison with a German divorcée suspected by the RCMP) becomes Canada's first political sex scandal (4 March). The Canada Pension Plan is established. The CBC introduces colour TV broadcasts (1 October).

1967: the Air Force, Army, and Navy are unified as the Canadian Armed Forces (25 April). World attention is turned to Expo '67 in Montréal (27 April). Centennial celebrations officially begin (1 July). The Order of Canada is founded. French President, Charles de Gaulle, controversially proclaims, *'Vive le Québec libre'* in Montréal (24 July).

1968: Pierre Trudeau succeeds Pearson as leader of the Liberals and wins a majority in the federal election (25 June). A royal commission on the status of women is appointed. Canadian divorce laws are reformed.

1969: postal reforms end Saturday deliveries (1 February). Abortion laws are liberalized (May). The Languages Act provides that all federal services shall be available in English and French (9 July). The Breathalyzer™ is put into use to test for drunken drivers (1 December).

1970: British trade commissioner James Cross is kidnapped by the FLQ (5 October), precipitating the October Crisis. Québec's labour and immigration minister, Pierre Laporte, is also kidnapped (10 October) and later found murdered. The War Measures Act is invoked by Premier Trudeau (16 October), banning the FLQ and leading eventually to nearly 500 arrests under martial law.

1971: the federal government officially adopts a policy of

multiculturalism. Gerhard Herzberg of the National Research Council wins the Nobel Prize for Chemistry for studies of smog.

1972: Canada wins the first hockey challenge against Soviet Russia. Trudeau's Liberals win a minority government by two seats.

1973: The House of Commons criticizes U.S. bombing of North Vietnam (5 January). Henry Morgentaler is acquitted of illegal abortion charges in Montréal (13 November). The separatist *Parti Québecois* becomes the official opposition in a provincial election.

1974: the Hydro-Electric Power Commission of Ontario changes its name to Ontario Hydro and begins to update its image (4 March). Soviet ballet dancer Mikhail Baryshnikov defects in Montréal (29 June). Trudeau's Liberals win a majority government (8 July).

1975: Toronto's CN Tower becomes the world's tallest free-standing structure (2 April). TV cameras are allowed in the House of Commons for the first time. Trudeau institutes wage and price controls to fight inflation (14 October).

1976: Canada announces a 200-mile (320-kilometre) coastal fishing zone (4 June). The death penalty, in abeyance for some years, is abolished (14 July). The Olympic Games are held in Montréal (17–31 July) under tight security. Team Canada wins the first Canada Cup (15 September). René Lévesque and the *Parti Québecois* win the provincial election (15 November). The Eaton Company discontinues catalogue sales after 92 continuous years.

1977: Québec passes Bill 101, restricting English schooling to children of parents who had been educated in English schools (26 August). Highway signs are changed to the metric system (6 September). VIA Rail is established to secure rail passenger services.

1978: the remains of a Soviet nuclear-powered satellite crash in the far north (24 January). Sun Life Assurance acknowledges that it moved its head office to Toronto because of Montréal's language laws and political instability.

1979: Conservatives under Joe Clark win a federal election (May 22). The first uniquely Canadian gold bullion coin, with a maple leaf motif, goes on sale (5 September). Most of Mississauga, Ontario, is evacuated following derailment of train cars containing chemicals (10 November). The Supreme Court of Canada declares unconstitutional the creation of officially monolingual legislatures in Manitoba and Québec (13 December). Clark's Conservatives lose a no-confidence vote on the budget (13 December), forcing their resignation.

1980: Ken Taylor, Canadian ambassador to Iran, helps six Americans escape Tehran (28 January). Canada boycotts Moscow's Olympic Games over the Soviet invasion of Afghanistan. A Québec referendum rejects sovereignty-association (22 May). 'O Canada' is officially adopted as Canada's national anthem (27 June). The Supreme Court recognizes the equal distribution of assets in failed common-law relationships. Terry Fox's cross-Canada 'Marathon of Hope' ends prematurely in Thunder Bay.

1981: Terry Fox dies of cancer (29 June). His example eventually raises about 25 million dollars. Québec bans public signs in English (23 September). All federal and provincial governments, except Québec, agree on a method to repatriate Canada's constitution (5 November).

1982: the offshore oil rig *Ocean Ranger* sinks, killing 84 (15 February). Bertha Wilson is the first woman appointed as a Justice of the Supreme Court (4 March). The Québec government demand for a veto over constitutional change is rejected (7 April). Canada gains a new constitution and charter of rights and freedoms (17 April). Marguerite Bourgeoys is canonized as Canada's first female saint.

1983: Pay TV begins operation (1 February). Public outcry opposes the government's approval of U.S. cruise missile testing in the west. Jeanne Sauvé is appointed Governor General – the first female to be appointed (23 December).

1984: John Turner succeeds Trudeau as Liberal Prime Minister (30 June) but is soon defeated by Brian Mulroney's Conservatives, by an even larger majority than Diefenbaker's in 1958 (4 September). Pope John Paul II visits Canada (9–20 September). Marc Garneau becomes the first Canadian in space, on the U.S. shuttle *Challenger* (5 October). The International Court of Justice defines fishing boundaries on George's Bank.

1985: U.S. icebreaker *Polar Sea* challenges Canada's Arctic sovereignty by making a traverse of the Northwest Passage. Premier Mulroney and U.S. President Ronald Reagan declare mutual support for Orbital Strategic Defence Initiatives (Star Wars) and Free Trade at the 'Shamrock Summit' in Québec City (2 December). Ontario Liberals under David Peterson end 40 years of Conservative premiership. Lincoln Alexander becomes Ontario's first black Lieutenant Governor.

1986: The Canadian dollar hits an all-time low of 70.2 U.S. cents on international money markets (31 January). The 'Supercontinental' crashes into a freight train west of Edmonton: 29 are killed (17 February). Expo '86 opens in Vancouver (2 May–13 October). The U.S. imposes tariffs on some imported Canadian wood products (22 May). Canada adopts sanctions against South Africa for its apartheid policies (5 August).Tamil refugees are found drifting off the coast of Newfoundland (11 August). Canada receives a United Nations award for sheltering foreign refugees (6 October). Canadian John Polanyi shares the Nobel Prize for Chemistry.

1987: Mulroney and the provincial premiers agree in principle to the Meech Lake Accord, designed to bring Québec into the new constitution (30 April).A tornado rips through Edmonton, killing 26 and injuring hundreds (20 July). Canadian sprinter, Ben Johnson, sets a new world record (30 August) for the 100-metre dash. The Canada–U.S. Free Trade Agreement is reached (3 October), but still requires ratification.

1988: the Supreme Court strikes down existing legislation against abortion as unconstitutional (28 January).The Winter Olympics open in Calgary (13 February). David See-Chai Lam, born in Hong Kong, becomes British Columbia's Lieutenant Governor (9 September). Ben Johnson sets a world sprint record and wins the gold medal at the Seoul Olympics in Korea (24 September).Testing positive for steroids, he is stripped of his medal two days later. The Supreme Court strikes down Québec's French-only sign law (15 December). Finding a constitutional loophole (the 'notwithstanding' clause) in the charter of rights and freedoms, the province reinstates the law (21 December). Manitoba Premier, Gary Filmon, slows the ratification of the Meech Lake Accord in reaction to Québec's move.The Canada–U.S. Free Trade Agreement is signed.

1989: free trade goes into effect (1 January). Heather Erxleben becomes Canada's first acknowledged female combat soldier. One-dollar bills are replaced by the one-dollar coin, featuring the loon, and popularly called the 'loonie'. The government announces cuts in the subsidy to VIA Rail, to much public outcry (5 June). The first woman to lead a federal political party,Audrey McLaughlin, replaces Ed Broadbent as head of the NDP (2 December). Fourteen female engineering students are murdered by a gunman at the École Polytechnique, Montréal (6 December).

1990: the Haggersville Tyre Depot in Ontario burns for 16 days (February). The 'Oka crisis' in Québec lasts 78 days as Mohawk Indians protest against a golf course being built over an ancestral burial ground. Newfoundland Premier, Clyde Wells, further slows down the signing of the Meech Lake Accord. Manitoba finally ends its chances when a native member of the provincial legislature, Elijah Harper, refuses to acknowledge Québec as Canada's principal, if not only, 'distinct society'. Following the Accord's failure to become law, the *Bloc Québecois* is formed (25 July). Bob Rae, with a large majority, becomes Ontario's first NDP premier (September). The Senate passes the unpopular Goods and Services Tax (December). An economic recession is officially announced.

1991:   the Goods and Services Tax comes into effect (1 January). Canadian forces join the multinational campaign to drive Saddam Hussein's Iraqi troops from Kuwait (15 January). British Columbia Premier, Bill Van Der Zalm, resigns in the midst of a real estate scandal. George Erasmus, leader of the Assembly of First Nations, resigns at the end of his second term (May); he is succeeded by Ovide Mercredi, whose popularity earns him the nickname of 'eleventh premier'. A new committee is set up to inquire into citizens' opinions on proposed constitutional reforms. David Schindler of the University of Alberta wins the first international Stockholm Water Prize for environmental research. In Brantford, Ontario, a Six Nations man is the first to be allowed to make a traditional native oath instead of swearing on the Bible (November). The Tungavik sign an agreement with Ottawa to create a new, semi-autonomous Inuit territory in the eastern Arctic.

1992:   the Miss Canada pageant is scrapped. Roberta Bondar is Canada's first female astronaut in space. Ontario lawyers vote to abandon the Oath to the Queen (January). Canada is the first country to sign the international biodiversity convention at the Earth Summit in Brazil (June). Canadians vote 'No' in a referendum seeking support for the Charlottetown Agreement, intended as a corrective to the Canadian constitution in the wake of the failed Meech Lake Accord (26 October). NAFTA free trade agreement signed with the U.S.A. and Mexico (December). Although the players are all American, the Toronto Blue Jays become the first Canadian team to win baseball's World Series.

1993:   Catherine Callbeck becomes the first woman premier, in Prince Edward Island. Environmental activists cause minor damage to government buildings in Victoria, British Columbia, during a demonstration (March). Kim Campbell replaces Brian Mulroney as the head of the Progressive Conservatives, becoming Canada's first woman Prime Minister (June). Part of northwest British Columbia is set aside as a world heritage conservation site. Protesters block loggers' access to ancient forests near Clayoquot Sound (July–August). The Toronto Blue Jays win the World Series for the second year in a row (23 October). The Liberals under Jean Chrétien are elected in a landslide victory, with the *Bloc Québecois* and Preston Manning's Reform Party only one seat apart in distant second and third places (25 October). The Progressive Conservatives, in power for nine years, are reduced to two seats in the House of Commons.

1994: trade barriers between provinces are reduced. Preparations go ahead for the establishment of devolved government for the Inuit. The *Parti Québecois* wins a narrow victory in provincial parliamentary elections. The Canadian pilot of a Korean airliner that crashed is arrested for endangering the lives of his passengers.

1995: a referendum on sovereignty in Québec narrowly fails to produce a majority in favour. Premier Parizeau is replaced by Lucien Bouchard. In Newfoundland, the government takes over control of church schools. A fishing 'war' over stocks breaks out between Canada and the European Community in the northwest Atlantic.

1996: a land claim agreement is settled with the Nisg'a people of British Columbia. The two-dollar coin is introduced (February). In British Columbia, Premier Harcourt resigns amid allegations of charity funds being directed to the NDP; Glen Clark takes over. The one billionth tonne of iron ore is dug at Labrador City (mine opened 1958).

1997: the 12.9-kilometre (8-mile) Confederation Bridge connecting Prince Edward Island to the mainland is opened. A salmon-fishing dispute over sea boundaries causes tension with the U.S.A. The Supreme Court accepts the legitimacy of oral history in the land claims of the native peoples.

1998: a massive ice storm fells power lines and disrupts electricity transmission in Ontario and Québec. The federal government formally apologizes to native peoples for past injustices, including the removal of children to residential schools. A Swissair MD-11 crashes in the sea off Peggy's Cove, Nova Scotia, with 229 deaths (September). The *National Post*, the first all-Canada daily newspaper, is launched.

1999: waves of illegal immigrants try to land in British Columbia. The McClean Lake and McArthur River uranium projects open. The Nunavut territory and government come into existence (April). Canadian troops are serving in Kosovo, East Timor, Sierra Leone, and Macedonia on peacekeeping missions.

2000: national controversy rages over mismanagement of billions of dollars in public grants. Yves Michaud causes controversy in Québec province by accusing Jewish and other ethnic groups of opposing sovereignty. Liberals win federal election (October) with 172 seats out of 301.

2001: a summit of the Americas at Québec agrees 2005 as date for

Algeria A huge country in northern Africa that fringes the Mediterranean Sea in the north. Over four-fifths of Algeria is covered by the Sahara Desert to the south. Near the north coastal area the Atlas Mountains run east-west in parallel ranges. The Chelif, at 450 miles (724 kilometres) long, is the country's main river, rising in the Tell Atlas and flowing to the Mediterranean. The climate in the coastal areas is warm and temperate with most of the rain falling in winter. The summers are dry and hot with temperatures rising to over 89°F (32°C). Inland beyond the Atlas Mountains conditions become more arid and temperatures range from 120°F (49°C) during the day to 50°F (10°C) at night. Most of Algeria is unproductive agriculturally, but it does possess one of the largest reserves of natural gas and oil in the world. Algeria's main exports are oil-based products, fruit, vegetables, tobacco, phosphates and cork, while imports include textiles, foodstuffs, machinery, iron and steel. In recent years, the country has been wracked by civil strife and terrorist attacks, with the various opposing forces unable to agree peace proposals.

Quick facts:

Area: 919,595 square miles (2,381,741 square kilometres)

Population: 29,168,000

Capital: Algiers (Alger)

Other cities: Oran, Constantine, Annaba

Form of government: Republic

Religion: Sunni Islam

Currency: Algerian Dinar

American Samoa *see* SAMOA, AMERICAN.

Andorra A tiny state, situated high in the eastern Pyrénées, between FRANCE and SPAIN. The state consists of deep valleys and high mountain peaks which reach heights of 9,843 feet (3,000 metres). Although only 12 miles (20 kilometres) wide and 19 miles (30 kilometres) long, the spectacular scenery and climate attract many tourists. About 10 million visitors arrive each year, during the cold weather when heavy snowfalls make for ideal skiing, or in summer when the weather is mild and sunny and the mountains are used for walking. Tourism and the duty-free trade are now Andorra's chief sources of income. Natives who are not involved in the tourist industry may raise sheep and cattle on the high pastures. Although Andorra has no airport or railroad, there is a good road system. The average life expectancy from birth is 95 for women, 86 for men and 91 years overall. In 1993 an Andorran government was elected and has its own Parliament after 715 years of being ruled by France's leader and the Spanish Bishop of Urgel.

Quick facts:

Area: 175 square miles (453 square kilometres)

Population: 65,900

Capital: Andorra la Vella

Form of government: Republic

Religion: Roman Catholicism

Currency: Euro

Angola Situated on the Atlantic coast of southern Africa, Angola lies about 10°S of the equator. It shares borders with CONGO, DEMOCRATIC REPUBLIC OF CONGO, ZAMBIA And NAMIBIA. Its climate is tropical with temperatures constantly between 68°F (20°C) and 77°F (25°C). The rainfall is heaviest in inland areas where there are vast equatorial forests. The country is also rich in minerals, however deposits of manganese, copper and phosphate are as yet unexploited. Diamonds are mined in the northeast and oil is produced near Luanda. Oil production is the most important aspect of the economy, making up about 90 per cent of exports which have traditionally included diamonds, fish, coffee and palm oil. Around 70 per cent of the workforce are engaged in agriculture. Since independence from Portugal in 1975, the United States is the main recipient of the country's exports. However, the Angolan economy has been severely damaged by the civil war of the 1980s and early 1990s.

Quick facts:
Area: 481,354 square miles (1,246,700 square kilometres)
Population: 11,185,000
Capital: Luanda
Other cities: Huambo, Lobito, Benguela, Lubango
Form of government: People's Republic
Religions: Roman Catholicism, African traditional religions
Currency: Kwanza

Anguilla An island in the Leeward Islands group of the Caribbean Sea, now a self-governing British dependency. From 1967 until 1980 it was in federation with ST CHRISTOPHER (ST KITTS) AND NEVIS. The country's main source of revenue is tourism and lobsters account for half of the island's exports.

Quick facts:
Area: 37 square miles (96 square kilometres)
Population: 12,400
Capital: The Valley
Form of government: British Overseas Territory
Religion: Christianity
Currency: East Caribbean Dollar

Antigua and Barbuda Located on the eastern side of the Leeward Islands, Antigua and Barbuda is a tiny state comprising three islands – Antigua, Barbuda and the uninhabited rocky islet of Redonda. Antigua's strategic position was recognised by the British in the 18th century when it was an important naval base and later by the USA who built the island's airport during World War II to defend the Caribbean and the Panama Canal. Although mainly low-lying, the country's highest point is Boggy Peak at 1,329 feet (405 metres). The climate is tropical although its average rainfall of 4 inches (100 millimetres) makes it drier than most of the other islands of the West Indies. Tourism is the main industry as its numerous sandy beaches make it an ideal destination. Barbuda is surrounded by coral reefs and the island is home to a wide range of wildlife. Cotton, sugar cane and fruits are cultivated and fishing is an important industry in Barbuda. Great damage was inflicted on Antigua and Barbuda in 1995 by Hurricane Luis when over 75 per cent of property was destroyed or damaged.

Quick facts:
Area: 171 square miles (442 square kilometres)
Population: 66,000
Capital: St John's
Form of government: Constitutional Monarchy
Religion: Christianity (mainly Anglicanism)
Currency: East Caribbean Dollar

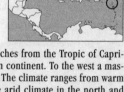

Argentina The world's eighth largest country, which stretches from the Tropic of Capricorn to Cape Horn on the southern tip of the South American continent. To the west a massive mountain chain, the Andes, forms the border with CHILE. The climate ranges from warm temperate over the Pampas in the central region, to a more arid climate in the north and west, while in the extreme south conditions although also dry are much cooler. The vast fertile plains of the Pampas are the main agricultural area and produce cereals and wheat, while in other irrigated areas sugar cane, fruit and grapes for wine are raised. Meat processing, animal products and livestock production are major industries and also feature prominently in export trade. A series of military regimes and ongoing political and economic crises have resulted in an unstable economy which fails to provide reasonable living standards for the population.

Quick facts:
Area: 1,073,518 square miles (2,780,400 square kilometres)
Population: 35,220,000
Capital: Buenos Aires
Other cities: Cordoba, Rosario, Mar del Plata, Mendoza, La Plata, Salta
Form of government: Federal Republic
Religion: Roman Catholicism
Currency: Peso

Armenia The smallest republic of the former USSR and part of the former kingdom of Armenia, which was divided between Turkey, Iran and the former USSR. It declared independence from the USSR in 1991. It is a landlocked Transcaucasian republic and its neighbours are Turkey, Iran, Georgia and Azerbaijan. The country is very mountainous, with many peaks over 9,900 feet (3,000 metres), the highest being Arragats Lerr at 13,435 feet (4,095 metres). Agriculture is mixed in the lowland areas. The main crops grown are grain, sugar beet and potatoes, and livestock reared include cattle, pigs and sheep. Mining of copper, zinc and lead is important, and to a lesser extent gold, aluminium and molybdenum, and industrial development is increasing. Hydroelectricity is produced from stations on the River Razdan as it falls 3,281 feet (1,000 metres) from Lake Sevan to its confluence with the River Araks. Territorial conflict with Azerbaijan over Nagorny Karabakh under a ceasefire since 1994 put a brake on economic development for many years.

Quick facts:
Area: 11,506 square miles (29,800 square kilometres)
Population: 3,893,000
Capital: Yerevan
Other major city: Kunmayr (Gyumri)
Form of government: Republic
Religion: Armenian Orthodox
Currency: Dram

Aruba A Caribbean island off the coast of Venezuela, until 1986 one of the Netherlands Antilles. It is a self-governing dependency of the Netherlands. The development of tourism began here in the 1980s.

Quick facts:
Area: 75 square miles (193 square kilometres)
Population: 87,000
Capital: Oranjestad
Form of government: Self-governing Dutch Territory
Religion: Christianity
Currency: Aruban Florin

Australia The world's smallest continental landmass is a vast and sparsely populated island state in the southern hemisphere and is comprised of seven states. The most mountainous region is the Great Dividing Range, which runs down the entire east coast. Because of its great size, Australia's climates range from tropical monsoon to cool temperate and also large areas of desert. The majority of the country's natural inland lakes are salt water and are the remnants of a huge inland sea. The Great Barrier Reef is approximately 1,250 miles (2,000 kilometres) long and is the largest coral formation known in the world. Central and south Queensland are subtropical while north and central New South Wales are warm temperate. Much of Australia's wealth comes from agriculture, with huge sheep and cattle stations extending over large parts of the interior known as the Outback. Australia is the world's leading producer of wool, particularly the fine merino wool. Cereal growing is dominated by wheat. Mining continues to be an important industry and produces coal, natural gas, oil, gold and iron ore. Australia is the largest producer of diamonds.

Quick facts:
Area: 2,988,902 square miles (7,741,220 square kilometres)
Population: 18,871,800
Capital: Canberra
Other cities: Adelaide, Brisbane, Melbourne, Perth, Sydney
Form of government: Federal Parliamentary State
Religion: Christianity
Currency: Australian Dollar

Austria A landlocked country in central Europe surrounded by seven nations. The wall of mountains that runs across the centre of the country dominates the scenery. In the warm summers tourists come to walk in the forests and mountains and in the cold winters skiers come to the mountains that now boast over 50 ski resorts. The main river is the Danube and there are numerous lakes, principally Lake Constance (Bodensee) and Lake Neusiedler. Agriculture is based on small farms, many of which are run by single families. Dairy products, beef and lamb from the hill farms contribute to exports. More than 37 per cent of Austria is covered in forest, resulting in the paper-making industry near Graz. There are mineral resources of lignite, magnesium, petroleum, iron ore and natural gas and high-grade graphite is exported. Unemployment is very low and its low strike record has attracted multinational companies in recent years. Attachment to local customs is still strong and in rural areas men still wear lederhosen and women the traditional dirndl skirt on feast days and special occasions.

Quick facts:
Area: 32,378 square miles (83,859 square kilometres)
Population: 8,106,000
Capital: Vienna (Wien)
Other cities: Graz, Linz, Salzburg, Innsbruck
Form of government: Federal Republic
Religion: Roman Catholicism
Currency: Euro

Azerbaijan A republic of the former USSR that declared itself independent in 1991. It is situated on the southwest coast of the Caspian Sea and shares borders with IRAN, ARMENIA, GEORGIA and the RUSSIAN FEDERATION. The Araks river separates Azerbaijan from the region known as Azerbaijan in northern Iran. The country is semi-arid and 70 per cent of the land is irrigated for the production of cotton, wheat, maize, potatoes, tobacco, tea and citrus fruits. It has rich mineral deposits of oil, natural gas, iron and aluminium. The most important mineral is oil, which is found in the Baku area from where it is piped to Batumi on the Black Sea. There are steel, synthetic rubber and aluminium works at Sumqayit just north of the capital, Baku. However, Azerbaijan is only minimally developed industrially and is hindered by its dispute with Armenia over the Nagorny-Karabakh region.

Quick facts:
Area: 33,436 square miles (86,600 square kilometres)
Population: 7,625,000
Capital: Baku
Other major city: Sumqayit
Form of government: Republic
Religions: Shia Islam, Sunni Islam, Russian Orthodox
Currency: Manat (= 100 gopik)

Bahamas, The The Bahamas consist of an archipelago of 700 islands located in the Atlantic Ocean off the southeast coast of Florida. The largest island is Andros (1,600 square miles/4,144 square kilometres) and the two most populated are Grand Bahama and New Providence where the capital, Nassau, lies. Winters in the Bahamas are mild and summers warm. Most rain falls in May, June, September and October and thunderstorms are frequent in summer. The islands are also subject to hurricanes and other tropical storms. The islands have few natural resources and for many years fishing and small-scale farming (citrus fruits and vegetables) were the only ways to make a living. Now, however, tourism, which employs almost half the workforce, is the most important industry and has been developed on a vast scale. Offshore banking is also a growing source of income. About three million tourists, mainly from North America, visit the Bahamas each year.

Quick facts:

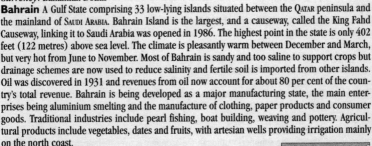

Area: 5,358 square miles (13,878 square kilometres)
Population: 284,000
Capital: Nassau
Other important city: Freeport
Form of government: Constitutional Monarchy
Religion: Christianity
Currency: Bahamian Dollar

Bahrain A Gulf State comprising 33 low-lying islands situated between the QATAR peninsula and the mainland of SAUDI ARABIA. Bahrain Island is the largest, and a causeway, called the King Fahd Causeway, linking it to Saudi Arabia was opened in 1986. The highest point in the state is only 402 feet (122 metres) above sea level. The climate is pleasantly warm between December and March, but very hot from June to November. Most of Bahrain is sandy and too saline to support crops but drainage schemes are now used to reduce salinity and fertile soil is imported from other islands. Oil was discovered in 1931 and revenues from oil now account for about 80 per cent of the country's total revenue. Bahrain is being developed as a major manufacturing state, the main enterprises being aluminium smelting and the manufacture of clothing, paper products and consumer goods. Traditional industries include pearl fishing, boat building, weaving and pottery. Agricultural products include vegetables, dates and fruits, with artesian wells providing irrigation mainly on the north coast.

Quick facts:

Area: 268 square miles (694 square kilometres)
Population: 599,000
Capital: Manama (Al Manamah)
Form of government: Hereditary Monarchy
Religions: Shia Islam, Sunni Islam
Currency: Bahrain Dinar

Bangladesh Formerly the eastern province of PAKISTAN, Bangladesh is the world's eighth most populated country. It is bounded almost entirely by INDIA and to the south by the Bay of Bengal. There is a wide variety of animal life, with the Sundarbans area being one of the last strongholds of the Bengal tiger. The country is extremely flat and is virtually a huge delta formed by the Ganges, Brahmaputra AND Meghna rivers. The country is subject to devastating floods and cyclones that sweep in from the Bay of Bengal. Most villages are built on mud platforms to keep them above water. The climate is tropical monsoon with heat, extreme humidity and heavy rainfall in the monsoon season (April to October) along with accompanying tornadoes. The short winter season is mild and dry. The combination of rainfall, sun and silt from the rivers makes the land productive and it is often possible to grow three crops a year. Bangladesh produces about 70 per cent of the world's jute and the production of jute-related products is a principal industry, with tea being an important cash crop. There are few mineral resources although natural gas, coal and peat are found.

Quick facts:

Area: 55,598 square miles (143,998 square kilometres)
Population: 120,073,000
Capital: Dhaka
Other cities: Chittagong, Khulna, Narayanganj, Saidpur
Form of government: Republic
Religion: Sunni Islam
Currency: Taka

Barbados The most easterly island of the West Indies, lying well outside the group of islands that make up the Lesser Antilles. Mainly surrounded by coral reefs, most of the island is low-lying and only in the north does it rise to 1,104 feet (336 metres) at Mount Hillaby. The climate is tropical, but the cooling effect of the northeast trade winds prevents the temperatures rising above 86°F (30°C). There are only two seasons, the dry and the wet, when rainfall is very heavy. At one time the economy depended almost exclusively on the production of sugar and its by-products, molasses and rum and although the industry is now declining, sugar is still the principal export. Tourism has now taken over as the main industry, employing approximately 40 per cent of the island's labour force, although there are industries manufacturing furniture, clothing, electrical and electronic equipment. More recently, deposits of natural gas and petroleum have been discovered and fishing is an important activity. The island is surrounded by pink and white sandy beaches and coral reefs that are visited by around 400,000 tourists each year.

Quick facts:

Area: 166 square miles (430 square kilometres)
Population: 265,000
Capital: Bridgetown
Form of government: Constitutional Monarchy
Religions: Anglicanism, Methodism
Currency: Barbados Dollar

Belarus (Belorussia, Byelorussia) A republic of the former USSR that declared itself independent in 1991. It borders POLAND to the west, UKRAINE to the south, LATVIA and LITHUANIA to the north, and the RUSSIAN FEDERATION to the east. The country consists mainly of a low-lying plain, and forests cover approximately one-third of the land. The climate is continental, with long severe winters and short warm summers. Although the economy is overwhelmingly based on industry, including oil refining, food processing, woodworking, chemicals, textiles and machinery, output has gradually declined since 1991 and problems persist in the supply of raw materials from other republics that previously were part of the USSR. Agriculture, although seriously affected by contamination from the Chernobyl nuclear accident of 1986, accounts for approximately 20 per cent of employment, the main crops being flax, potatoes and hemp. The main livestock raised are cattle and pigs. Extensive forest areas also contribute in the supply of raw materials for woodwork and paper-making. Peat is the fuel used to provide power for industry and the country's power plants. Belarus has a good transport system of road, rail, navigable rivers and canals.

Quick facts:

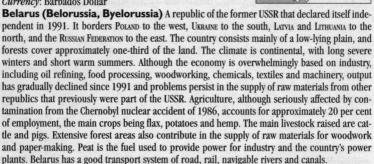

Area: 80,155 square miles (207,600 square kilometres)
Population: 10,203,000
Capital: Minsk
Other cities: Homyel (Gomel), Vitsyebsk, Mahilyov
Form of government: Republic
Religions: Russian Orthodox, Roman Catholicism
Currency: Rouble

Belau *see* PALAU.

Belgium A highly industrialised, relatively small country in northwest Europe with a short coastline on the North Sea. The Meuse river divides Belgium into two distinct geographical regions. To the north of the river the land slopes continuously for 93 miles (150 kilometres) until it reaches the North Sea where the coastlands are flat and grassy. To the south of the river is the forested plateau area of the Ardennes. Between these two regions lies the Meuse valley. Belgium is a densely populated country with few natural resources. Agriculture, which uses about 45 per cent of the land for cultivation or rearing of livestock, employs only 3 per cent of the workforce. About one-fifth of the country is covered with forests, with the wooded areas mainly used for recreation. The metal-working industry, originally based on the small mineral deposits in the Ardennes, is the most important industry, and in the northern cities new textile industries are producing carpets and clothing. Nearly all raw materials are now imported through the main port of Antwerp. There are three officially recognised languages in Belgium – Dutch, French and German.

Quick facts:
Area: 11,783 square miles (30,519 square kilometres)
Population: 10,159,000
Capital: Brussels
Other cities: Antwerp, Charleroi, Ghent, Liège, Oostende
Form of government: Constitutional Monarchy
Religion: Roman Catholicism
Currency: Euro

Belize A small Central American country on the southeast of the Yucatan Peninsula in the Caribbean Sea. Its coastline on the Gulf of Honduras is approached through some 550 kilometres (342 miles) of coral reefs and keys (cayo). The coastal area and north of the country are low-lying and swampy with dense forests inland. In the south the Maya Mountains rise to 1100 metres (3609 feet). The subtropical climate is warm and humid and the trade winds bring cooling sea breezes. Rainfall is heavy, particularly in the south and hurricanes may occur in summer. The dense forests that cover most of the country provide valuable hardwoods such as mahogany. Most of the population make a living from forestry, fishing, or agriculture, although only 5 per cent of the land is cultivated. The main crops grown for export are sugar cane, citrus fruits (mainly grapefruit), bananas and coconuts. Industry is very underdeveloped, causing many people to emigrate to find work. The official language is English although many others are spoken, including Mayan, Carib and Spanish.

Quick facts:
Area: 8,763 square miles (22,696 square kilometres)
Population: 222,000
Capital: Belmopan
Other major city: Belize City
Form of government: Constitutional Monarchy
Religions: Roman Catholicism, Protestantism
Currency: Belize Dollar

Belorussia *see* BELARUS.

Benin An ice cream cone-shaped country with a very short coastline on the Bight of Benin on the southern coast of West Africa. The coastal area has white sandy beaches backed by lagoons and low-lying fertile lands known as barre country. In the northwest the Atakora Mountains are grassy plateaus that are deeply cut into steep forested valleys and on the grasslands sheep, cattle and goats are reared. The main rivers of Benin are the Donga, Couffo and Niger with its tributaries. The climate in the north is tropical and in the south equatorial. There are nine rainy months each year so crops rarely fail. Farming is predominantly subsistence and accounts for around 60 per cent of employment, with yams, cassava, maize, rice, groundnuts and vegetables forming most of the produce. The country is very poor, although since the late 1980s economic reforms have been towards a market economy and Western financial aid has been sought. The main exports are palm oil, palm kernels and cotton. Tourism is now being developed but as yet facilities for this are few except in some coastal towns.

Quick facts:
Area: 43,484 square miles (112,622 square kilometres)
Population: 5,563,000
Capital: Porto-Novo
Other major city: Cotonou
Form of government: Republic
Religions: African traditional religions, Roman Catholicism,
Sunni Islam, Christian
Currency: CFA Franc

95

Bermuda A country consisting of a group of 150 small islands in the western Atlantic Ocean. It lies about 572 miles (920 kilometres) east of Cape Hatteras on the coast of the United States. The hilly limestone islands are the caps of ancient volcanoes rising from the sea bed. The main island, Great Bermuda, is linked to the other islands by bridges and causeways. The climate is warm and humid, with rain spread evenly throughout the year but with the risk of hurricanes from June to November. Bermuda's chief agricultural products are fresh vegetables, bananas and citrus fruit, but 80 per cent of food requirements are imported. Many foreign banks and financial institutions operate from the island, taking advantage of the lenient tax laws. Other industries include ship repair and pharmaceuticals. Its proximity to the USA and the pleasant climate have led to a flourishing tourist industry.

Quick facts:
Area: 20 square miles (53 square kilometres)
Population: 64,000
Capital: Hamilton
Form of government: British Overseas Territory
Religions: Protestantism, Roman Catholicism
Currency: Bermuda Dollar

Bhutan A country that is surrounded by INDIA to the south and CHINA to the north. It rises from foothills overlooking the Brahmaputra river to the southern slopes of the Himalayas. The Himalayas, which rise to over 24,600 feet (7,500 metres) in Bhutan, make up most of the country. The climate is hot and wet on the plains but temperatures drop progressively with altitude, resulting in glaciers and permanent snow cover in the north. The valleys in the centre of the country are wide and fertile, and about 95 per cent of the workforce are farmers growing wheat, rice, potatoes and corn. Fruit such as plums, pears, apples and also cardamom are grown for export. There are many monasteries, with about 6,000 monks. Yaks reared on the high pasture land provide milk, cheese and meat. Vast areas of the country still remain forested as there is little demand for new farmland. Bhutan is one of the world's poorest and least developed countries. It has little contact with the rest of the world although tourism has been encouraged in recent years. There are no railways but roads join many parts of the country.

Quick facts:
Area: 18,147 square miles (47,000 square kilometres)
Population: 1,812,000
Capital: Thimphu
Form of government: Constitutional Monarchy
Religions: Buddhism, Hinduism
Currency: Ngultrum

Bolivia A landlocked republic of central South America through which the great mountain range of the Andes runs. It is in the Andes that the highest navigable lake in the world, Lake Titicaca, is found. On the undulating depression south of the lake, the Altiplano, is the highest capital city in the world, La Paz. To the east and northeast of the mountains is a huge area of lowland containing tropical rainforests (the Llanos) and wooded savanna (the Chaco). The northeast has a heavy rainfall while in the southwest it is negligible. Temperatures vary with altitude, from extremely cold on the summits to cool on the Altiplano, where at least half the population lives. Although rich in natural resources such as lead, silver, copper, zinc, oil and tin, Bolivia remains a poor country because of lack of funds for their extraction, lack of investment and political instability. Bolivia is self-sufficient in petroleum and exports natural gas. Agriculture produces soya beans, sugar cane and cotton for export, and increased production of coca, from which cocaine is derived, has resulted in an illicit economy.

Quick facts:
Area: 424,165 square miles (1,098,581 square kilometres)
Population: 8,140,000
Capital: La Paz (administrative), Sucre (legal)
Other cities: Cochabamba, Santa Cruz, Oruro, Potosi
Form of government: Republic
Religion: Roman Catholicism
Currency: Boliviano

Bosnia and Herzegovina A republic of former Yugoslavia that was formally recognised as an independent state in March 1992. It is a very mountainous country and includes part of the Dinaric Alps, which are densely forested and deeply cut by rivers flowing northwards to join the Sava river. Half the country is forested, and lumber is an important product of the northern areas. One quarter of the land is cultivated, and corn, wheat and flax are the principal products of the north. In the south, tobacco, cotton, fruits and grapes are the main products. Bosnia and Herzegovina has large deposits of lignite, iron ore and bauxite, and its metallurgical plants create air pollution. Water is also polluted around these, with a shortage of drinking water, the Sava river being severely affected. Despite the natural resources the economy has been devastated by civil war, which began in 1991 following the secession of Croatia and Slovenia from the former Yugoslavia. Dispute over control of Bosnia and Herzegovina continued, leading to United Nations intervention in an attempt to devise a territorial plan acceptable to all factions. A peace agreement signed in late 1995 has resulted in the division of the country into two self-governing provinces. The population of the state was significantly diminished when refugees from the civil war fled between 1992 and 1993.

Quick facts:
Area: 19,735 square miles (51,129 square kilometres)
Population: 4,510,000
Capital: Sarajevo
Other cities: Banja Luka, Mostar, Tuzla
Form of government: Republic
Religions: Eastern Orthodox, Sunni Islam, Roman Catholicism
Currency: Dinar

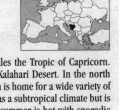

Botswana A landlocked republic in southern Africa that straddles the Tropic of Capricorn. Much of the west and southwest of the country forms part of the Kalahari Desert. In the north there is a huge area of marshland around the Okavango Delta, which is home for a wide variety of wildlife. With the exception of the desert area, most of the country has a subtropical climate but is subject to drought. In winter, days are warm and nights cold while summer is hot with sporadic rainfall. The people are mainly farmers and cattle rearing is the main activity. After independence in 1966, the exploitation of minerals started. In 1972 the first diamond mine was set up at Orapa, and diamonds quickly became the country's most important export, and copper from the nickel/copper complex at Selebi-Pikwe was also exported. Exploitation of these mineral resources has facilitated a high rate of economic growth within the country. Coal is also mined but the majority is for domestic use. About 17 per cent of the land is set aside for wildlife preservation in national parks, game reserves, game sanctuaries and controlled hunting areas.

Quick facts:
Area: 224,607 square miles (581,730 square kilometres)
Population: 1,490,000
Capital: Gaborone
Other cities: Francistown, Molepolole, Mahalapye
Form of government: Republic
Religions: African traditional religions, Christian
Currency: Pula

Brazil A huge South American country bounded to the north, south and east by the Atlantic ocean. It is the fifth largest country in the world and covers nearly half of South America. The climate is mainly tropical, but altitude, distance from the sea and prevailing winds cause many variations. The Amazon river basin occupies a huge area of land, over one-third of the country's area, and much of this is covered by tropical rainforests. In the tropical areas winters are dry and summers wet and droughts may occur in the northeast where it is hot and arid. About 14 per cent of the population is employed in agriculture, which occupies only about 7 per cent of the land area, and the main products exported are coffee, soya beans, orange juice and cocoa. Brazil is rich in minerals and is the only source of high grade quartz crystal in commercial quantities. It is also a major producer of chrome ore, and it is now developing what is thought to be the richest iron ore deposits in the world. Since improvement of facilities, fishing is now an important industry, mainly of lobsters, shrimp and sardines.

Quick facts:
Area: 3,300,171 square miles (8,547,403 square kilometres)
Population: 157,872,000
Capital: Brasília
Other cities: Balem, Belo Horizonte, Curitiba, Porto Alegre, Recife, Rio de Janeiro, Salvador, São Paulo
Form of government: Federal Republic
Religion: Roman Catholicism
Currency: Cruzeiro

Brunei A sultanate located on the northwest coast of the island of Borneo in Southeast Asia. It is bounded on all sides by the Sarawak territory of MALAYSIA, which splits the sultanate into two separate parts. Broad tidal swamplands cover the coastal plains, and inland Brunei is hilly and covered with tropical rainforests that occupy almost half the country's land area. The climate is tropical marine, hot and moist, with cool nights. Rainfall is heavy (98 inches/2,500 millimetres) at the coast but even heavier (197 inches/5,000 millimetres) inland. The main crops grown are rice, vegetables and fruit, but economically the country depends on its oil industry, which employs 7 per cent of the working population. Cloth weaving and metalwork are also small local industries. Oil production began in the 1920s and now oil and natural gas account for almost all exports. Other minor products are rubber, pepper, gravel and animal hides.

Quick facts:
Area: 2,226 square miles (5,765 square kilometres)
Population: 300,000
Capital: Bandar Seri Begawan
Other cities: Kuala Belait, Seria
Form of government: Monarchy (Sultanate)
Religion: Sunni Islam
Currency: Brunei Dollar

Bulgaria A southeast European republic located on the east Balkan peninsula and with a coast on the Black Sea. It is bounded to the north by ROMANIA, to the west by Serbia and the Former Yugoslav Republic of MACEDONIA, and to the south by GREECE and TURKEY. The centre of Bulgaria is crossed from west to east by the Balkan Mountains. The south of the country has a Mediterranean climate with hot dry summers and mild winters. Farther north the temperatures become more extreme and rainfall is higher in summer. The main river in Bulgaria is the Danube, and about a third of the country is covered by forests. Traditionally Bulgaria is an agricultural country and a revolution in farming during the 1950s led to great increases in output. This was because of the collectivisation of farms and the use of more machinery, fertilisers and irrigation. Increased mechanisation led to more of the workforce being available to work in mines and industry. However, the country suffered very high rates of inflation and unemployment in the early 1990s after the break-up of the former Soviet Union, with whom Bulgaria had very close trade links and industrial pollution affects its rivers, soils and the Black Sea coastline, an area that is extremely important for tourism, with over 10,000,000 people visiting the Black Sea resorts annually.

Quick facts:
Area: 42,823 square miles (110,912 square kilometres)
Population: 8,356,000
Capital: Sofiya
Other cities: Burgas, Plovdiv, Ruse, Varna
Form of government: Republic
Religion: Eastern Orthodox
Currency: Lev

Burkina Faso (Burkina) A landlocked state in West Africa, Burkina (formerly called Upper Volta) lies on the fringe of the Sahara, to the north. It comprises a plateau region in the north which gives way southwards to an area of plains. The northern part of the country is arid and is more or less an extension of the Sahara Desert. The south is less dry and has savanna-type vegetation and scattered trees. Precipitation is generally low, the heaviest rain falling in the southwest, while the rest of the country is semi-desert. The dusty grey plains in the north and west have infertile soils that have been further impoverished by overgrazing and over-cultivation. About 85 per cent of the people live by subsistence farming and food crops include sorghum, millet, pulses, corn and rice. The main industries are textiles, metal products and the processing of agricultural products and production of consumer items such as footwear and soap. Cotton is the main export, along with minerals such as gold and animal products. There is great poverty and shortage of work and many of the younger population go to GHANA and CÔTE D'IVOIRE for employment. During the 1970s the country was severely affected by drought and this was followed by political instability in the 1980s. The situation has improved since 1992.

Quick facts:
Area: 105,792 square miles (274,000 square kilometres)
Population: 10,780,000
Capital: Ouagadougou
Other cities: Bobo-Dioulasso, Koudougou
Form of government: Republic
Religions: African traditional religions, Sunni Islam
Currency: CFA Franc

Burma *see* MYANMAR.

Burundi A small, densely populated country in central east Africa, bounded by RWANDA to the north, TANZANIA to the east and south and the Democratic Republic of CONGO to the west. One of the poorest nations in the world, Burundi consists mainly of an upland plateau at an elevation of 4,600–5,900 feet (1,400–1,800 metres). The climate is equatorial but modified by altitude. The savanna in the east is several degrees hotter than the plateau and there are two wet seasons. The soils are not rich but there is enough rain to grow crops in most areas for subsistence farming. The main food crops are bananas, sweet potatoes, peas, lentils and beans. Cassava is grown near the shores of Lake Tanganyika which is in the Great Rift Valley. The main cash crop is coffee, which accounts for 90 per cent of Burundi's export earnings. Cotton and tea are also cultivated for export. There is a little commercial fishing on Lake Tanganyika, otherwise industry is very basic. Since 1994 Burundi has been afflicted by ethnic conflict between the majority Hutu and minority Tutsi. Between 1994 and 1995 it is estimated that 150,000 were killed as a result of ethnic violence and the political situation remains highly volatile.

Quick facts:
Area: 10,747 square miles (27,834 square kilometres)
Population: 6,088,000
Capital: Bujumbura
Form of government: Republic
Religion: Roman Catholicism
Currency: Burundi Franc

Byelorussia *see* BELARUS.

Cambodia A southeast Asian state bounded by THAILAND, LAOS and VIETNAM, with its southern coast lying on the Gulf of Thailand. The country was devastated by its involvement in the Vietnam War (1960–75) followed by the brutal regime of the Khymer Rouge under Pol Pot (1975–79). The heart of the country is saucer-shaped, and gently rolling alluvial plains are drained by the Mekong river. The Dangrek Mountains form the frontier with Thailand in the northwest. In general Cambodia has a tropical monsoon climate and about half the land is tropical forest. During the rainy season the Mekong swells and backs into the Tônlé Sap (Great Lake), increasing its size threefold to about 4,015 square miles (10,400 kilometres). This seasonal flooding means the area is left with rich silt when the river recedes. Crop production depends entirely on the rainfall and floods but production was badly disrupted during the civil war when there was widespread famine, and yields still remain low. The cultivation of rice accounts for about 80 per cent of agricultural land and the other main crop is rubber, which grows in the eastern plateau. Despite the gradual rebuilding of the infrastructure in the early 1990s, Cambodia remains one of the world's poorest nations.

Quick facts:

Area: 69,898 square miles (181,035 square kilometres)
Population: 10,273,000
Capital: Phnom-Penh
Other cities: Battambang, Kampong Cham
Form of government: People's Republic
Religion: Buddhism
Currency: Riel

Cameroon A triangular-shaped country of diverse landscapes in west central Africa. It stretches from Lake Chad at its apex to the northern borders of EQUATORIAL GUINEA, GABON and the CONGO in the south. The landscape ranges from low-lying lands, through the semi-desert Sahel to dramatic mountain peaks and then to the grassy savanna, rolling uplands, steaming tropical forests and hardwood plantations. Cameroon's jungles contain not only commercially valuable trees but also an immense diversity of other plants, many of which have been identified as useful for their medicinal properties. Farther south are the volcanoes, including the sporadically active Mount Cameroon, the highest peak at 1,250 feet (4,100 metres) and the palm beaches at Kribi and Limbe. The climate is equatorial with high temperatures and plentiful rain. The majority of the population are farmers who live in the south and in central Cameroon where they grow maize, millet, cassava and vegetables. In the drier north, where drought and hunger are well known, life is harder and this area is populated by semi-nomadic herders. Bananas, coffee and cocoa are the major exports although oil, gas and aluminium are becoming increasingly important.

Quick facts:

Area: 183,569 square miles (475,442 square kilometres)
Population: 13,560,000
Capital: Yaoundé
Other major city: Douala
Form of government: Republic
Religions: African traditional religions, Roman Catholicism, Sunni Islam
Currency: CFA Franc

Canada The second largest country in the world and the largest in North America. Canada is a land of great climatic and geographical extremes. It lies to the north of the UNITED STATES and has Pacific, Atlantic and Arctic coasts. The country has the highest number of inland waters and lakes in the world, including the Great Lakes on the border with the USA. The Rocky Mountains and Coast Mountains run down the west side and the highest point, Mount Logan (19,524 feet/6,050 metres), is in the Yukon. Climates range from polar conditions in the north to cool temperate in the south, with considerable differences from west to east. More than 80 per cent of its farmland is in the prairies that stretch from Alberta to Manitoba. Wheat and grain crops cover three-quarters of the arable land. Canada is rich in forest reserves, which cover more than half the total land area.

The most valuable mineral deposits (oil, gas, coal and iron ore) are found in Alberta. Most industry in Canada is associated with processing its natural resources and it is one of the main exporters of food products.

Quick facts:
Area: 3,848,900 square miles (9,984,670 square kilometres)
Population: 31,414,000
Capital: Ottawa
Other cities: Calgary, Toronto, Montréal, Vancouver, Québec City, Winnipeg
Form of government: Federal Parliamentary State
Religions: Roman Catholicism, United Church of Canada, Anglicanism
Currency: Canadian Dollar

Cape Verde One of the world's smallest nations, situated in the Atlantic Ocean about 400 miles (640 kilometres) northwest of SENEGAL. It consists of ten islands and five islets and there is an active volcano on Fogo, one of the islands. The islands are divided into the Windward group and the Leeward group. Over 50 per cent of the population live on São Tiago on which is Praia, the capital. The climate is arid with a cool dry season from December to June and warm dry conditions for the rest of the year. Rainfall is sparse and the islands suffer from periods of severe drought. Agriculture is mostly confined to irrigated inland valleys and the chief crops are coconuts, sugar cane, potatoes, cassava and dates. Bananas and some coffee are grown for export. Fishing for tuna and lobsters is an important industry but in general the economy is shaky and Cape Verde relies heavily on foreign aid. Because of its lack of natural resources and droughts, large numbers of its people have emigrated for many years. Tourism is being encouraged although the number of visitors is at present relatively low.

Quick facts:
Area: 1,557 square miles (4,033 square kilometres)
Population: 396,000
Capital: Praia
Form of government: Republic
Religion: Roman Catholicism
Currency: Cape Verde Escudo

Cayman Islands A group of three low-lying coral islands in the Caribbean Sea, 149 miles (240 kilometres) south of Cuba. They are a British overseas territory. The group comprises Grand Cayman, by far the largest of the three, Cayman Brac and Little Cayman (the name is derived from the Carib Indian word for 'crocodile'). The Cayman Islands are a popular destination for cruise liners and a tax haven.

Quick facts:
Area: 102 square miles (264 square kilometres)
Population: 38,000
Capital: George Town, on Grand Cayman
Form of government: British Overseas Territory
Religion: Christianity
Currency: Cayman Islands Dollar

Central African Republic A landlocked country in central Africa bordered by CHAD in the north, CAMEROON in the west, SUDAN in the east and the CONGO and Democratic Republic of CONGO in the south. The terrain consists of 2,000–3,000 feet (610–915 metres) high undulating plateaus with dense tropical forest in the south and a semi-desert area in the east. The climate is tropical with little variation in temperature throughout the year. The wet months are May, June, October and November. Floods and tornadoes can occur at the beginning of the rainy season. Most of the population live in the west and in the hot, humid south and southwest. Over 86 per cent of the working population are subsistence farmers and the main crops grown are cassava, groundnuts, bananas, plantains, millet and maize. Livestock rearing is small-scale because of the prevalence of the tsetse fly. Gems and industrial diamonds are mined and deposits of uranium, iron ore, lime, zinc and gold have been discovered, although they remain relatively undeveloped. The country's main exports are coffee, diamonds, cotton, tobacco and lumber, although this is hampered by the distance from a port. Since the country's independence in 1960, its political and economic fortunes have been mixed, with widespread corruption and violence.

Quick facts:

Area: 240,535 square miles (622,984 square kilometres)
Population: 3,344,000
Capital: Bangui
Other cities: Bambari, Bangassou
Form of government: Republic
Religions: African traditional religions, Roman Catholicism
Currency: CFA Franc

Chad A landlocked country in the centre of northern Africa that extends from the edge of the equatorial forests in the south to the middle of the Sahara Desert in the north. It lies more than 944 miles (1,600 kilometres) from the nearest coast. The climate is tropical, with adequate rainfall in the south, but the north experiences semi-desert conditions. In the far north of the country the Tibesti Mountains rise from the desert sand more than 11,200 feet (3,415 metres). The southern part of Chad is the most densely populated and its relatively well-watered savanna has always been the country's most arable region. Unless there is drought, this area is farmed for cotton (the main cash crop along with livestock exports), millet, sorghum, groundnuts, rice and vegetables. Fishing is carried out in the rivers and in Lake Chad. Cotton ginning and manufacture of peanut oil are the principal industries. As a result of drought and civil war, Chad remains one of the poorest countries in the world. The country was torn by civil strife for much of the latter part of the 20th century but a ceasefire has been in place since 1994.

Quick facts:

Area: 495,755 square miles (1,284,000 square kilometres)
Population: 6,515,000
Capital: N'Djamena
Other cities: Sarh, Moundou, Abéché
Form of government: Republic
Religions: Sunni Islam, African traditional religions
Currency: CFA Franc

Chile A country that lies like a backbone down the Pacific coast of the South American continent with the Andes Mountains extending its length. Its Pacific coastline is 2,600 miles (4,184 kilometres) long and the country is liable to volcanic explosions and earthquakes. Because of its enormous range in latitude it has almost every kind of climate, from desert conditions to icy wastes. The north, in which lies the Atacama Desert, is extremely arid. The Atacama Desert is rich in mineral deposits and has large quantities of nitrates. The climate of the central region is Mediterranean and that of the south cool temperate. Sixty per cent of the population live in the central valley where the climate is similar to that of southern California. The land here is fertile and the principal crops grown are grapes, wheat, apples, sugar beet, maize, tomatoes and potatoes. There is also a significant wine-making industry. It is also in the central valley that the vast copper mine of El Teniente is located. This is one of the largest copper mines in the world and accounts for Chile's most important source of foreign exchange.

Quick facts:

Area: 292,135 square miles (756,626 square kilometres)
Population: 14,419,000
Capital: Santiago
Other cities: Arica, Concepcion, Valparaiso, Viña del Mar
Form of government: Republic
Religion: Roman Catholicism
Currency: Chilean Peso

China The third largest country in the world, which covers a large area of East Asia and also includes over 3,400 islands. In western China most of the terrain is very inhospitable. In the northwest there are deserts that extend into MONGOLIA and the RUSSIAN FEDERATION, and much of the southwest consists of the ice-capped peaks of TIBET. The southeast has a green and well-watered landscape comprising terraced hillsides and paddy fields, and its main rivers are the Yangtze, Huang He and Xi Jiang. Most of China has a temperate climate but in such a large country wide ranges of latitude and altitudes produce local variations. China is an agricultural country, and intensive cultivation and horticulture are necessary to feed its population of over one billion. After the death of Mao Tse-tung in 1976 and under the leadership of Deng Xiaoping, China experienced a huge modernisation of agriculture and industry as a result of the supply of expertise, capital and technology from Japan and the West. The country was opened up to tourists and, to a degree, adopted the philosophy of free enterprise, resulting in a dramatic improvement in living standards for a significant proportion of the population. The change towards a market economy, however, created internal political problems. Pro-democracy demonstrations in 1989 resulted in the Tianmen Square massacre, which was condemned throughout the world and raised questions regarding China's approach to human rights.

Quick facts:
Area: 3,705,408 square miles (9,596,961 square kilometres)
Population: 1,246,872,000
Capital: Beijing (Peking)
Other cities: Chengdu, Guangzhou, Harbin, Shanghai, Tianjin, Wuhan
Form of government: People's Republic
Religions: Buddhism, Confucianism, Taoism
Currency: Yuan

Colombia A country situated in the north of South America, most of it lying between the equator and 10 degrees north. The Andes, which split into three ranges (the Cordilleras) in Colombia, run north along the west coast and gradually disappear towards the Caribbean Sea. Half of Colombia lies east of the Andes and much of this region is covered in tropical grassland. Towards the Amazon Basin the vegetation changes to tropical forest. The climates in Colombia include equatorial and tropical, according to altitude. Very little of the country is under cultivation although much of the soil is fertile. The range of climates results in an extraordinary variety of crops, of which coffee is the most important and includes cocoa beans, sugar cane, bananas, cotton and tobacco. Colombia is rich in minerals such as gold, silver, platinum and copper and produces about half of the world's emeralds. It is South America's leading producer of coal and petroleum is the country's most important foreign revenue earner.

Quick facts:
Area: 439,737 square miles (1,138,914 square kilometres)
Population: 35,626,000
Capital: Bogotá
Other cities: Barranquilla, Cali, Cartagena, Medellin
Form of government: Republic
Religion: Roman Catholicism
Currency: Colombian Peso

Comoros, The A country that consists of three volcanic islands in the Indian Ocean, situated between mainland Africa and MADAGASCAR. Physically, four islands make up the group but the island of Mayotte remained a French dependency when the three western islands became a federal Islamic republic in 1975. The islands are mostly forested and the tropical climate is affected by Indian monsoon winds from the north. There is a wet season from November to April that is accompanied by cyclones. Only small areas of the islands are cultivated and most of this land belongs to foreign plantation owners. The chief product was formerly sugar cane but now vanilla, copra, maize, cloves and essential oils are the most important products. The forests provide lumber for building and there is a small fishing industry. The coelacanth (a primitive bony fish), previously thought to have been extinct for millions of years, was discovered living in the seas off the Comoros in 1938.

Quick facts:

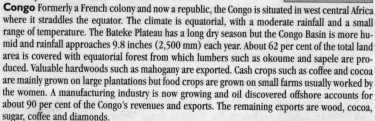

Area: 720 square miles (1,865 square kilometres) excluding Mayotte
Population: 538,000
Capital: Moroni
Other cities: Dornoni, Fomboni, Mutsamudu, Mitsamiouli
Form of government: Federal Islamic Republic
Religion: Sunni Islam
Currency: Comorian Franc

Congo Formerly a French colony and now a republic, the Congo is situated in west central Africa where it straddles the equator. The climate is equatorial, with a moderate rainfall and a small range of temperature. The Bateke Plateau has a long dry season but the Congo Basin is more humid and rainfall approaches 9.8 inches (2,500 mm) each year. About 62 per cent of the total land area is covered with equatorial forest from which lumbers such as okoume and sapele are produced. Valuable hardwoods such as mahogany are exported. Cash crops such as coffee and cocoa are mainly grown on large plantations but food crops are grown on small farms usually worked by the women. A manufacturing industry is now growing and oil discovered offshore accounts for about 90 per cent of the Congo's revenues and exports. The remaining exports are wood, cocoa, sugar, coffee and diamonds.

Quick facts:

Area: 132,047 square miles (342,000 square kilometres)
Population: 2,668,000
Capital: Brazzaville
Other major city: Pointe-Noire
Form of government: Republic
Religions: Christian, African traditional religions
Currency: CFA Franc

Congo, Democratic Republic of A vast country, formerly known as Zaire, situated in west central Africa. It has a short coastline of only 25 miles (40 kilometres) on the Atlantic Ocean. Rainforests, which cover about 55 per cent of the country, contain valuable hardwoods such as mahogany and ebony. The country is drained by the Congo (Zaire) river, which is largely navigable and its main tributaries. There is enormous potential for hydroelectricity, but this is not yet exploited. Mountain ranges and plateaus surround the Congo basin, and in the east the Ruwenzori Mountains overlook the lakes in the Great Rift Valley. In the central region the climate is hot and wet all year but elsewhere there are well-marked wet and dry seasons. Agriculture employs 75 per cent of the population yet less than 3 per cent of the country can be cultivated. Grazing land is limited by the infestation of the tsetse fly. Cassava is the main subsistence crop, and coffee, tea, cocoa, rubber and palms are grown for export. The country's huge mineral resources have fuelled the ongoing civil war and ethnic conflict in the region, and the government has no control over large parts of the country.

Quick facts:

Area: 905,355 square miles (2,344,858 square kilometres)
Population: 46,812,000
Capital: Kinshasa
Other cities: Bukavu, Lubumbashi, Matadi, Mbuji-Mayi, Kananga, Kisangani
Form of government: Republic
Religions: Roman Catholicism, Protestantism, Islam
Currency: Congolese Franc

Cook Islands A group of 15 islands in the South Pacific, independent since 1965 but associated with New Zealand.

Quick facts:

Area: 93 square miles (240 square kilometres)
Population: 18,500
Capital: Avarua, on Rarotonga
Form of government: Self-governing in association with New Zealand
Religion: Christianity
Currency: Cook Islands Dollar/New Zealand Dollar.

Costa Rica With the Pacific Ocean to the south and west and the Caribbean Sea to the east, Costa Rica is sandwiched between the Central American countries of Nicaragua and Panama. Much of the country consists of volcanic mountain chains that run northwest to southeast. The climate is tropical with a small temperature range and abundant rain. The dry season is from December to April. The most populated area is the Valle Central in which the Spanish settled in the 16th century. The upland areas have rich volcanic soils that are good for coffee growing and the slopes provide lush pastures for cattle. Coffee and bananas are grown commercially and are the major agricultural exports. Costa Rica's mountainous terrain provides hydroelectric power, which makes it almost self-sufficient in electricity, and attractive scenery for its growing tourist industry. The country has a high literacy rate (around 92 per cent) and its culture reflects its Spanish heritage.

Quick facts:

Area: 19,730 square miles (51,100 square kilometres)
Population: 3,398,000
Capital: San José
Other cities: Alajuela, Límon, Puntarenas
Form of government: Republic
Religion: Roman Catholicism
Currency: Colón

Côte d'Ivoire A former French colony in West Africa, Côte d'Ivoire is located on the Gulf of Guinea with Ghana to the east and Liberia and Guinea to the west. The southwest coast has rocky cliffs but farther east there are coastal plains, which are the country's most prosperous region. The climate is tropical and affected by distance from the sea. The coastal area has two wet seasons, but in the north there is only the one. Côte d'Ivoire is basically an agricultural country with about 55 per cent of the workforce involved in producing cocoa, coffee, rubber, bananas and pineapples. It is the world's largest producer of cocoa and the fourth largest producer of coffee. These two crops bring in half the country's export revenue although lumber production is also of economic importance. Since independence was achieved in 1960, industrialisation has developed rapidly, particularly food processing, textiles and sawmills. Oil was discovered offshore in the late 1970s and there is mining for gold and diamonds.

Quick facts:

Area: 124,504 square miles (322,463 square kilometres)
Population: 14,781,000
Capital: Yamoussoukro
Other cities: Abidjan, Bouaké, Daloa
Form of government: Republic
Religions: African traditional religions, Sunni Islam, Roman Catholicism
Currency: CFA Franc

Croatia (Hrvatska) A republic of former Yugoslavia that made a unilateral declaration of independence on 25 June 1991. Sovereignty was not formally recognised by the international community until early in 1992. Located in southeast Europe, it is bounded to the west by the Adriatic Sea, to the north by Slovenia and Romania and to the south by Bosnia-Herzegovina. Western Croatia lies in the Dinaric Alps. The eastern region, drained by the Rivers Sava and Drava, which both flow into the Danube, is low-lying and agricultural. The chief farming region is the Pannonian Plain. Over one-third of the country is forested, with beech and oak trees being predominant, and lumber is a major export. Deposits of coal, bauxite, copper, petroleum, oil and iron ore are substantial, and most of the republic's industry is based on their processing. In Istria in the northwest and on the Dalmatian coast tourism was a major industry until Croatia became embroiled in the Serbo-Croat war prior to its secession in 1992. Following the formal recognition of Croatia's independence by the international community, the fighting abruptly ceased; however, the tourism industry continued to suffer from the effects of the ongoing hostilities in other parts of the former Yugoslavia. More recently, tourists are returning although there is a need to rebuild the infrastructure.

Quick facts:

Area: 21,824 square miles (56,538 square kilometres)
Population: 4,501,000
Capital: Zagreb
Other cities: Osijek, Rijeka, Split
Form of government: Republic
Religions: Roman Catholicism, Eastern Orthodox
Currency: Kuna

Cuba The largest and most westerly of the Greater Antilles group of islands in the West Indies. It is strategically positioned at the entrance to the Gulf of Mexico and lies about 87 miles (140 kilometres) south of the tip of Florida. Cuba is as big as all other Caribbean islands put together and is home to a third of the whole West Indian population. The climate is warm and generally rainy, and hurricanes are liable to occur between June and November. It possesses unusual natural subsurface limestone caverns and its rivers tend to be short and unnavigable. The island consists mainly of extensive plains and the soil is fertile. The most important agricultural product is sugar and its byproducts, and the processing of these is the most important industry. Tobacco is also of commercial significance, with Havana cigars being known internationally. Most of Cuba's trade was with other communist countries, particularly the former USSR, and the country's economy has suffered as a result of a US trade embargo.

Quick facts:

Area: 42,804 square miles (110,861 square kilometres)
Population: 11,019,000
Capital: Havana (La Habana)
Other cities: Camaguey, Holguin, Santa Clara, Santiago de Cuba
Form of government: Socialist Republic
Religion: Roman Catholicism
Currency: Cuban Peso

Cyprus An island that lies in the eastern Mediterranean about 53 miles (85 kilometres) south of Tur-KEY. It has a long thin panhandle and is divided from west to east by two parallel ranges of mountains that are separated by a wide central plain open to the sea at either end. The highest point is Mount Olympus (6,401 feet/1,951 metres) in the southwest. The climate is Mediterranean, with very hot dry summers and warm damp winters. This contributes towards the great variety of crops grown, such as early potatoes, vegetables, cereals, tobacco, olives, bananas and grapes, and these account for about 17 per cent of the land. The grapes are used for the strong wines and sherries for which Cyprus is famous. The main mineral found is copper while asbestos, gypsum and iron pyrites are also found. Fishing is a significant industry, but above all the island depends on visitors and it is the tourist industry that has led to a recovery in the economy since 1974, when it was invaded by Turkey, which still occupies the northern third of the island. There are no railways on the island although it does possess three international airports.

Quick facts:

Area: 3,572 square miles (9,251 square kilometres)
Population: 756,000
Capital: Nicosia
Other cities: Famagusta, Limassol, Larnaca
Form of government: Republic
Religions: Greek Orthodox, Sunni Islam
Currency: Cyprus Pound

Czech Republic, The A country that was newly constituted on 1 January 1993 with the dissolution of the 74-year-old federal republic of Czechoslovakia. It is landlocked, at the heart of central Europe, bounded by SLOVAKIA, GERMANY, POLAND and AUSTRIA. Natural boundaries are formed by the Sudeten Mountains in the north, the Erzgebirge, or Ore Mountains, to the northwest, and the Bohemian Forest in the southwest. The climate is humid continental, with warm summers and cold winters. Most rain falls in summer and thunderstorms are frequent. Agriculture, although accounting for only a small percentage of the national income, is highly developed and efficient. The main crops are sugar beet, wheat and potatoes. Over a third of the labour force is employed in industry, which has to import its raw materials and energy. The most important industries are iron and steel, coal, machinery, cement and paper, but industrialisation has caused serious environmental problems. The Czech Republic was considered to be the most polluted country in eastern Europe in the early 1990s. Recently investment has gone into electronics factories and research establishments. Tourism has increased post-Communism, with the country's many resorts, historic cities and winter sports facilities attracting visitors.

Quick facts:

Area: 30,450 square miles (78,864 square kilometres)
Population: 10,315,000
Capital: Prague (Praha)
Other cities: Brno, Olomouc, Ostrava, Plzen
Form of government: Republic
Religions: Roman Catholicism, Protestantism
Currency: Koruna

Denmark A small European state lying between the North Sea and the entrance to the Baltic. It consists of a western peninsula and an eastern archipelago of more than 500 islands, 100 of which are inhabited. The country is very low-lying and the proximity of the sea combined with the effect of the Gulf Stream result in warm sunny summers and cold cloudy winters. The scenery is flat and monotonous and the acidic soils need a great deal of fertilisation for a wide variety of crops to be grown. It is an agricultural country and three-quarters of the land is cultivated, mostly by the rotation of grass, barley, oats and sugar beet. Animal husbandry is, however, a particularly important activity, its produce including the famous bacon and butter. Danish beer and lager are also famous throughout the world. It is estimated that 85 per cent of the population live in the towns and cities. Despite Denmark's limited range of raw materials, it produces a wide range of manufactured goods and is famous for its imaginative design of ceramics, furniture, silverware and porcelain. Denmark is a wealthy country and the standard of living is high.

Quick facts:

Area: 16,639 square miles (43,094 square kilometres)
Population: 5,262,000 (excluding the FAEROE ISLANDS)
Capital: Copenhagen (København)
Other cities: Ålborg, Århus, Odense
Form of government: Constitutional Monarchy
Religion: Lutheranism
Currency: Danish Krone

Djibouti A country that is situated in northeast Africa and is bounded almost entirely by ETHIOPIA except in the southeast where it shares a border with SOMALIA and in the northwest where it shares a border with ERITREA. Its coastline is on the Gulf of Aden. Djibouti was formerly a French overseas territory but achieved independence in 1977. The land, which is mainly basalt plains, has some mountains rising to about 5,000 feet (1,500 metres). The climate is hot, among the world's hottest and extremely dry. Less than a tenth of the land can be farmed even for grazing so it has great difficulty supporting its modest population. The native population is mostly nomadic, moving from oasis to oasis or across the border to Ethiopia in search of grazing land. Crops raised include fruits, vegetables and dates. Most foodstuffs for the urban population in Djibouti city are imported. The capital is linked to Addis Ababa by a railway. Cattle, hides and skins are the main exports. There are small deposits of copper, iron ore and gypsum but these are not mined.

Quick facts:
Area: 8,958 square miles (23,200 square kilometres)
Population: 617,000
Capital: Djibouti
Form of government: Republic
Religion: Sunni Islam
Currency: Djibouti Franc

Dominica Discovered by Columbus, Dominica is the most northerly of the Windward Islands in the West Indies. It is situated between the islands of Martinique and Guadeloupe. The island is very rugged and with the exception of 87 square miles (225 square kilometres) of flat land, it consists of three inactive volcanoes, the highest of which is 4,747 feet (1,447 metres). There are many unnavigable rivers, and Boiling Lake, situated in the south, often gives off sulphurous gases. The climate is tropical and even on the leeward coast it rains two days out of three. The wettest season is from June to October when hurricanes often occur. The steep slopes are difficult to farm but agriculture provides almost all Dominica's exports. Bananas are the main agricultural export, but copra, citrus fruits, cocoa, coconuts, bay leaves, cinnamon and vanilla are also revenue earners. Industry is mostly based on the processing of the agricultural products.

Quick facts:
Area: 290 square miles (751 square kilometres)
Population: 74,000
Capital: Roseau
Form of government: Republic
Religion: Roman Catholicism
Currency: East Caribbean Dollar

Dominican Republic A country that forms the eastern portion of the island of Hispaniola in the West Indies. It covers two-thirds of the island, the smaller portion consisting of HAITI. The climate is semi-tropical, and occasionally hurricanes occur, causing great destruction. The west of the country is made up of four almost parallel mountain ranges, and between the two most northerly is the fertile Cibao Valley. The southeast is made up of fertile plains. Although well endowed with fertile land, only about 30 per cent is cultivated. Sugar is the main crop and mainstay of the country's economy and is grown mainly on plantations in the southeast plains. Other crops grown are rice, coffee, bananas, cocoa and tobacco. Mining of gold, silver, platinum, nickel and aluminium is carried out, but the main industries are food processing and manufacture of consumer goods. Fishing is also carried out but not to any great extent because of lack of equipment and refrigeration facilities. The island has fine beaches and the tourism industry is now very important to the economy.

Quick facts:
Area: 18,816 square miles (48,734 square kilometres)
Population: 8,052,000
Capital: Santo Domingo
Other cities: Barahona, Santiago, San Pedro de Macoris
Form of government: Republic
Religion: Roman Catholicism
Currency: Dominican Republic Peso

East Timor A country at the eastern end of the Lesser Sunda Islands in the Malay archipelago in southeast Asia, consisting of the eastern part of the island of Timor, a coastal enclave on the northwest and the islands of Ataúro and Jaco. Formerly a Portuguese overseas province, Portuguese Timor (Timor Timur) was illegally annexed by Indonesia in 1975, a claim that was never recognised by the UN. East Timor was the site of much civil unrest in its fight for independence, and its independence movement was violently suppressed by Indonesia. A referendum in 1999 officially ended Indonesia's occupation, and after a transitional period under the administration of the UN, it became an independent country in May of 2002. West Timor is under the administration of Indonesia. The official languages are Portuguese, Tetun and English. The economy is mainly supported by the export of maize and coffee.

Quick facts:
Area: 5,743 sq mi (14,874 sq km)
Population: 857,000
Capital: Dili
Form of government: Republic
Religions: Roman Catholicism
Currency: US dollar

Ecuador An Andean country situated in the northwest of the South American continent. It is bounded to the north by Colombia and to the east and south by Peru. It also includes the Galapagos Islands, which are located about 600 miles (965 kilometres) west of the mainland. The country contains over 30 active volcanoes, with Mount Cotopaxi at 19,340 feet (5,895 metres) the highest active volcano on Earth. Running down the middle of Ecuador are two ranges of the Andes that are divided by a central plateau. The coastal area consists of plains and the eastern area is made up of tropical jungles. The climate varies from equatorial through warm temperate to mountain conditions according to altitude. It is in the coastal plains that plantations of bananas, cocoa, coffee and sugar cane are found. In contrast to this, the highland areas are adapted to grazing, dairying and cereal growing. The fishing industry is important on the Pacific Coast and processed fish such as tuna and shrimp are main exports. Ecuador is one of the world's leading producers of balsawood. Oil is produced in the eastern region and petroleum is Ecuador's most important export. The official language is Spanish although many people in rural areas speak Quecha, the Incan language.

Quick facts:
Area: 109,484 square miles (283,561 square kilometres)
Population: 11,698,000
Capital: Quito
Other cities: Ambato, Guayaquil, Cuenca, Machala
Form of government: Republic
Religion: Roman Catholicism
Currency: Sucre

Egypt A country situated in northeast Africa, acting as the doorway between Africa and Asia. Its outstanding physical feature is the Tiver Nile, the valley and delta of which cover about 13 737 square miles (35,580 square kilometres). The climate is mainly dry but there are winter rai s along the Mediterranean coast. The temperatures are comfortable in winter but summer temperatures are extremely high, particularly in the south. The rich soils deposited by floodwaters along the banks of the Nile can support a large population and the delta is one of the world's most fertile agricultural regions. Around 99 per cent of the population live in the delta and Nile valley where the main crops are rice, cotton, sugar cane, maize, tomatoes and wheat. This concentration makes it one of the most densely populated areas in the world. The main industries are food processing and textiles. The economy has been boosted by the discovery of oil and is enough to supply the country's needs and leave surplus for export. Natural gas production is increasing for domestic use and Egypt has a significant fishing industry, mainly in the shallow lakes and Red Sea. The Suez Canal, shipping and tourism connected with the ancient sites are also important revenue earners.

Quick facts:
Area: 386,662 square miles (1,001,449 square kilometres)
Population: 60,603,000
Capital: Cairo (El Qâhira)
Other cities: Alexandria, Giza, Port Said, Suez
Form of government: republic
Religions: Sunni Islam, Christianity
Currency: Egyptian Pound

El Salvador The smallest and most densely populated state in Central America. It is bounded north and east by Honduras and has a Pacific coast to the south. Two volcanic ranges run from east to west across the country. The Lempa river cuts the southern ranges in the centre of the country and opens as a large sandy delta to the Pacific Ocean. Although fairly near the equator, the climate tends to be warm rather than hot and the highlands have a cooler temperate climate. The country is predominantly agricultural and 32 per cent of the land is used for crops such as coffee (the major crop and revenue earner), cotton, maize, beans, rice and sorghum, and a slightly smaller area is used for grazing cattle, pigs, sheep and goats. Fishing is carried out, the most important being shrimp, although tuna, mackerel and swordfish are also caught. A few industries such as food processing, textiles and chemicals are found in the major towns. The country suffers from a high rate of inflation and unemployment and is one of the poorest countries in the west.

Quick facts:

Area: 8,124 square miles (21,041 square kilometres)
Population: 5,796,000
Capital: San Salvador
Other cities: Santa Ana, San Miguel
Form of government: Republic
Religion: Roman Catholicism
Currency: Colón

Equatorial Guinea A country that lies about 124 miles (200 kilometres) north of the equator on the hot humid coast of west Africa. The country consists of a square-shaped mainland area (Mbini), with its few small offshore islets, and the islands of Bioko and Pagalu (Annobon). The climate is tropical and the wet season in Bioko and Pegalu lasts from December to February. Bioko is a very fertile volcanic island, and it is here that the capital, Malabo, is situated beside a volcanic crater flooded by the sea. It is also the centre of the country's cocoa production. Coffee and lumber are produced for export on the mainland. The country now relies heavily on foreign aid. Spanish is the official language although a variant of Bantu, Fang, is most commonly used. There is, however, much potential for a tourist industry.

Quick facts:

Area: 10,830 square miles (28,051 square kilometres)
Population: 410,000
Capital: Malabo
Other major city: Bata
Form of government: Republic
Religion: Roman Catholicism
Currency: CFA Franc

Eritrea Formerly an autonomous province of ETHIOPIA that gained independence in May 1993, shortly after a landslide vote in favor of sovereignty. Bounded by DJIBOUTI, SUDAN and ETHIOPIA, Eritrea has acquired Ethiopia's entire coastline along the Red Sea. The small Eritrean port of Aseb, in the southeast corner of the country has, however, been designated a "free port" guaranteeing the right of access for the now landlocked Ethiopia. Eritrea's climate is hot and dry along its desert coast but is colder and wetter in its central highland regions. Most of the population depend on subsistence farming. Future revenues may come from developing fishing, tourism and oil industries. Eritrea's natural resources include gold, potash, zinc, copper, salt, fish and probably oil. Deforestation and the consequent erosion are partly responsible for the frequent droughts and resultant famines that have blighted this area in recent years. Because of the famines and war with Ethiopia, a great many of the population were either displaced or were living as refugees in Sudan.

Quick facts:

Area: 45,406 square miles (117,600 square kilometres)
Population: 3,280,000
Capital: Asmara
Other cities: Mitsiwa, Keren, Nak'fa, Ak'ordat
Form of government: Republic
Religions: Sunni Islam, Christianity
Currency: Ethiopian Birr

Estonia A country that has over 1,500 islands and lies to the northwest of the RUSSIAN FEDERATION and is bounded to the north by the Gulf of Finland, to the west by the Baltic Sea and to the south by LATVIA. It is the smallest of the three previous Soviet Baltic Republics. Agriculture and dairy farming are the chief occupations and there are nearly three hundred agricultural collectives and state farms. The main products are grain, potatoes, flax, vegetables, meat, milk and eggs. Livestock includes cattle, sheep, goats and pigs. Almost 22 per cent of Estonia is forested, mainly with aspen, pine, birch and fir, and this provides material for sawmills, furniture, match and pulp industries. The country has rich, high quality shale deposits and phosphorous has been found near Tallinn. Peat deposits are substantial and supply some of the electric power stations. Estonia has about 72 per cent of its population living in urban areas, with almost a third living in the capital city. The economy is currently undergoing a major transformation to a free market system. Tourism and investment from the West have greatly contributed to the country's economy.

Quick facts:
Area: 17,413 square miles (45,227 square kilometres)
Population: 1,453,800
Capital: Tallinn
Other cities: Tartu, Narva, Pärnu
Form of government: Republic
Religions: Eastern Orthodox, Lutheranism
Currency: Kroon

Ethiopia A landlocked, East African country with borders with SUDAN, KENYA, SOMALIA, DJIBOUTI and ERITREA. Most of the country consists of highlands that drop sharply toward SUDAN in the west. Because of the wide range of latitudes, Ethiopia has many climatic variations between the high temperate plateau and the hot humid lowlands. The country is very vulnerable to drought but in some areas thunderstorms can erode soil from the slopes, reducing the area available for crop planting. Around 80 per cent of the population are subsistence farmers, and there are mineral deposits of copper, iron, petroleum, platinum and gold, which have been exploited. Coffee is the main source of rural income and teff is the main food grain. The droughts in 1989–90 brought much famine. Employment outside agriculture is confined to a small manufacturing sector in Addis Ababa. The country is wrecked with environmental, economic and political problems that culminated in May 1993 when one of ETHIOPIA's provinces, ERITREA, became independent.

Quick facts:
Area: 426,373 square miles (1,104,300 square kilometres)
Population: 58,506,000
Capital: Addis Ababa (Adis Abeba)
Other cities: Dire Dawa, Gonder, Jima
Form of government: Federation
Religions: Ethiopian Orthodox, Sunni Islam
Currency: Ethiopian Birr

Faeroe (Faroe) Islands (Føroyar) A self-governing part of DENMARK since 1948. They consist of a group of 18 basaltic islands and are situated in the North Atlantic, approximately halfway between the Shetland Islands and Iceland. The landscape of these islands is characterised by steep, stepped peaks rising out of the sea to nearly 3,000 feet (900 metres) and glaciated, trough-shaped valleys. Although the islands are inhabited, poor agricultural conditions compel the population to seek their living at sea. Fishing, including some whaling, is the main occupation and exports comprise fish and associated products.

Quick facts:
Area: 540 square miles (1,399 square kilometres)
Population: 47,000
Capital: Tørshavn
Form of government: Self-governing Region of Denmark
Religion: Lutheranism
Currency: Danish Krone

Falkland Islands A British Crown Colony situated in the South Atlantic, consisting of two large islands (West and East Falkland), separated by the 10-mile (16-kilometre) wide Falkland Sound and surrounded by some 200 smaller islands. Lying about 410 miles (650 kilometres) east of southern Argentina, these islands were invaded by Argentina in 1982. Argentina had long laid claim to these "Islas Malvinas" but they were recaptured by a British marine task force a few months later. The main economic activity is sheep farming, with open grazing on the wind-swept, treeless, rugged moorland that rises to over 2,295 feet (705 metres) on both main islands. The highest point is Mount Usborne at 2,313 feet (705 metres). Over recent years, substantial income has been gained from the sales of licenses to permit foreign trawlers to fish in the Falklands exclusion zone. There are also considerable off-shore oil reserves available.

Quick facts:
Area: 4,700 square miles (12,173 square kilometres)
Population: 2,200
Capital: Stanley
Form of government: British Crown Colony
Religion: Christianity
Currency: Falkland Islands Pound

Fiji One of the largest nations in the western Pacific, consisting of some 800 islands and atolls of which only about 100 are inhabited. It is situated around the 180-degree International Date Line and lies about 17 degrees south of the equator. Fiji has high rainfall, high temperatures and plenty of sunshine all year round. The two main islands, Viti Levu and Vanua Levu, are extinct volcanoes, and most of the islands in the group are fringed with coral reefs. The southeast of the islands have tropical rainforests but a lot of lumber has been felled and soil erosion is a growing problem. The main cash crop is sugar cane although copra, ginger and fish are also exported. Tourism is now a major industry and source of revenue although it was adversely affected by political coups in the late 1980s. In 1993, Cyclone Kina caused great destruction to agriculture and the general infrastructure.

Quick facts:
Area: 7,056 square miles (18,274 square kilometres)
Population: 797,000
Capital: Suva
Form of government: Republic
Religions: Christianity, Hinduism
Currency: Fijian Dollar

Finland A Scandinavian country that shares borders with Sweden, Norway and the RUSSIAN FEDERATION. Its coastline lies along the Gulf of Bothnia and the Gulf of Finland, both of which are arms of the Baltic Sea. Some 30,000 islands and islets line Finland's coast. Finnish Lapland in the north lies within the Arctic Circle. Most of mainland Finland is low-lying, becoming more hilly towards the north. Almost three-quarters of the country is forested, comprising mainly coniferous trees such as spruce and pine, and there are many thousands of lakes. The climate has great extremes between summer and winter. Winter is very severe and lasts about six months but only for three months in the south. Summers are short but quite warm, with light rain throughout the country. Finland is largely self-sufficient in food and produces great surpluses of dairy produce. Most crops are grown in the southwest. In the north reindeer are herded and forests yield great quantities of lumber for export. Just under 20 per cent of the electricity was supplied by its hydroelectric power stations in the early 1990s. Major industries are lumber products, wood pulp and paper, machinery and shipbuilding, which developed because of the country's great need for an efficient fleet of ice-breakers. Finland has an efficient transport system utilising canals, road, rail and air services.

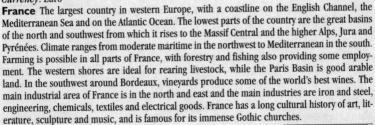

Quick facts:
Area: 130,559 square miles (338,145 square kilometres)
Population: 5,125,000
Capital: Helsinki (Helsingfors)
Other cities: Turku, Tampere
Form of government: Republic
Religion: Lutheranism
Currency: Euro

France The largest country in western Europe, with a coastline on the English Channel, the Mediterranean Sea and on the Atlantic Ocean. The lowest parts of the country are the great basins of the north and southwest from which it rises to the Massif Central and the higher Alps, Jura and Pyrénées. Climate ranges from moderate maritime in the northwest to Mediterranean in the south. Farming is possible in all parts of France, with forestry and fishing also providing some employment. The western shores are ideal for rearing livestock, while the Paris Basin is good arable land. In the southwest around Bordeaux, vineyards produce some of the world's best wines. The main industrial area of France is in the north and east and the main industries are iron and steel, engineering, chemicals, textiles and electrical goods. France has a long cultural history of art, literature, sculpture and music, and is famous for its immense Gothic churches.

Quick facts:
Area: 212,935 square miles (551,500 square kilometres)
Population: 58,375,000
Capital: Paris
Other cities: Bordeaux, Lyon, Marseille, Nantes, Nice, Toulouse,
    Strasbourg
Form of government: Republic
Religion: Roman Catholicism
Currency: Euro

French Guiana *see* GUIANA.

French Polynesia A total of about 130 islands in the South Pacific Ocean administered as overseas territories by FRANCE. The islands include the Society Islands, the Tuamotu group, the Gambier group, the Tubual Islands and the Marquesas Islands.

Quick facts:
Area: 1,544 square miles (4,000 square kilometres)
Population: 223,000
Capital: Papeete
Form of government: Overseas Territory of France
Religions: Protestantism, Roman Catholicism
Currency: Franc

Gabon A small country in west central Africa that straddles the equator. It has a low narrow coastal plain and the rest of the country comprises a low plateau. Three-quarters of Gabon is covered by dense tropical forest. The climate is hot, humid and typically equatorial, with little seasonal variation. It was in Lambaréné that Albert Schweitzer, the medical missionary, had his hospital. Until the 1960s lumber was virtually Gabon's only resource and then oil was discovered. By the mid-1980s it was Africa's sixth largest oil producer and other minerals, such as manganese, uranium and iron ore, were being exploited. Deposits of lead and silver have also been discovered. Much of the earnings from these resources has been squandered and around two-thirds of the Gabonese people remain subsistence farmers, growing cassava, sugar cane, plantains and yams. It is believed that the original inhabitants of the country were Pygmies but only a small number of them remain. The country has great tourist potential but because of the dense hardwood forests, transport links with the uninhabited interior are very difficult.

Quick facts:
Area: 103,347 square miles (267,668 square kilometres)
Population: 1,106,000
Capital: Libreville
Other major city: Port Gentile
Form of government: Republic
Religions: Roman Catholicism, African traditional religions
Currency: CFA Franc

Gambia The smallest country in Africa, which pokes like a crooked finger into SENEGAL. The country is divided along its entire length by the River Gambia, which can be crossed at only two main ferry crossings. On the coast there are pristine beaches and sand cliffs backed by mangrove swamps, with tropical jungle clothing much of the river banks away from the coast. Gambia has two very different seasons. In the dry season there is little rainfall, then the southwest monsoon sets in, with spectacular storms producing heavy rain for four months. Most Gambians live in villages with a few animals and grow enough millet and sorghum to feed themselves. Groundnuts are the main and only export crop of any significance. The river provides a thriving local fishing industry and the white sandy beaches on the coast are becoming increasingly popular with foreign tourists, although a military takeover in 1994 dealt tourism and trade a severe blow.

Quick facts:
Area: 4,361 square miles (11,295 square kilometres)
Population: 1,141,000
Capital: Banjul
Form of government: Republic
Religions: Sunni Islam, Christianity
Currency: Dalasi

Georgia A republic in the southwest of the former USSR, occupying the central and western parts of the Caucasus. It shares borders with TURKEY, ARMENIA, AZERBAIJAN and the RUSSIAN FEDERATION. It is bounded to the west by the Black Sea. Almost 40 per cent of the country is covered by forests. Agriculture, which is the main occupation of the population, includes tea cultivation and fruit growing, especially citrus fruits and viticulture. The republic is rich in minerals, especially manganese, but imports the majority of its energy needs. Industries include coal, lumber, machinery, chemicals, silk, food processing and furniture. In the past, the Black Sea tourist trade exploited the country's wealth of thermal and mineral springs very successfully and tourism should again become an economic mainstay. Georgia declared itself independent in 1991. A struggle for regional autonomy by ethnic minorities led to much disruption and violent conflict. Elections were held in 1995, heralding some progress and reform.

Quick facts:
Area: 26,911 square miles (69,700 square kilometres)
Population: 5,411,000
Capital: T'bilisi
Other cities: Kutaisi, Rustavi, Batumi
Form of government: Republic
Religions: Georgian and Russian Orthodox, Islam
Currency: Lari

Germany A large populous country in northern central Europe that comprises the former East and West German republics, reunified in 1990. In the north is the North German Plain, which merges with the North Rhinelands in the west. Farther south, a plateau that stretches across the country from east to west is divided by the River Rhine. In the southwest the Black Forest separates the Rhine Valley from the fertile valleys and scarplands of Swabia. More recently, coniferous forests have suffered from acid rain caused by industrial pollution. The Bohemian Uplands and Erz Mountains mark the border with the CZECH REPUBLIC. Generally the country has warm summers and cold winters. Agricultural products include wheat, rye, barley, oats, potatoes and sugar beet, although agriculture accounts for only a small percentage of employment and a third of the country's food has to be imported. The main industrial and most densely populated areas are in the Ruhr Valley. Products of the principal manufacturing industries include iron and steel, motor vehicles, mechanical and electrical equipment, aircraft, ships, computers, electronic and technical goods, chemicals and petrochemicals, pharmaceuticals, textiles, clothing and footwear, foods, beer, optical and high precision instruments.

Quick facts:
Area: 137,735 square miles (356,733 square kilometres)
Population: 81,912,000
Capital: Berlin
Other cities: Bonn, Cologne, Dortmund, Düsseldorf, Essen, Frankfurt, Hamburg, Leipzig, Munich, Stuttgart
Form of government: Republic
Religions: Lutheranism, Roman Catholicism
Currency: Euro

Ghana A country located on the southern coast of West Africa between CÔTE D'IVOIRE and TOGO. In 1957, as the former British Gold Coast, it became the first black African state to achieve independence from European colonial rule. It has palm-fringed beaches of white sand along the Gulf of Guinea and where the great River Volta meets the sea there are peaceful blue lagoons. The climate on the coast is equatorial and towards the north there are steamy tropical evergreen forests which give way in the far north to tropical savanna. The landscape becomes harsh and barren near the border with BURKINA FASO. Most Ghanaians are village dwellers whose homes are made of locally available materials. The south of the country has been most exposed to European influence and it is here that cocoa, rubber, palm oil and coffee are grown. Ghana's most important crop is cocoa and others include coffee, palm kernels, coconut oil, copra, shea nuts and bananas which are all exported. Fishing is also of major importance and has increased in recent years. Ghana has important mineral resources, notably gold, diamonds, manganese and bauxite. Most of Ghana's towns are in the south but rapid growth has turned many of them into unplanned sprawls.

Quick facts:
Area: 92,100 square miles (238,537 square kilometres)
Population: 17,459,350
Capital: Accra
Other cities: Sekondi-Takoradi, Kumasi, Tamale
Form of government: Republic
Religions: Protestantism, African traditional religions, Roman Catholicism
Currency: Cedi

Gibraltar A self-governing British Crown colony on the southwestern tip of SPAIN, where a limestone hill called the Rock of Gibraltar rises to 1,394 feet (425 metres). Its strategic importance, guarding as it does the western approaches to the Mediterranean and separated from MOROCCO by the narrow Straits of Gibraltar, has resulted in it being occupied at various periods of history by Phoenicians, Carthaginians, Romans, Visigoths, Moors, Spaniards and the British. In 1713, the Treaty of Utrecht awarded Gibraltar to Britain but Spain has never relinquished its claim to the Rock and relations have at times been difficult. English is the official language, although Spanish is also spoken. The British armed forces, tourism, banking and construction are the main sources of employment and most imports are from Britain. The Mediterranean climate and many sites of natural and historical interest attract numerous visitors each year.

Quick facts:
Area: 2.5 square miles (6.5 square kilometres)
Population: 27,100
Capital: Gibraltar
Form of government: Self-governing British Colony
Religion: Christianity
Currency: Gibraltar Pound

Greece The Greek peninsula is the most southeasterly extension of Europe and has over 1,400 islands lying off its coast and scattered throughout the Aegean Sea. Mainland Greece shares borders with ALBANIA in the northwest, MACEDONIA and BULGARIA in the north and TURKEY in the northeast. The northwestern and central regions of the country are rugged and mountainous, the main chain being the Pindus Mountains. About 70 per cent of the land is hilly, with harsh mountain climates and poor soils and there are few natural resources of economic value although there are deposits of petroleum and natural gas found under the Aegean Sea. The Greek islands and coastal regions have a typical Mediterranean climate, with mild rainy winters and hot dry summers. Winter in the northern mountains is severe, with deep snow and heavy precipitation. About 21 per cent of the people are engaged in agriculture, mostly on small family farms. Forestry and fishing are carried out on a small scale. Greece has undergone a rapid process of industrialisation since the Second World War and pollution is a serious problem in some areas. Tourism is a major source of revenue for the country along with shipping.

Quick facts:

Area: 50,949 square miles (131,957 square kilometres)
Population: 10,475,000
Capital: Athens (Athínai)
Other cities: Iráklian, Lárisa, Patras, Piraeus, Thessaloníki
Form of government: Republic
Religion: Greek Orthodox
Currency: Euro

Greenland (Kalaallit Nunaat) The largest island in the world (discounting continental land masses). It lies mainly within the Arctic Circle, off the northeast coast of Canada. Its vast interior is mostly covered with a permanent ice cap that has a known thickness of up to 11,000 feet (3,300 metres). The ice-free coastal strips are characterised by largely barren mountains, rising to Gunnbjorn at 12,140 feet (3,700 metres) in the southeast. Glaciers flow into deeply indented fjords which are fringed by many islands, islets and icebergs. Of the small ice-free fringe, only about a third (58,000 square miles/150,000 square kilometres) can be classed as being inhabited, mainly in the southwest. The largely Inuit population is heavily dependent on fishing for its livelihood, and fish account for 95 per cent of exports. There is some sheep farming and mining of coal and mineral resources as well as iron ore, lead, zinc, uranium and molybdenum.

Quick facts:

Area: 840,000 square miles (2,175,600 square kilometres)
Population: 58,200
Capital: Gothåb (Nuuk)
Form of government: Self-governing Region of Denmark
Religion: Lutheranism
Currency: Danish Krone

Grenada The most southerly of the Windward Islands chain in the Caribbean and its territory includes the southern Grenadine Islands to the north. The main island consists of the remains of extinct volcanoes and has an attractive wooded landscape. The highest peak is Mount St Catherine at 2,750 feet (838 metres). In the dry season the typical climate is very pleasant, with warm days and cool nights, but in the wet season it is hot day and night. Agriculture is the island's main industry and the chief crops grown for export are citrus fruits, cocoa, nutmegs, bananas and mace. Other crops grown are cloves, cotton, coconuts and cinnamon. Apart from the processing of its crops, Grenada has little manufacturing industry although tourism is an important source of foreign revenue. It is a popular port of call for cruise ships.

Quick facts:

Area: 133 square miles (344 square kilometres)
Population: 92,000
Capital: St George's
Form of government: Independent State within the Commonwealth
Religions: Roman Catholicism, Anglicanism, Methodism
Currency: East Caribbean Dollar

Guadeloupe A small group of islands in the Caribbean lying in the middle of the Lesser Antilles, with some islands in the Leeward Islands and some in the Windward Islands. Since 1946 Guadeloupe has been an overseas department of FRANCE. Ninety per cent of the population live on the two main islands of Basse Terre and Grande Terre. Basse Terre is mountainous, covered with rainforest and dominated by the Soufrière volcano at 4,318 feet (1,467 metres). Grande Terre is flat and dry with white sandy beaches. The other islands include Marie Galante, La Désirade, Iles des Saints, St Barthélémy and St Martin. The islands have a warm and humid climate with rainfall heaviest between May and November. Main exports include bananas, sugar and rum.

Quick facts:

Area: 658 square miles (1,705 square kilometres)
Population: 431,000
Capital: Basse Terre
Other main town: Pointe-à-Pitre
Form of government: French Overseas Department
Religion: Roman Catholicism
Currency: Euro

Guam Guam is the most southerly and the largest of the Mariana Islands in the northwest Pacific. It consists mainly of a high, coraline limestone plateau with some low volcanic mountains in the south of the island. Guam's climate is tropical with a rainy season from July to December. An unincorporated territory of the USA, its economy depends to a large extent on government activities and military installations account for some 35 per cent of the land area of the island. Exports include copra, palm oil and processed fish. The country has also become a financial centre, particularly for mainland and Asian banks and tourism has come to play an important role in its economy.

Quick facts:

Area: 212 square miles (549 square kilometres)
Population: 153,000
Capital: Agana
Form of government: Unincorporated territory of the USA
Religion: Roman Catholicism
Currency: US dollar

Guatemala A country situated between the Pacific Ocean and the Caribbean Sea where North America meets Central America. It is mountainous, with a ridge of volcanoes running parallel to the Pacific coast. It has a tropical climate with little or no variation in temperature and a distinctive wet season. The Pacific slopes of the mountains are exceptionally well watered and fertile and it is here that most of the population is settled. Coffee-growing on the lower slopes dominates the economy, although bananas, sugar, cardamom, petroleum and shellfish are exported. The forested area of the country, about 36 per cent, plays an important part in the country's economy and produces balsam, cabinet woods, chicle and oils. There are also deposits of petroleum and zinc, while lead and silver are mined. Industry is mainly restricted to the processing of the agricultural products. Guatemala is politically a very unstable country and civil conflict has practically destroyed tourism.

Quick facts:

Area: 42,042 square miles (108,889 square kilometres)
Population: 10,928,000
Capital: Guatemala City
Other cities: Cobán, Puerto Barrios, Quezaltenango
Form of government: Republic
Religion: Roman Catholicism
Currency: Quetza

Guiana (French) or Guyane Situated on the northeast coast of South America and still an overseas department of FRANCE, Guiana is bounded to the south and east by BRAZIL and to the west by SURINAM. The climate is tropical with heavy rainfall. Guiana's economy relies almost completely on subsidies from France. It has little to export apart from shrimps and the small area of land that is cultivated produces rice, manioc and sugar cane. Recently the French have tried to develop the tourist industry and exploit the extensive reserves of hardwood in the jungle interior. This has led to a growing sawmill industry and the export of logs. Natural resources, in addition to lumber, include bauxite, cinnabar (mercury ore) and gold (although this is in scattered deposits). The Ariane rocket launch site of the European Space Agency is located at Kourou.

Quick facts:
Area: 34,749 square miles (90,000 square kilometres)
Population: 153,000
Capital: Cayenne
Form of government: French Overseas Department
Religion: Roman Catholicism
Currency: Euro

Guinea Formerly a French West African territory, Guinea is located on the coast at the 'bulge' in Africa. It is a lush green beautiful country about the same size as the UNITED KINGDOM. It has a tropical climate with constant heat and a high rainfall near the coast. Its principal rivers are the Gambia and the Bafing while the Niger rises in the forests of the Guinea Highlands. Guinea has great agricultural potential and many of the coastal swamps and forested plains have been cleared for the cultivation of rice, cassava, yams, maize and vegetables. Around 80 per cent of the population are subsistence farmers. Although the country has eight national languages, the official language is French. Farther inland on the plateau of Fouta Djallon, dwarf cattle are raised and in the valleys bananas and pineapples are grown. Coffee and kola nuts are important cash crops grown in the Guinea Highlands to the southwest. Minerals such as bauxite, of which there are substantial reserves, iron ore, diamonds, gold and uranium are mined but development is hampered by lack of transport.

Quick facts:
Area: 94,926 square miles (245,857 square kilometres)
Population: 7,518,000
Capital: Conakry
Other cities: Kankan, Kindia, Labé
Form of government: Republic
Religion: Sunni Islam
Currency: Guinea Franc

Guinea-Bissau Formerly a Portuguese territory but granted independence in 1974, Guinea-Bissau is located south of SENEGAL on the Atlantic coast of West Africa. The republic's territory includes over 60 coastal islands, including the archipelago of Bijagós. It is a country of stunning scenery and rises from a deeply indented and island-fringed coastline to a low inland plateau and hills on the border with neighbouring GUINEA. The climate is tropical, with abundant rain from June to November but hot dry conditions for the rest of the year. Years of Portuguese rule and civil war have left Guinea-Bissau impoverished and it is one of the poorest West African states. The country's main aim is to become self-sufficient in food and the main crops grown by the subsistence farmers are rice, groundnuts, cassava, sugar cane, plantains, maize and coconuts. Fishing is an important export industry although cashew nuts are the principal export. Peanuts, palm products and cotton are also a source of export revenue.

Quick facts:
Area: 13,948 square miles (36,125 square kilometres)
Population: 1,091,000
Capital: Bissau
Form of government: Republic
Religions: African traditional religions, Sunni Islam
Currency: Peso

Guyana The only English-speaking country in South America, situated on the northeast coast of the continent on the Atlantic Ocean. Guyana was formerly called British Guiana but achieved independence in 1966. The country is intersected by many rivers and the coastal area comprises tidal marshes and mangrove swamps. It is on this narrow coastal area that rice is grown and vast plantations produce sugar. The jungle in the southwest has potential for the production of minerals, hardwood and hydroelectric power, but 90 per cent of the population live in the coastal area where the climate is moderated by sea breezes. Sugar and its by-products and rice are the mainstay of the country's economy, while tropical fruits and vegetables, such as coconuts, citrus, coffee and corn, are grown mainly for home consumption. Large numbers of livestock including cattle, sheep, pigs and chickens are also raised. Guyana's principal mineral is bauxite, with gold, manganese and diamonds also being produced.

Quick facts:

Area: 83,000 square miles (214,969 square kilometres)
Population: 838,000
Capital: Georgetown
Other cities: Linden, New Amsterdam
Form of government: Cooperative Republic
Religions: Hinduism, Protestantism, Roman Catholicism
Currency: Guyana Dollar

Guyane *see* GUIANA.

Haiti Occupying the western third of the large island of Hispaniola in the Caribbean, Haiti is a mountainous country consisting of five different ranges, the highest point reaching 8,793 feet (2,680 metres) at Pic La Selle. The mountain ranges are separated by deep valleys and plains. The climate is tropical but semi-arid conditions can occur in the lee of the central mountains. Hurricanes and severe thunderstorms are a common occurrence. Only a third of the country is arable, yet agriculture is the chief occupation, with around 80 per cent of the population concentrated in rural areas. Many farmers grow enough to feed only their own families, and the export crops of coffee, sugar and sisal are grown on large estates. Severe soil erosion caused by extensive forest clearance has resulted in a decline in crop yields and environmental damage has been caused. The country has only limited amounts of natural resources, bauxite not now being commercially profitable, although deposits of salt, copper and gold exist. Haiti is the poorest country in the Americas and has experienced many uprisings and attempted coups.

Quick facts:

Area: 10,714 square miles (27,750 square kilometres)
Population: 7,336,000
Capital: Port-au-Prince
Other towns: Cap-Haïtien, Les Cayes, Gonaïves
Form of government: Republic
Religions: Roman Catholicism, Voodooism
Currency: Gourde

Honduras A fan-shaped country in Central America that spreads out towards the Caribbean Sea at the Gulf of Honduras. Four-fifths of the country is covered by mountains that are indented with river valleys running towards the very short Pacific coast. There is little change in temperatures throughout the year and rainfall is heavy, especially on the Caribbean coast where temperatures are also higher than inland. The highlands are covered with forests, mainly of oak and pine, while palms and mangroves grow in the coastal areas. The country is sparsely populated and, although agricultural, only about 25 per cent of the land is cultivated. Honduras was once the world's leading banana exporter and although that fruit is still its main export, agriculture is now more diverse. Grains, coffee and sugar are important crops, and these are grown mainly on the coastal plains of the Pacific and Caribbean. Forestry is one of the principal industries, producing mahogany, pine, walnut, ebony and rosewood. Industry has increased in recent years, producing cotton, cement and sugar products for export.

Quick facts:
Area: 43,277 square miles (112,088 square kilometres)
Population: 6,140,000
Capital: Tegucigalpa
Other cities: San Pedro Sula, La Ceiba, Puerto Cortès
Form of government: Republic
Religion: Roman Catholicism
Currency: Lempira

Hong Kong Formerly a British Dependent Territory, on 1 July 1997 it became a Special Autonomous Province of China. Hong Kong is located in the South China Sea and consists of Hong Kong Island (once a barren rock), the peninsula of Kowloon and about 386 square miles (1,000 square kilometres) of adjacent land known as the New Territories. Hong Kong is situated at the mouth of the Pearl River, about 81 miles (130 kilometres) southeast of Guangzhou (Canton). The climate is warm subtropical with cool dry winters and hot humid summers. Hong Kong has no natural resources, even its water comes from reservoirs across the Chinese border. Its main assets are its magnificent natural harbor and its position close to the main trading routes of the Pacific. Hong Kong's economy is based on free enterprise and trade, an industrious work force and an efficient and aggressive commercial system. Hong Kong's main industries are textiles, clothing, tourism and electronics.

Quick facts:
Area: 415 square miles (1,075 square kilometres)
Population: 6,687,200
Form of government: Special Autonomous Province of China
Religions: Buddhism, Taoism, Christianity
Currency: Hong Kong Dollar

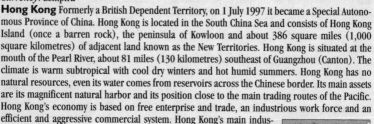

Hungary Landlocked in the heartland of Europe, Hungary is dominated by the great plain to the east of the River Danube, which runs north-south across the country, its tributaries including the Tisza, the longest river. In the west lies the largest lake in Central Europe, Lake Balaton. Winters are severe, but the summers are warm and although wet in the west, summer droughts often occur in the east. Hungary experienced a modest boom in its economy in the 1970s and 1980s. The government invested money in improving agriculture by mechanising farms, using fertilisers, and bringing new land under cultivation. Yields of cereals for bread-making and rice have since soared, and large areas between the Danube and Tisza rivers are now used to grow vegetables. However, the use of these artificial fertilisers has caused water pollution. Industries have been carefully developed where adequate natural resources exist, such as bauxite, which is the country's main resource. New industries like electrical and electronic equipment are now being promoted and tourism is fast developing around Lake Balaton.

Quick facts:
Area: 35,920 square miles (93,032 square kilometres)
Population: 10,193,000
Capital: Budapest
Other cities: Debrecen, Miskolc, Pécs, Szeged
Form of government: Republic
Religions: Roman Catholicism, Calvinism, Lutheranism
Currency: Forint

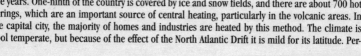

Iceland A large island situated in a tectonically unstable part of the North Atlantic Ocean, just south of the Arctic Circle. The island has over 100 volcanoes, at least one of which erupts every five years. One-ninth of the country is covered by ice and snow fields, and there are about 700 hot springs, which are an important source of central heating, particularly in the volcanic areas. In the capital city, the majority of homes and industries are heated by this method. The climate is cool temperate, but because of the effect of the North Atlantic Drift it is mild for its latitude. Permanent daylight occurs for three months in summer and the beautiful Aurora Borealis (Northern Lights) can be seen from the end of August. The southwest corner is the most densely populated area as the coast here is generally free from ice. Very little of the land can be cultivated and the main crops are root vegetables such as turnip and potatoes. Fishing and fish processing are the mainstay of the Icelandic economy, with much of the catch being exported. Aluminium and ferrosilicon, nitrates for fertilisers, cement and chemicals are produced for export. Other manufactured goods include paints, textiles, clothing, footwear and knitted products. Tourism is also of growing importance to the island.

Quick facts:

Area: 39,769 square miles (103,000 square kilometres)
Population: 275,300
Capital: Reykjavík
Other cities: Akureyri, Kópavogur
Form of government: Republic
Religion: Lutheranism
Currency: Icelandic Króna

India A vast country in South Asia that is dominated in the extreme north by the world's youngest and highest mountains, the Himalayas, which extend about 1,500 miles (about 2,400 kilometres) along India's northern and eastern borders. The range contains Mount Everest and K2. At the foot of the Himalayas, a huge plain, drained by the Indus and Ganges rivers, is one of the most fertile areas in the world and the most densely populated part of India. Farther south the ancient Deccan plateau extends to the southern tip of the country. India generally has four seasons, the cool, the hot, the rainy and the dry. About 70 per cent of the population depend on agriculture for their living and the lower slopes of the Himalayas represent one of the world's best tea-growing areas. Rice, sugar cane and wheat are grown in the Ganges plain, and there is a comprehensive system of irrigation to aid agriculture. India is self-sufficient in all its major food crops and main exports include precious stones, jewelry, engineering products, clothes and chemicals. Since becoming a republic in 1950, India has been troubled by internal dissent and external disputes, particularly with Pakistan over the status of Kashmir.

Quick facts:

Area: 1,269,346 square miles (3,287,590 square kilometres)
Population: 970,930,000
Capital: New Delhi
Other cities: Ahmadabad, Bangalore, Bombay, Calcutta, Delhi,
  Madras, Hyderabad, Kanpur
Form of government: Federal Republic, Secular Democracy
Religions: Hinduism, Islam, Sikkism, Christianity, Jainism, Buddhism
Currency: Rupee

Indonesia A country made up of 13,667 islands that are scattered across the Indian and Pacific Oceans in a huge crescent. It is the world's fourth most highly populated country. Its largest landmass is the province of Kalimantan, which is part of the island of Borneo. Sumatra is the largest individual island. Java, however, is the dominant and most densely populated island. The climate is generally tropical monsoon and temperatures are high all year round. The country has 130 active volcanoes and earthquakes are frequent in the southern islands. Overpopulation is a big problem, especially in Java where its fertile rust-coloured soil is in danger of becoming exhausted. Rice, maize and cassava are the main crops grown. Indonesia has the largest reserves of tin in the world and is one of the world's leading rubber producers. Other mineral resources found are bauxite, natural gas, nickel and copper. Oil production is also important. Indonesia's resources are not as yet fully developed but the country's economy is now expanding and needs to create over two million jobs annually to keep pace with the expanding population. Ongoing political instability and human rights abuse are hampering this process.

Quick facts:
Area: 735,358 square miles (1,904,569 square kilometres)
Population: 196,813,000
Capital: Jakarta
Other cities: Bandung, Medan, Palembang, Semarang, Surabaya
Form of government: Republic
Religions: Sunni Islam, Christianity, Hinduism
Currency: Rupiah

Iran, Islamic Republic of Lying across The Gulf from the Arabian Peninsula and stretching from the Caspian Sea to the Arabian Sea, Iran is a land dominated by mountains in the north and west, with a huge expanse of desert in its centre. The climate is hot and dry, although more temperate conditions are found on the shores of the Caspian Sea. In winter, terrible dust storms sweep the deserts and almost no life can survive. Most of the population live in the north and west, where Tehran is situated. The only good agricultural land is on the Caspian coastal plains, where wheat, barley, potatoes and rice are grown. Fresh and dried fruit are the country's main exports apart from petroleum. About 5 per cent of the population are nomadic herdsmen who wander in the mountains. Most of Iran's oil is in the southwest, and other valuable minerals include coal, iron ore, copper and lead. Precious stones are found in the northeast. Main exports are petrochemicals, carpets and rugs, textiles, raw cotton and leather goods. There was a rapid expansion in the economy from petroleum industry revenue. After the Islamic revolution in the late 1970s, however and war with Iraq, the economy slowed dramatically and is only gradually beginning to pick up again.

Quick facts:
Area: 634,293 square miles (1,648,195 square kilometres)
Population: 61,128,000
Capital: Tehran
Other cities: Esfahan, Mashhad, Tabriz
Form of government: Islamic Republic
Religion: Shia Islam
Currency: Rial

Iraq Located in southwest Asia, wedged between The Gulf and Syria, Iraq is almost landlocked except for its outlet to the Gulf at Shatt al Arab. Its two great rivers, the Tigris and the Euphrates, flow from the northwest into the Gulf at this point. The climate is arid, with very hot summers and cold winters. The high mountains on the border with Turkey are snow-covered for six months of the year, and desert in the southwest covers nearly half the country. The only fertile land in Iraq is in the basins of the Tigris and Euphrates, where wheat, barley, rice, tobacco and cotton are grown, with the country being primarily an agricultural one. The country is a large producer of dates. Oil was the main export. Iraq profited from the great oil boom of the 1970s, but during the war with Iran, oil terminals in the Gulf were destroyed and the Trans-Syrian Pipeline closed. Iraq invaded Kuwait in 1990, leading to the Gulf War in 1991 in which Iraq was defeated by United Nation forces. In a state of economic crisis since then, the regime of Saddam Hussein, President since 1979, collapsed in April 2003, three weeks into a major US-led military campaign to rid the country of weapons of mass destruction.

Quick facts:
Area: 169,235 square miles (438,317 square kilometres)
Population: 20,607,000
Capital: Baghdad
Other cities: Al-Basrah, Al Mawsil
Form of government: Republic
Religions: Shia Islam, Sunni Islam
Currency: Iraqi Dinar

Ireland, Republic of One of Europe's most westerly countries, situated in the Atlantic Ocean and separated from Great Britain by the Irish Sea. It has an equable climate, with mild southwest winds, which makes temperatures uniform over most of the country. The Republic extends over four-fifths of the island of Ireland and the west and southwest are mountainous, with the highest peak reaching 3,416 feet (1,041 metres) at Carrauntoohil. The central plain is largely limestone covered by boulder clay, which provides good farmland and pasture with about 80 per cent of the land being under agriculture. The main rivers are the Erne and the Shannon. Livestock production is the most important, including cattle, sheep, pigs and horses. The rural population have tended to migrate to the cities, mainly Dublin, which is the main industrial centre and the focus of radio, television, publishing and communications. Lack of energy resources and remoteness from major markets did slow industrial development, but by taking full advantage of membership of the European Union the economy has improved markedly in recent years, particularly tourism.

Quick facts:

Area: 27,137 square miles (70,284 square kilometres)

Population: 3,626,000

Capital: Dublin (Baile Atha Cliath)

Other cities: Cork, Galway, Limerick, Waterford

Form of government: Republic

Religion: Roman Catholicism

Currency: Euro

Israel Occupying a long narrow stretch of land in the southeast of the Mediterranean, Israel's eastern boundary is formed by the Great Rift Valley through which the River Jordan flows to the Dead Sea. The south of the country is made up of a triangular wedge of the Negev desert, which ends at the Gulf of Aqaba. The Negev desert has mineral resources, such as copper, phosphates and manganese, plus commercial amounts of natural gas and petroleum. Other assets are the vast amounts of potash, bromine and other minerals found in the Dead Sea. The climate in summer is hot and dry; in winter it is mild with some rain. The south of the country is arid and barren. Most of the population live on the coastal plain bordering the Mediterranean where Tel Aviv (Tel Aviv-Yafo) is the country's main commercial centre. Israel's agriculture is based on collective settlements known as kibbutz. The country is virtually self-sufficient in foodstuffs and a major exporter of its produce. A wide range of products is processed or finished in the country and main exports include finished diamonds, textiles, fruit, vegetables, chemicals, machinery and fertilisers. Tourism also makes an important contribution to the economy.

Quick facts:

Area: 8,130 square miles (21,056 square kilometres)

Population: 6,100,000

Capital: Jerusalem (UN recognised capital is Tel Aviv)

Other cities: Haifa

Form of government: Republic

Religions: Judaism, Sunni Islam, Christianity

Currency: New Israeli Shekel

Italy A republic in southern Europe that comprises a large peninsula and the two main islands of Sicily and Sardinia. The Alps form a natural boundary with its northern and western European neighbours and the Adriatic Sea to the east separates it from the countries of former Yugoslavia. The Apennine Mountains form the backbone of Italy and extend the full length of the peninsula. Between the Alps and the Apennines lies the Po Valley, a great fertile lowland. Sicily and Sardinia are largely mountainous. Much of Italy is geologically unstable and it has four active volcanoes, including Etna, Vesuvius and Stromboli. Italy enjoys warm dry summers and mild winters. In the south farms are small and traditional. Industries in the north include motor vehicles, textiles, clothing, leather goods, glass and ceramics. Although there is a lack of natural resources, almost 60 per cent of the land is under crops and pasture and there is an abundance of building stone, particularly marble. The coastal waters are rich in marine life, with anchovy, sardine and tuna being of commercial importance. Tourism is an important source of foreign currency.

Quick facts:
Area: 116,320 square miles (301,268 square kilometres)
Population: 57,339,000
Capital: Rome (Roma)
Other cities: Milan, Naples, Turin, Genoa, Palermo, Florence
Form of government: Republic
Religion: Roman Catholicism
Currency: Euro

Jamaica An island state in the Caribbean Sea about 93 miles (150 kilometres) south of Cuba. The centre of the island comprises a limestone plateau and this is surrounded by narrow coastal flatlands and palm-fringed beaches. The highest mountains, the Blue Mountains, are in the east of the island. The climate is tropical, with high temperatures at the coast and slightly cooler and less humid conditions in the highlands. Jamaica suffers from severe earthquakes and thermal springs can be found in areas of the country. The island lies right in the middle of the hurricane zone. The traditional crops grown are sugar cane, bananas, peppers, ginger, cocoa and coffee and new crops such as winter vegetables, fruit and honey are being developed for export. The mining of bauxite and alumina plays a very important part in Jamaica's economy and accounts for around 60 per cent of its total yearly exports. Industrialisation has been encouraged and clothing, footwear, cement and agricultural machinery are now produced. Tourism is a particularly important industry, with over one million visitors annually.

Quick facts:
Area: 4,243 square miles (10,990 square kilometres)
Population: 2,491,000
Capital: Kingston
Other town: Montego Bay
Form of government: Constitutional Monarchy
Religions: Anglicanism, Roman Catholicism, Protestantism
Currency: Jamaican Dollar

Japan Located on the eastern margin of Asia and consisting of four major islands, Honshu, Hokkaido, Kyushu and Shikoku and many small islands, Japan is separated from the mainland of Asia by the Sea of Japan. The country is made up of six chains of steep serrated mountains, which contain about 60 active volcanoes. Earthquakes are frequent and widespread and often accompanied by giant waves (tsunami). A devastating earthquake occurred in 1995 when more than 5,000 people died and over 300,000 were left homeless. Summers are warm and humid and winters mild, except on Hokkaido, which is covered in snow in winter. Japan's agriculture is highly advanced, with extensive use made of fertilisers and miniature machinery for the small fields. Fishing is very important, both for domestic consumption and export. Heavy industries, such as iron and steel, shipbuilding, chemicals and petrochemicals, used to account for almost three-quarters of Japan's export revenue, but now it has to rely on the success of its manufacturing industry which produces automobiles, televisions, videos, electronic equipment, cameras, watches, clocks, robots and textiles. Japan's financial markets have experienced some problems in recent years, which has introduced some uncertainty into what was a very secure economy.

Quick facts:
Area: 145,870 square miles (377,801 square kilometres)
Population: 125,761,000
Capital: Tokyo
Other cities: Osaka, Nagoya, Sapporo, Kobe, Kyoto, Yokohama
Form of government: Constitutional Monarchy
Religions: Shintoism, Buddhism, Christianity
Currency: Yen

Jordan Almost landlocked except for a short coastline on the Gulf of Aqaba, Jordan is bounded by SAUDI ARABIA, SYRIA, IRAQ and ISRAEL. Almost 80 per cent of the country is desert and the rest comprises the East Bank Uplands and Jordan Valley, part of the Great Rift Valley. In general, summers are hot and dry and winters cool and wet, with variations related to altitude. The east has a desert climate. Since under 5 per cent of the land is arable and only part of this is irrigated, production of grain is insufficient for the country's needs although some fruits and vegetables are grown for export. The capital, Amman, is the main industrial centre of the country and the industries include phosphates, petroleum products, cement, iron and fertilisers. The rich Arab states such as Saudi Arabia give Jordan substantial economic aid and the country has a modern network of roads that link the cities. In 1994 an historic peace agreement was signed with Israel that ended 46 years of hostilities.

Quick facts:

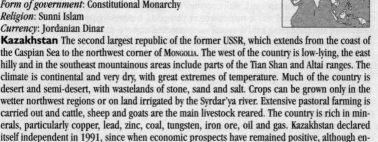

Area: 37,738 square miles (97,740 square kilometres)
Population: 5,581,000
Capital: Amman
Other cities: Aqaba, Irbid, Zarqa
Form of government: Constitutional Monarchy
Religion: Sunni Islam
Currency: Jordanian Dinar

Kazakhstan The second largest republic of the former USSR, which extends from the coast of the Caspian Sea to the northwest corner of MONGOLIA. The west of the country is low-lying, the east hilly and in the southeast mountainous areas include parts of the Tian Shan and Altai ranges. The climate is continental and very dry, with great extremes of temperature. Much of the country is desert and semi-desert, with wastelands of stone, sand and salt. Crops can be grown only in the wetter northwest regions or on land irrigated by the Syrdar'ya river. Extensive pastoral farming is carried out and cattle, sheep and goats are the main livestock reared. The country is rich in minerals, particularly copper, lead, zinc, coal, tungsten, iron ore, oil and gas. Kazakhstan declared itself independent in 1991, since when economic prospects have remained positive, although environmental problems have been left as a legacy of past Soviet exploitation and have still to be tackled (e.g. the overdraining of the Aral Sea). Parts of the country, particularly the mountainous regions, are subject to earthquakes and the former capital, Almaty, has been largely rebuilt following extensive damage. In 1997 the capital was moved to Astana, located in a more stable geological region.

Quick facts:

Area: 1,049,156 square miles (2,717,300 square kilometres)
Population: 15,671,000
Capital: Astana
Other major city: Almaty
Form of government: Republic
Religion: Sunni Islam
Currency: Tenge

Kenya Located in East Africa, Kenya straddles the equator and extends from Lake Victoria in the southwest to the Indian Ocean in the southeast. Highlands run north to south through central Kenya and are divided by the steep-sided Great Rift Valley. The coastal lowlands have a hot humid climate but in the highlands it is cooler and rainfall heavier. In the east it is very arid. The southwestern region is well watered, with huge areas of fertile soil and this accounts for the bulk of the population and almost all its economic production. A wide variety of crops are grown for domestic consumption, such as wheat, maize and cassava. Tea, coffee, sisal, sugar cane and cotton are grown for export. Oil refining at Mombasa is the country's largest single industry and other industry includes food processing and textiles. Mining is carried out on a small scale for soda ash, gold and limestone, but large quantities of silver and lead exist near Mombasa. Tourism is an important source of foreign revenue, the many wildlife and game reserves being a major attraction.

Quick facts:
Area: 224,081 square miles (580,367 square kilometres)
Population: 31,806,000
Capital: Nairobi
Other towns: Mombasa, Eldoret, Kisumu, Nakuru
Form of government: Republic
Religions: Roman Catholicism, Protestantism, other Christianity,
  African traditional religions
Currency: Kenya Shilling

Kiribati Formerly known as the Gilbert and Ellice Islands, Kiribati comprises three groups of coral atolls and one isolated volcanic island spread over a large expanse of the central Pacific Ocean. The group includes the former Gilbert Islands, the Phoenix Islands (now Rawaki) and the southern Line Islands. The largest island is Kiritimati, formerly known as Christmas island. The climate is maritime equatorial, with a rainy season from October to March. Most islanders are involved in subsistence agriculture. The principal tree is the coconut, which grows well on all the islands. There are palm and breadfruit trees and bananas and papaws to be found. Tuna fishing is an important industry, with coconuts and palm products being the main cash crops. Ocean Island (Banaba) was a rich source of phosphate deposits (guano) but these are now exhausted and the mining has left severe environmental damage, causing most Banabans to re-settle elsewhere. Tourism is becoming increasingly important but the country is heavily dependent on overseas aid.

Quick facts:
Area: 280 square miles (726 square kilometres)
Population: 80,000
Capital: Tarawa
Government: Republic
Religions: Roman Catholicism, Protestantism
Currency: Australian Dollar

Korea, Democratic People's Republic of A country occupying the northern half of the Korean peninsula in east Asia and formerly known as North Korea. The Yala and Tumen rivers form its northern border with CHINA and the RUSSIAN FEDERATION. Its southern border with the Republic of KOREA is just north of the 38th parallel. It is a mountainous country, three-quarters of which is forested highland or scrubland, with Paektu-San the highest peak at 9,003 feet (2,737 metres). The climate is warm temperate, although winters can be cold in the north. Most rain falls during the summer. Nearly 90 per cent of its arable land is farmed by cooperatives that employ over 40 per cent of the labour force and rice is the main crop grown. North Korea is quite well endowed with fuel and minerals such as magnesite, zinc, copper, lead, tungsten, gold and silver. Deposits of coal and hydroelectric power generate electricity and substantial deposits of iron ore are found near Pyongyang and Musan. Sixty per cent of the labour force is employed in industry, the most important of which are metallurgical, building, cement and chemicals. Fishing is carried on, with the main catches being tuna, anchovy and seaweeds.

Quick facts:
Area: 46,540 square miles (120,538 square kilometres)
Population: 22,466,000
Capital: Pyongyang
Other cities: Chongjin, Wonsan, Hamhung
Form of government: Socialist Republic
Religions: Buddhism, Confucianism, Chondogyo (a combination
  of Taoism and Confucianism)
Currency: Won

Korea, Republic of Formerly South Korea, the country occupies the southern half of the Korean peninsula in eastern Asia. It is bordered in the north by a demilitarised zone which acts as a buffer between the former South and North Koreas. Most of the country is hilly or mountainous, with the highest ranges running north to south along the east coast. The west is lowland and extremely densely populated. The extreme south has a humid warm temperate climate while farther north it is more continental. Most rain falls in summer. Cultivated land represents only 23 per cent of the country's total area and the main crops are rice, onions, potatoes, barley and maize. An increasing amount of fruit, such as melons, apples and peaches, is now produced. The country has few natural resources but does produce coal, graphite and iron ore. It has a flourishing manufacturing industry and is the world's leading supplier of ships and footwear. Other important industries are electronic equipment, electrical goods, steel, petrochemicals, motor vehicles and toys. Its people enjoy a reasonably high standard of living brought about by hard work and determination.

Quick facts:

Area: 38,368 square miles (99,373 square kilometres)
Population: 46,430,000
Capital: Seoul (Soul)
Other cities: Pusan, Taegu
Form of government: Republic
Religions: Buddhism, Christianity, Confucianism, Chondogyo
(a combination of Taoism and Confucianism), Unification Church
Currency: Won

Kuwait A tiny Arab state on The Gulf, comprising the city of Kuwait at the southern entrance of Kuwait Bay, a small undulating desert wedged between Iraq and Saudi Arabia and nine small offshore islands. It has a dry desert climate, cool in winter but very hot and humid in summer. There is little agriculture because of lack of water. The major crops produced are melons, tomatoes, onions and dates. The country's water comes from the desalination of seawater. Shrimp fishing is becoming an important industry. Large reserves of petroleum and natural gas are the mainstay of the economy although this wealth is limited. It has about 950 oil wells, but 600 were fired during the Iraqi occupation in 1991 and are unlikely to resume production for several years. Apart from oil, industry includes boat-building, plastics, petrochemicals, gases, cement and building materials. Although there are no railways, there are over 2,000 miles (3,220 kilometres) of roads and an international airport near the capital.

Quick facts:

Area: 6,880 square miles (17,818 square kilometres)
Population: 1,866,100
Capital: Kuwait City (Al Kuwayt)
Government: Constitutional Monarchy
Religions: Sunni Islam, Shia Islam
Currency: Kuwaiti Dinar

Kyrgyzstan A central Asian republic of the former USSR, independent since 1991. It is located on the border with northwest China. Much of the country is occupied by the Tian Shan Mountains, which rise to spectacular peaks. The highest is Pik Pobedy at 24,406 feet (7,439 metres), lying on the border with China. In the northeast of the country is Issyk Kul, a large lake heated by volcanic action, so it never freezes in winter. Most of the country is semi-arid or desert, but climate is greatly influenced by altitude. Soils are badly leached except in the valleys, where some grains are grown. Grazing of sheep, horses and cattle is extensive. Industries include non-ferrous metallurgy, machine building, coal mining, tobacco, food processing, textiles, gold mining and hydroelectricity. The country has large mineral deposits of gold, coal and uranium, while deposits of natural gas and oil have not, as yet, been developed. Parts of Kyrgyzstan are threatened by environmental pollution caused by storage of toxic waste and radioactive material which are the by-products of mining, former nuclear tests and the overuse of chemicals, especially fertilisers. The government is making efforts to address this problem and encourage foreign visitors.

Quick facts:
Area: 76,641 square miles (198,500 square kilometres)
Population: 4,575,000
Capital: Bishkek
Other major city: Osh
Form of government: Republic
Religion: Sunni Islam
Currency: Som

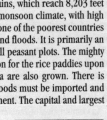

Laos A landlocked country in Southeast Asia that is ruggedly mountainous, apart from the Mekong river plains along its border with THAILAND. The Annam Mountains, which reach 8,203 feet (2,500 metres), form a natural border with VIETNAM. It has a tropical monsoon climate, with high temperatures throughout the year and heavy rains in summer. Laos is one of the poorest countries in the world and its development has been retarded by war, drought and floods. It is primarily an agricultural country, with rice being the principal crop grown on small peasant plots. The mighty Mekong river provides the main means of transport as well as irrigation for the rice paddies upon which the people's subsistence depends. Corn, potatoes and cassava are also grown. There is some export of lumber, coffee, tin and electricity. All manufactured goods must be imported and are mainly food, machinery, petroleum products and electrical equipment. The capital and largest city, Vientiane, is the country's main trade outlet via Thailand.

Quick facts:
Area: 91,429 square miles (236,800 square kilometres)
Population: 5,035,000
Capital: Vientiane
Other cities: Luang Prabang, Savannakhét, Paksé
Form of government: People's Republic
Religion: Buddhism
Currency: New Kip

Latvia A Baltic state that regained its independence in 1991 with the break-up of the former Soviet Union. It is located in northeast Europe on the Baltic Sea and is sandwiched between ESTONIA and LITHUANIA. It has cool summers, wet summers and long, cold winters. Latvians traditionally lived by forestry, fishing and livestock rearing. The chief agricultural occupations are cattle and dairy farming and the main crops grown are oats, barley, rye, potatoes and flax. Latvia's population is now over 70 per cent urban and agriculture is no longer the mainstay of the economy. It has a well-developed industrial base and produces electric railway carriages, electronic and electrical equipment (radios and refrigerators), paper, cement, chemicals, textiles, woolen goods, furniture and foodstuffs. Latvia has abundant deposits of peat and gypsum but lacks other fossil fuels and minerals, which has made it heavily dependent on imports of oil, gas and electricity. Hydroelectric plants on the Daugava river supply over half of the domestic production of electricity, which in total amounts to about 50 per cent of overall consumption. Economic development was difficult in the years following independence but the situation is gradually improving and Latvia is seeking full membership of the European Union.

Quick facts:
Area: 24,942 square miles (64,600 square kilometres)
Population: 2,491,000
Capital: Riga
Other cities: Liepaja, Daugavpils
Form of government: Republic
Religion: Lutheranism
Currency: Lat

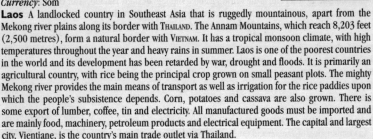

Lebanon A mountainous country in the eastern Mediterranean. A narrow coastal plain runs parallel to its 149-mile (240-kilometre) Mediterranean coast and gradually rises to the spectacular Lebanon Mountains, which are snow-covered in winter. The Anti-Lebanon Mountains form the border with SYRIA and between the two ranges lies the Beqaa Valley. The climate is Mediterranean, with short warm winters and long hot and rainless summers. Rainfall can be torrential in winter and snow falls on high ground. Lebanon is an agricultural country, the main regions of production being the Beqaa Valley and the coastal plain, although erosion is a common problem in the uplands. Main products include olives, grapes, bananas, citrus fruits, apples, cotton, tobacco and sugar beet. Industry is small scale and manufactures include cement, fertilisers and jewelry. There are oil refineries at Tripoli and Sidon. Lebanon's main economy is based on commercial services such as banking, but civil war, invasion by Israel and factional fighting have created severe problems for the economy, causing high inflation and unemployment.

Quick facts:

Area: 4,015 square miles (10,400 square kilometres)
Population: 3,084,900
Capital: Beirut (Beyrouth)
Other important cities: Tripoli, Sidon
Form of government: Republic
Religions: Shia Islam, Sunni Islam, Christianity
Currency: Lebanese Pound

Lesotho A small, landlocked kingdom entirely surrounded by the Republic of SOUTH AFRICA. Snow-capped mountains and treeless uplands, cut by spectacular gorges, cover two-thirds of the country. The climate is pleasant with variable rainfall. Winters are generally dry with heavy frosts in lowland areas and frequent snow in the highlands. Because of the mountainous terrain, only one-eighth of the land can be cultivated and the main crop is maize. Yields are low because of soil erosion on the steep slopes and overgrazing by herds of sheep and cattle. Wool and mohair are exported but most foreign exchange comes from money sent home by Lesotho workers in South Africa. Tourism is beginning to flourish, with skiing and pony trails on hardy Lesotho ponies in the mountains two of the main attractions.

Quick facts:

Area: 11,720 square miles (30,355 square kilometres)
Population: 2,078,000
Capital: Maseru
Form of government: Constitutional Monarchy
Religions: Roman Catholicism, other Christianity
Currency: Loti

Liberia Located in West Africa, Liberia has a 348-mile (560-kilometres) coast stretching from SIERRA LEONE to CÔTE D'IVOIRE. It is the only African country never to be ruled by a foreign power. It has a treacherous coast, with rocky cliffs and lagoons enclosed by sand bars. Inland the land rises to a densely forested plateau dissected by deep, narrow valleys. Farther inland still, there are beautiful waterfalls and the Nimba Mountains rise to a maximum height of 5,748 feet (1,752 metres). Agriculture employs three-quarters of the labour force and produces cassava and rice as subsistence crops and rubber, coffee and cocoa for export. Forest and animal reserves are magnificent and the beaches and lagoons are beautiful. The Nimba Mountains are rich in iron ore, which accounts for 70 per cent of export earnings and wood, rubber, diamonds and coffee are also exported. Liberia has a very large delivery tanker fleet, most of which have foreign owners. In the early 1990s the economy suffered greatly because of civil war, with food shortages and the drying up of foreign investment. The situation remains uncertain, leaving Liberia with considerable problems to overcome.

Quick facts:

Area: 43,000 square miles (111,369 square kilometres)
Population: 2,820,000
Capital: Monrovia
Other major city: Buchanan
Form of government: Republic
Religions: African traditional religions, Sunni Islam, Christianity
Currency: Liberian Dollar

Libya A large North African country that stretches from the south coast of the Mediterranean to and in some parts beyond, the Tropic of Cancer. The Sahara covers much of the country, extending right to the Mediterranean coast at the Gulf of Sirte. The only green areas are the scrublands found in the northwest and the forested hills near Benghazi. The coastal area has mild wet winters and hot dry summers, but the interior has had some of the highest recorded temperatures of anywhere in the world. Around 18 per cent of the people work on the land, the main agricultural region being in the northwest, near Tripoli, but this is dependent on rainfall. The main crops produced are wheat, tomatoes, fruits and barley. Many sheep, goats and cattle are reared and there is an export trade in skins, hides and hairs. Libya is one of the world's largest producers of oil and natural gas and also produces potash and marine salt. Other industries include food processing, textiles, cement and handicrafts. The majority of consumer products are imported.

Quick facts:

Area: 679,362 square miles (1,759,540 square kilometres)
Population: 4,389,739
Capital: Tripoli (Tarabulus)
Other cities: Benghazi, Misrāta
Form of government: Socialist People's Republic
Religion: Sunni Islam
Currency: Libyan Dinar

Liechtenstein The principality of Liechtenstein is a tiny central European state situated on the east bank of the River Rhine, bounded by AUSTRIA to the east and SWITZERLAND to the west. To the east and south lie the foothills of the Austrian Alps. The highest peak, on the border with Switzerland, is Grauspitz at 8,527 feet (2,599 metres). The climate is mild alpine. Approximately one-third of the country is covered by forests and there are deer, fox, chamois and badger. Once an agricultural country, Liechtenstein has rapidly moved into industry in the last 30 years, with a variety of light industries such as textiles, high quality metal goods, precision instruments, ceramics and pharmaceuticals. It is a popular location for the headquarters of foreign companies in order that they can benefit from the favorable tax laws. Tourism also thrives, beautiful scenery and good skiing being the main attractions. Other income is derived from international banking and financial services and the sale of postage stamps.

Quick facts:

Area: 62 square miles (160 square kilometres)
Population: 31,320
Capital: Vaduz
Form of government: Constitutional Monarchy (Principality)
Religion: Roman Catholicism
Currency: Swiss Franc

Lithuania A country that lies to the northwest of the RUSSIAN FEDERATION and BELARUS and is bounded to the north by LATVIA and west by POLAND. It is the largest of the three former Soviet Baltic republics. Before 1940 Lithuania was a mainly agricultural country but has since been considerably industrialised, with shipbuilding, food processing and electrical machinery production being the most significant industries. Most of the land is lowland, covered by forest and swamp and the main products are rye, barley, sugar beet, flax, meat, milk and potatoes. About 20 per cent of the population is engaged in agriculture, principally dairy farming and livestock production. Oil production has started from a small field at Kretinga in the west of the country, 10 miles (16 kilometres) north of Klaipeda. Amber is found along the Baltic coast and used by Lithuanian craftsmen for making jewelry. Financial scandals involving government members and banking institutions troubled the economy during the 1990s.

Quick facts:
Area: 25,174 square miles (65,200 square kilometres)
Population: 3,701,300
Capital: Vilnius
Other cities: Kaunas, Klaipeda, Siauliai
Form of government: Republic
Religion: Roman Catholicism
Currency: Litas

Luxembourg, Grand Duchy of A small independent landlocked country bounded by BEL-GIUM on the west, FRANCE on the south and GERMANY on the east. In the north of the duchy a wooded plateau, the Oesling, rises to 1,804 feet (550 metres) and in the south a lowland area of valleys and ridges is known as the Gutland. Northern winters are cold and raw, with snow covering the ground for almost a month, but in the south winters are mild and summers cool. In the south the land is fertile and crops grown include maize, roots, tubers and potatoes, with livestock also being raised. It is in the south, also, that (declining) beds of iron ore are found and these form the basis of the country's iron and steel industry. The country is very industrialised, with the financial sector playing an increasingly important part in the country's economy, as is tourism. In the east, Luxembourg is bordered by the Moselle river in whose valley grapes are produced for wine. The capital, Luxembourg City, is the seat of the European Court of Justice.

Quick facts:
Area: 998 square miles (2,586 square kilometres)
Population: 412,000
Capital: Luxembourg City
Other cities: Esch-sur-Algette, Differdange, Dudelange
Form of government: Constitutional Monarchy (Duchy)
Religion: Roman Catholicism
Currency: Euro

Macao *or* Macau Formerly a Portuguese colony, Macao reverted to China in 1999, becoming a special administrative region under Chinese sovereignty. China has promised 50 years of non-interference in its economic and social systems. One of the most densely populated places in the world, Macao consists of a rocky, hilly peninsula, connected by a sandy isthmus to China's Zhongshan (Tangjiahuan) island and the two small islands of Taipa and Coloâne. A free port, it is a leading trade, fishing and tourist centre with gambling casinos and textile, clothing, toy, plastics, fireworks and food processing industries.

Quick facts:
Area: 7 square miles (18 square kilometres)
Population: 440,000
Capital: Macao
Form of government: Special Administrative Region under
Chinese Sovereignty
Religions: Buddhism, Roman Catholicism
Currency: Pataca

Macedonia, The Former Yugoslav Republic of (FYROM) A country that, under the name of Macedonia, declared its independence from YUGOSLAVIA in November 1991. However GREECE, angered at the use of "Macedonia" – also the name of the neighbouring Greek province –imposed a trade embargo and convinced the United Nations not to recognise the nation's independence. In 1993, Macedonia was admitted to the UN after changing its official name to the Former Yugoslav Republic of Macedonia. In 1995 an agreement was reached with Greece whereby both countries would respect the territory, sovereignty and independence of the other, with Macedonia agreeing to adopt a new flag. A landlocked country, Macedonia shares its borders with ALBANIA, BULGARIA, Greece and Yugoslavia. Its terrain is mountainous, covered by deep valleys, with several large lakes. The River Vardar is the country's longest river and divides the country, flowing into Greece and eventually emptying into the Aegean Sea. The climate consists of hot, dry summers and cold winters with considerable snow. It is the poorest of the six former Yugoslav republics but sustains itself through agriculture and the coal industries. Some of its natural resources include chromium, lead, zinc, nickel, iron ore and lumber. Tourism has been badly affected by fighting in the region in the early 1990s.

Quick facts:

Area: 9,928 square miles (25,713 square kilometres)
Population: 2,174,000
Capital: Skopje
Other cities: Kumanovo, Ohrid
Form of government: Republic
Religions: Eastern Orthodox, Islam
Currency: Dinar

Madagascar An island state situated off the southeast coast of Africa, separated from the mainland by the Mozambique Channel. Madagascar is the fourth largest island in the world and the centre of it is made up of high savanna-covered plateaus. In the east, forested mountains fall steeply to the coast and in the southwest the land falls gradually through dry grassland and scrub. The staple food crop is rice and although only 5 per cent of the land is cultivated, 80 per cent of the population grow enough to feed themselves. Cassava, potatoes, maize, beans and bananas are also grown, but some 58 per cent of the land is pasture and there are more cattle than people. The main export earners are coffee, vanilla, cloves and sugar cane. There is mining for chromite, graphite, mica and salt and an oil refinery at Toamasina on the east coast. Upon independence in 1960, Madagascar became known as the Malagasy Republic, but was changed back by referendum in 1975. Due to Madagascar's isolation from mainland Africa, there are several species of plants and animals that are quite different from mainland species. As a result, many tourists come to Madagascar to explore this aspect of the country's fauna and flora.

Quick facts:

Area: 226,658 square miles (587,041 square kilometres)
Population: 15,353,000
Capital: Antananarivo
Other cities: Fianarantsoa, Mahajanga, Toamasina, Toliara
Form of government: Republic
Religions: African traditional religions, Roman Catholicism, Protestantism
Currency: Franc Malgache

Malawi A country that lies along the southern and western shores of the third largest lake in Africa, Lake Malawi. To the south of the lake the Shire river flows through a valley overlooked by wooded, towering mountains. The tropical climate has a dry season from May to October and a wet season for the remaining months. Agriculture is the predominant occupation and many Malawians live off their own crops. Exports include tea grown on the terraced hillsides in the south and tobacco on the central plateau plus peanuts and sugar, with maize also being an important crop. Malawi has bauxite and coal deposits but because of the inaccessibility of their locations, mining is limited. Hydroelectricity is now being used for manufacturing but imports of manufactured goods remain high and the country remains one of the poorest in the world. Malawi was formerly the British colony of Nyasaland, a name meaning "Land of the Lake," which was given to it by the 19th-century explorer David Livingstone.

Quick facts:

Area: 45,747 square miles (118,484 square kilometres)
Population: 10,114,000
Capital: Lilongwe
Other cities: Blantyre, Zomba
Form of government: Republic
Religions: African traditional religions, Roman Catholicism, Presbyterianism
Currency: Kwacha

Malaysia The Federation of Malaysia lies in the South China Sea in southeast Asia and comprises peninsular Malaysia on the Malay Peninsula and the states of Sabah and Sarawak on the island of

Borneo. Malaysia is affected by the monsoon climate. The northeast monsoon brings rain to the east coast of peninsular Malaysia in winter and the southwest monsoon brings rain to the west coast in summer. Throughout the country the climate is generally tropical and temperatures are uniformly hot throughout the year. Peninsular Malaysia has always had thriving rubber-growing and tin-dredging industries and now oil palm-growing is also important on the east coast. Sabah and Sarawak have grown rich by exploiting their natural resources, the forests. There is also some offshore oil and around the capital, Kuala Lumpur, new industries such as electronics are expanding. In recent years tourism has become an important industry and there are plans for a new international airport and a large dam for hydroelectric production. Malaysia was hit by economic recession in 1997 and implemented a series of measures designed to restore confidence in its economy.

Quick facts:
Area: 127,320 square miles (329,758 square kilometres)
Population: 20,581,000
Capital: Kuala Lumpur
Other cities: Ipoh, George Town, Johor Baharu
Form of government: Federal Constitutional Monarchy
Religion: Islam
Currency: Ringgit or Malaysian Dollar

Maldives, Republic of A country that lies 398 miles (640 kilometres) southwest of Sri Lanka in the Indian Ocean and comprises 1,200 low-lying coral islands grouped into 12 atolls. Roughly 202 of the islands are inhabited, and the highest point is only 5 feet (1.5 metres) above sea level. Independence was gained in 1965, with a republic being formed three years later. The climate is hot and humid and affected by monsoons from May to August. The islands are covered by coconut palms and some millet, cassava, yams and tropical fruit are grown. However, rice, the staple diet of its islanders, is imported. The most important natural resource is marine life and fishing is an important occupation. The chief export is now canned or frozen tuna. Tourism is now developing fast and has taken over from fishing as the major foreign currency earner.

Quick facts:
Area: 115 square miles (298 square kilometres)
Population: 263,000
Capital: Malé
Form of government: Republic
Religion: Sunni Islam
Currency: Rufiyaa

Mali A landlocked state in West Africa. The country mainly comprises vast plains and plateaus. It rises to 3,790 feet (1,155 metres) in the Adrar des Iforas range in the northeast. The Sahara in the north of the country is encroaching southwards. Mali is one of the poorest countries in the world. In the south there is some rain and plains are covered by grassy savanna and a few scattered trees. The River Niger runs through the south of the country and small steamboats use it for shipping between Koulikoro and Gao. Fish are plentiful in the river and its water is used to irrigate the land. Only a fifth of the land can be cultivated. Rice, cassava and millet are grown for domestic consumption and cotton for export. Droughts in the 1970s and mid-1980s resulted in thousands of cattle dying and in crop failure, with famine and disease killing many of the population. The country's main exports include cotton, gold, foodstuffs, livestock and mangoes. Iron ore and bauxite have been discovered but have yet to be exploited.

Quick facts:
Area: 478,841 square miles (1,240,192 square kilometres)
Population: 11,134,000
Capital: Bamako
Other towns: Gao, Kayes, Ségou, Mopti, Sikasso
Form of government: Republic
Religions: Sunni Islam, African traditional religions
Currency: CFA Franc

133

Malta A small republic in the middle of the Mediterranean Sea, lying just south of the island of Sicily. It comprises three islands, Malta, Gozo and Comino, which are made up of low limestone plateaus with little surface water. The climate is Mediterranean, with hot, dry sunny summers and little rain. Lack of water has led to the production of desalination plants that produce up to 70 per cent of the country's needs. Winters are cooler and wetter. Malta is virtually self-sufficient in agricultural products and exports potatoes, vegetables, wine and cut flowers. The British military base on Malta was once the mainstay of the economy but after the British withdrew in the late 1970s, the naval dockyard was converted for commercial shipbuilding and repairs, which is now one of the most important industries. Tourism has also boomed and the island has become popular for retirement in the sunshine with low taxes. Malta has a long history of civilisation, with remains found from Stone and Bronze Age peoples.

Quick facts:
Area: 122 square miles (316 square kilometres)
Population: 376,500
Capital: Valletta
Form of government: Republic
Religion: Roman Catholicism
Currency: Maltese Pound

Marshall Islands Formerly part of the United States-administered United Nations territory, this self-governing republic comprises a scattering of over 1,000 coral atolls and islets, arranged in two parallel chains, Ratak and Ralik, located in eastern Micronesia in the western Pacific Ocean and lying to the northwest of KIRIBATI. The climate is tropical maritime, with little variation in temperature and rainfall that is heaviest from July to October. The republic remains in free association with the USA and the economy is almost totally dependent on US-related payments for use of the islands as bases. The Bikini Atoll was used as a nuclear testing area in 1946. The main occupations are fishing and agriculture, with the chief export being copra. Attempts are being made to diversify the economy before US aid finishes in 2001.

Quick facts:
Area: 70 square miles (181 square kilometres)
Population: 58,000
Capital: Dalag-Uliga-Darrit (on Majuro atoll)
Form of government: Republic in free association with the USA
Religion: Protestantism
Currency: US Dollar

Martinique One of the larger of the islands in the Windward Islands group in the southern Caribbean, lying between Dominica and St Lucia. It is administered as a department of FRANCE. The centre of the island is mountainous, while the quality of its beaches has played a role in its development as a tourist resort. It has a volcano, Mont Pelée (4,750 feet /1,448 metres), that erupted in 1902, wiping out the town of St Pierre and killing all but one of its inhabitants. Martinique is periodically subjected to hurricanes that can cause considerable damage. The island's economy relies mainly on tourism with sugar, bananas, pineapples, citrus fruits, nutmeg and spices being grown in some parts of the island.

Quick facts:
Area: 425 square miles (1,102 square kilometres)
Population: 384,000
Capital: Fort-de-France
Form of government: Overseas Department of France
Religion: Roman Catholicism
Currency: Euro

Mauritania or the Islamic Republic of Mauritania A country nearly twice the size of France located on the west coast of Africa. About 47 per cent of the country is desert, the Sahara covering much of the north. The only settlements found in this area are around oases, where a little millet, dates and vegetables can be grown. The main agricultural regions are in the Senegal river valley in the south. The rest of the country is made up of the drought-stricken Sahel grasslands. The majority of the people are traditionally nomadic herdsmen, but severe droughts since the late 1960s and early 1970s have killed about 70 per cent of the nation's animals and the population has settled along the Senegal river. As a result, vast shanty towns have sprung up around all the towns. Production of iron ore and other deposits provide the country's main exports and development of these and the fishing industry on the coast form the only hope for a brighter future as the country's economy is very reliant on foreign aid. Mauritania has also experienced some internal political unrest and been involved in disputes with its neighbours. Conditions appear to have become more settled in recent years with a new constitution adopted in 1991.

Quick facts:
Area: 395,956 square miles (1,025,520 square kilometres)
Population: 2,351,000
Capital: Nouakchott
Other cities: Kaédi, Nouadhibou
Form of government: Republic
Religion: Sunni Islam
Currency: Ouguiya

Mauritius A beautiful island with tropical beaches, lying about 20 degrees south in the Indian Ocean, 497 miles (800 kilometres) east of MADAGASCAR and which gained independence in 1968. The islands of Rodrigues and Agalega are also part of Mauritius. Mauritius is a volcanic island with many craters surrounded by lava flows. The central plateau rises to over 2,625 feet (800 metres), then drops sharply to the south and west coasts. The climate is hot and humid, southwesterly winds bringing heavy rain in the uplands and there is the possibility of cyclones during December to April. The island has well-watered fertile soil, ideal for the sugar plantations that cover 45 per cent of the island. Although the export of molasses and sugar still dominate the economy, diversification is being encouraged. Other crops such as tea, tobacco, peanuts and vegetables are grown. The clothing and electronic equipment industries are becoming increasingly important and tourism is now the third largest source of foreign exchange.

Quick facts:
Area: 788 square miles (2,040 square kilometres)
Population: 1,160,000
Capital: Port Louis
Form of government: Republic
Religions: Hinduism, Roman Catholicism, Sunni Islam
Currency: Mauritian Rupee

Mexico The most southerly country in North America. It has its longest border with the UNITED STATES to the north, a long coast on the Pacific Ocean and a smaller coast in the west of the Gulf of Mexico. It is a land of volcanic mountain ranges and high plateaus. The highest peak is Citlaltepetl, 18,697 feet (5,699 metres), which is permanently snow-capped. Coastal lowlands are found in the west and east. Its wide range of latitude and relief produce a variety of climates. In the north there are arid and semi-arid conditions while in the south there is a humid tropical climate. Thirty per cent of the labour force is involved in agriculture, growing maize, wheat, kidney beans and rice for subsistence and coffee, cotton, fruit and vegetables for export, although some irrigation is needed. Mexico has substantial and varied mineral deposits, such as silver, coal, phosphates, gold and uranium, as well as large reserves of oil and natural gas. Forests cover around a quarter of the country with trees such as ebony, mahogany and walnut. Developing industries are petrochemicals, textiles, motor vehicles and food processing. Tourism also makes an important contribution to the country's economy.

Quick facts:
Area: 756,066 square miles (1,958,201 square kilometres)
Population: 96,578,000
Capital: México City
Other cities: Guadalajara, León, Monterrey, Puebla, Tijuana
Form of government: Federal Republic
Religion: Roman Catholicism
Currency: Mexican Peso

Micronesia, Federated States of Formerly part of the United States administered United Nations Trust Territory of the Pacific, known as the Caroline Islands, this self-governing republic became independent in 1990. It comprises an archipelago of over 600 islands, including Pohnpei (Ponape), Truk (Churk) Islands, Yap Islands and Kosrae. Mostly uninhabited, they are located in the western Pacific Ocean, about 2,500 miles (4,025 kilometres) southwest of Hawaii. The climate is tropical maritime, with high temperatures and rainfall all year round but a pronounced precipitation peak between July and October. Micronesia is still closely linked to the USA, with a heavy reliance on aid. Attempts are being made to diversify the economy, the exports of which are mainly fishing and copra. There are significant phosphate deposits but the island's isolation restricts development. Tourism is a growing trade but the economy of the region remains fragile.

Quick facts:
Area: 271 square miles (702 square kilometres)
Population: 109,000
Capital: Palikir
Form of government: Republic
Religion: Christianity
Currency: US Dollar

Moldova (Moldavia) A Soviet socialist republic from 1940 until 1991 when it became independent of the former USSR. It is bounded to the west by ROMANIA and to the north, east and south by UKRAINE. The republic consists of a hilly plain with an average height of around 500 feet (150 metres). Its main rivers are the Prut in the west and the Dnister in the north and east. Moldova's soils are fertile and crops grown include wheat, corn, barley, tobacco, sugar beet, soybeans and sunflowers. There are also extensive fruit orchards, vineyards and walnut groves. Wildlife is abundant, such as roe deer, weasels, martens and badgers. Beekeeping and silkworm breeding are widespread throughout the country. Food processing is the main industry, particularly sugar refining and wine making. Other industries include metal-working, engineering and the manufacture of electrical equipment. After independence, the economy declined, inflation soared and assistance was gained from the International Monetary Fund and others.

Quick facts:
Area: 13,012 square miles (33,700 square kilometres)
Population: 4,327,000
Capital: Chisinau
Other cities: Tiraspol, Tighina, Bel'tsy
Form of government: Republic
Religion: Russian Orthodox
Currency: Leu

Monaco A tiny principality on the Mediterranean Sea, surrounded landwards by the Alpes Maritimes department of FRANCE. It comprises a rocky peninsula and a narrow stretch of coast. It has mild moist winters and hot dry summers. The ancient fortified town of Monaco is situated on a rocky promontory and houses the royal palace and the cathedral. The Monte Carlo district has its world-famous casino and La Condamine has thriving businesses, stores, banks and attractive residential areas. Fontvieille is an area reclaimed from the sea where marinas and light industry are now located. Light industry includes chemicals, plastics, electronics, engineering and paper, but it is tourism that is the main revenue earner. The sale of stamps, tobacco, insurance and banking industries also contribute to the economy. Well-known annual events such as the Monte Carlo Rally and Monaco Grand Prix are held in the principality.

Quick facts:
Area: 0.4 square mile (1 square kilometre)
Population: 32,000
Capital: Monaco
Form of government: Constitutional Monarchy
Religion: Roman Catholicism
Currency: Euro

Mongolia A landlocked country in northeast Asia that is bounded to the north by the RUSSIAN FEDERATION and by CHINA to the south, west and east. Most of Mongolia is mountainous. In the northwest are the Hangayn Mountains and the Altai, rising to 14,312 feet (4,362 metres). In the south there are grass-covered steppes and the desert wastes of the Gobi. The climate is very extreme and dry, with long, very cold winters and short, mild summers. Agriculture, particularly the rearing of livestock, is the main economic activity and source of employment in Mongolia. Under Communism, all cultivation and livestock rearing was state-controlled but Mongolia has now started to move towards a free market economy. Crops grown include cereals (wheat, barley and oats), potatoes and some other vegetables but cultivation is heavily dependent on irrigation. Mongolia has valuable reserves of iron ore, coal, copper, molybdenum, fluorspar, tungsten, uranium, gold and silver. Manufacturing industries are generally on a small scale and include the processing of wool, hides, leather, furs, meat and dairy produce, textiles, wooden goods, agricultural equipment and building products. The collapse of trade with the former Soviet Union has created severe economic problems for Mongolia and it is increasingly looking to Japan and China for trade and economic assistance.

Quick facts:
Area: 604,829 square miles (1,566,500 square kilometres)
Population: 2,354,000
Capital: Ulaanbaatar
Other cities: Altay, Saynshand, Hovd, Choybalsan, Tsetserleg
Form of government: Republic
Religions: Buddhism, Shamanism, Islam
Currency: Tughrik

Montenegro *see* YUGOSLAVIA.

Morocco A country in northwest Africa strategically placed at the western entrance to the Mediterranean Sea. It is a land of great contrasts, with high rugged mountains, the arid Sahara AND green Atlantic and Mediterranean coasts. The country is split from southwest to northeast by the Atlas Mountains. The north has a pleasant Mediterranean climate with hot dry summers and mild moist winters. Farther south winters are warmer and summers even hotter. Snow often falls in winter on the Atlas Mountains. Morocco is mainly a farming country, wheat, barley and maize being the main food crops and it is one of the world's chief exporters of citrus fruit although agriculture accounts for less than 20 per cent of the land use. Morocco's main wealth comes from phosphates, reserves of which are the largest in the world, while coal, lead, iron and manganese ores are also produced. The economy is very mixed. Morocco is self-sufficient in textiles, has automobile assembly plants, soap and cement factories and a large sea fishing industry. Tourism is a major source of revenue, as are remittances sent home by Moroccans who work abroad.

Quick facts:
Area: 172,414 square miles (446,550 square kilometres)
Population: 27,623,000
Capital: Rabat
Other cities: Casablanca, Fès, Marrakech, Tangier
Form of government: Constitutional Monarchy
Religion: Sunni Islam
Currency: Dirham

Mozambique A republic located in southeast Africa and one of the world's poorest. A coastal plain covers most of the southern and central territory, giving way to the western highlands and north to a plateau including the Nyasa Highlands. The Zambezi river separates the high plateaus in the north from the lowlands in the south. The country has a humid tropical climate with highest temperatures and rainfall in the north. Normally conditions are reasonably good for agriculture but a drought in the early 1980s, followed a few years later by severe flooding, resulted in famine and more than 100,000 deaths. A lot of industry was abandoned when the Portuguese left the country and was not taken over by the local people because of lack of expertise. The economy is now on the upturn although the drought and subsequent costs of the civil war, such as rehoming the many displaced persons, have severely hampered matters. This has also led to a black market that now accounts for a sizable part of the economy. Forestry is mainly unexploited while fishing for lobster and shrimp is an important source of export revenue.

Quick facts:

Area: 309,496 square miles (799,380 square kilometres)
Population: 16,916,000
Capital: Maputo
Other towns: Beira, Nampula
Form of government: Republic
Religions: African traditional religions, Roman Catholicism, Sunni Islam
Currency: Metical

Myanmar, Union of Formerly Burma, the second largest country in Southeast Asia. The heartland of the country is the valley of the Irrawaddy. The north and west of the country are mountainous and in the east the Shan Plateau runs along the border with THAILAND. The climate is equatorial at the coast, changing to tropical monsoon over most of the interior. The Irrawaddy river flows into the Andaman Sea, forming a huge delta area that is ideal land for rice cultivation. Rice is the country's staple food and accounts for half the country's export earnings. Tropical fruits such as bananas, mangoes, citrus and guavas grow well in the fertile coastal regions. Myanmar is rich in lumber and mineral resources such as natural gas, petroleum, jade and natural rubies, but because of poor communications, lack of development and unrest among the ethnic groups, the resources have not been fully exploited which has at least contributed to the preservation of the country's natural environment.

Quick facts:

Area: 261,228 square miles (676,578 square kilometres)
Population: 45,922,000
Capital: Rangoon (Yangon)
Other cities: Mandalay, Moulmein, Pegu
Form of government: Republic
Religion: Buddhism
Currency: Kyat

Namibia A country situated on the Atlantic coast of southwest Africa. There are three main regions in the country. Running down the entire Atlantic coastline is the Namib Desert, east of which is the Central Plateau of mountains, rugged outcrops, sandy valleys and poor grasslands. East again and north is the Kalahari Desert. Namibia has a poor rainfall, the highest falling at Windhoek, the capital. Even here it only amounts to 8–10 inches (200–250 millimetres) per year. It is essentially a stock-rearing country, with sheep, cattle and goats raised with subsistence agriculture mainly in the north. Diamonds are mined just north of the River Orange, as are other minerals such as silver, lead, uranium and copper. Namibia's output of diamonds amounts to almost a third of the world's total. One of Africa's richest fishing grounds lies off the coast of Namibia and mackerel, anchovies and pilchards are an important export although production has dropped in recent years because of overfishing.

Quick facts:
Area: 318,261 square miles (824,292 square kilometres)
Population: 1,575,000
Capital: Windhoek
Form of government: Republic
Religions: Lutheranism, Roman Catholicism, other Christianity
Currency: Namibian Dollar

Nauru The world's smallest republic. It is an island situated just 25 miles (40 kilometres) south of the equator and is halfway between AUSTRALIA and Hawaii. It is an oval-shaped coral island only 12 miles (20 kilometres) in diametre and is surrounded by a reef. The centre of the island comprises a plateau that rises to 197 feet (60 metres) above sea level. Most of the population live along a narrow coastal belt of fertile land. The climate is tropical with a high and irregular rainfall. The country is rich, due entirely to the deposits of high quality phosphate rock in the central plateau. This is sold for fertiliser to Australia, NEW ZEALAND, JAPAN and KOREA. Phosphate deposits are likely to be exhausted in the near future but the government is investing overseas and attempting to diversify to ensure the economic future of the country. Since around 80 per cent of the land will be uninhabitable once the mines are exhausted, considerable rehabilitation will be required.

Quick facts:
Area: 8 square miles (21 square kilometres)
Population: 11,000
Capital: Nauru
Form of government: Republic
Religions: Protestantism, Roman Catholicism
Currency: Australian Dollar

Nepal, Kingdom of A long narrow rectangular country, landlocked between CHINA and INDIA on the flanks of the eastern Himalayas. Its northern border runs along the mountain tops. In this border area is Mount Everest, at 29,028 feet (8,848 metres) the highest mountain in the world and Nepal also has the six other highest mountains within its borders. The climate is subtropical in the south and all regions are affected by the monsoon. Nepal is one of the world's poorest and least developed countries, with most of the population trying to survive as peasant farmers. Some mineral deposits, such as copper, iron ore, mica and ochre, exist but, because of the country's inaccessible terrain, have not been completely charted. With Indian and Chinese aid, however, roads have been built from the north and south to Kathmandu. The construction of hydroelectric power schemes is underway, although at a high cost. Nepal's main exports are carpets, foodstuffs, clothing and leather goods, with principal sources of foreign revenue being tourism and Gurkha soldiers' foreign earnings. Nepal now attracts thousands of visitors each year, many of whom belong to trekking and climbing expeditions.

Quick facts:

Area: 56,827 square miles (147,181 square kilometres)
Population: 21,127,000
Capital: Kathmandu
Other city: Biratnagar
Form of government: Constitutional Monarchy
Religion: Hinduism, Buddhism
Currency: Nepalese Rupee

Netherlands, The Situated in northwest Europe, the Netherlands (also known as Holland) is bounded to the north and west by the North Sea. Around half of the Netherlands is below sea level and the Dutch have tackled some huge reclamation schemes to add some land area to the country. One such scheme is the Ijsselmeer, where four large reclaimed areas (polders) have added an extra 637 square miles (1,650 square kilometres) for cultivation and an overspill town for Amsterdam. The Netherlands has mild winters and cool summers. Natural vegetation is now confined mainly to grasses and heathers, with small areas of beech, ash, pine and oak forests being carefully maintained. Migratory birds visit the new habitats created by land reclamation. Agriculture and horticulture are highly mechanised and the most notable feature is the sea of glass under which salad vegetables, fruit and flowers are grown. Manufacturing industries include chemicals, machinery, petroleum, refining, metallurgy and electrical engineering. The main port of the Netherlands, Rotterdam, is the largest in the world.

Quick facts:

Area: 15,770 square miles (40,844 square kilometres)
Population: 15,517,000
Capital: Amsterdam
Seat of government: The Hague (s'Gravenhage)
Other cities: Rotterdam, Eindhoven
Form of government: Constitutional Monarchy
Religions: Roman Catholicism, Dutch Reformed, Calvinism
Currency: Euro

Netherlands Antilles An overseas division of the NETHERLANDS, spread over the southern Caribbean Sea and consisting of two sets of islands, the Southern Netherlands Antilles (Bonaire and Curaçao) and the Northern Netherlands Antilles (Saba, St Maarten and St Eustatius). Saba is the highest island in the group rising to 2,854 feet (870 metres) at Mount Scenery. ARUBA was part of the group until 1986. The islands have a tropical climate. Oil refining and tourism are the most important economic activities.

Quick facts:

Area: 309 square miles (800 square kilometres)
Population: 207,300
Capital: Willemstad
Form of government: Self-governing Dutch Territory
Religion: Roman Catholicism
Currency: Netherlands Antilles Guilder

New Caledonia or Nouvelle Calédonie The most southerly of the Melanesian countries in the Pacific Ocean. It is a French overseas territory but there has been ongoing unrest in the country between the indigenous Melanesians and the French settlers over the question of independence. The main island, Nouvelle Calédonie, is 248 miles (400 kilometres) long and rises to a height of 5,377 feet (1,639 metres) at Mount Panie. The island is divided into two natural regions by the mountain range that runs down its centre: a dry west coast covered with gum tree savanna and a tropical east coast. It has a Mediterranean-type climate with rainfall at its heaviest between December and March. The country is rich in mineral resources, particularly nickel, which accounts for 90 per cent of its exports. Other exports include coffee and copra. The main tourist resorts are on the east coast of Nouvelle Calédonie.

Quick facts:

Area: 7,172 square miles (18,575 square kilometres)
Population: 189,000
Capital: Noumea
Form of government: French Overseas Territory
Religion: Roman Catholicism
Currency: Franc

New Zealand A country that lies southeast of AUSTRALIA in the South Pacific. It comprises two large islands (North Island and South Island), Stewart Island and the Chatham Islands and many smaller islands. The vast majority of the population live on North Island. New Zealand enjoys very mild winters with regular rainfall and no extremes of heat or cold. North Island is hilly, with isolated mountains, active volcanoes, hot mineral springs and geysers. Earthquakes occur, and in 1987 considerable damage was caused by one at Edgecumbe. On South Island, the Southern Alps run north to south, and the highest point is Mount Cook at 12,313 feet (3,753 metres). The Canterbury Plains lie to the east of the mountains. Two-thirds of New Zealand is suitable for agriculture and grazing. Meat, wool and dairy goods are the main products. Forestry supports the pulp and paper industry, and a considerable source of hydroelectric power produces cheap electricity for the manufacturing industry, which now accounts for 30 per cent of New Zealand's exports. Mining is also an important industry, with petroleum, natural gas, limestone, gold and iron ore being exploited.

Quick facts:
Area: 104,454 square miles (270,534 square kilometres)
Population: 3,681,546
Capital: Wellington
Other cities: Auckland, Christchurch, Dunedin, Hamilton
Form of government: Constitutional Monarchy
Religions: Anglicanism, Roman Catholicism, Presbyterianism
Currency: New Zealand Dollar

Nicaragua A country that lies between the Pacific Ocean and the Caribbean Sea, on the isthmus of Central America, and is sandwiched between HONDURAS to the north and COSTA RICA to the south. The east coast contains forested lowland and is the wettest part of the country. Behind this is a range of volcanic mountains, and the west coast is a belt of savanna lowland running parallel to the Pacific coast. The western region, which contains the two huge lakes, Nicaragua and Managua, is where most of the population live. The whole country is subject to devastating earthquakes. Nicaragua is primarily an agricultural country and 65 per cent of the labour force work on the land. The main export crops are coffee, bananas, cotton, meat and gold. There are mineral deposits of gold, copper and silver, with gold being of prime importance, but the country's economy is dependent on foreign aid.

Quick facts:
Area: 50,193 square miles (130,668 square kilometres)
Population: 4,663,000
Capital: Managua
Form of government: Republic
Religion: Roman Catholicism
Currency: Córdoba Oro

Niger A landlocked republic in West Africa, just south of the Tropic of Cancer. Over half the country is covered by the encroaching Sahara in the north, and the south lies in the drought-stricken Sahel. In the extreme southwest corner, the River Niger flows through the country, and in the extreme southeast lies Lake Chad, but the rest of the country is very short of water. The people in the southwest fish and farm their own food, growing rice and vegetables on land flooded by the river. Farther from the river, crops have failed as a result of successive droughts since 1968. Niger is an agricultural country, mainly of subsistence farmers, with the raising of livestock being the major activity. It has recovered from disastrous droughts and exports cotton and cowpeas, although uranium mined in the Aïr Mountains is Niger's main export. More recently, there has been further unrest involving the Tuareg people who wish for an independent state.

Quick facts:
Area: 489,191 square miles (1,267,000 square kilometres)
Population: 9,465,000
Capital: Niamey
Other cities: Agadez, Maradi, Tahoua, Zinder
Form of government: Republic
Religion: Sunni Islam
Currency: CFA Franc

Nigeria A large and populous country in West Africa. From the Gulf of Guinea it extends north to the border with NIGER. It has a variable landscape, from the swampy coastal areas and tropical forest belts of the interior, to the mountains and savanna of the north. The two main rivers are the Niger and the Benue, and just north of their confluence lies the Jos Plateau. The climate is hot and humid, and rainfall, heavy at the coast, gradually decreases inland. The dry far north is affected by the Harmattan, a hot dry wind blowing from the Sahara. About three-quarters of the land is suitable for agriculture and a wide variety of crops is raised by the subsistence farmers, mainly on small, family-owned farms. The main agricultural products are cocoa, rubber, groundnuts and cotton, with only cocoa being of any export significance. The country depends on revenue from its crude petroleum exports, which have a low sulphur content and therefore produce less air pollution, making it attractive to American and European countries. Full independence was achieved by Nigeria in 1960 but due to several factors, including the complex ethnic make-up of the country, the country's progress has frequently been interrupted by strife and internal dissent.

Quick facts:

Area: 356,669 square miles (923,768 square kilometres)

Population: 115,120,000

Capital: Abuja

Other cities: Lagos, Onitsha, Enugu, Ibadan, Kano, Ogbomosho

Form of government: Federal Republic

Religions: Sunni Islam, Christianity

Currency: Naira

Northern Mariana Islands The islands are situated in the northwest Pacific Ocean. In 1986, the islanders voted for Commonwealth status in union with the USA and they were granted US citizenship. The country consists of mainly volcanic islands with coral limestone and lava shores. Tourism is the main industry.

Quick facts:

Area: 179 square miles (464 square kilometres)

Population: 49,000

Capital: Saipan

Form of government: Commonwealth in union with the USA

Religion: Roman Catholicism

Currency: US Dollar

Norway A country that occupies the western half of the Scandinavian peninsula in northern Europe and is surrounded to the north, west and south by water. It shares most of its eastern border with SWEDEN and almost one-third of the country is north of the Arctic Circle. It is a country of spectacular scenery, of fjords, cliffs, rugged uplands and forested valleys. It has some of the deepest fjords in the world and has a huge number of glacial lakes. The climate is temperate as a result of the warming effect of the Gulf Stream. Summers are mild and although the winters are long and cold, the waters off the west coast remain ice-free. The country's longest river is the Glåma. Some southern lakes are affected by acid rain, which concerns the country's environmentalists. Agriculture is chiefly concerned with dairying and fodder crops. Fishing is an important industry and the large reserves of forest, which cover just over a quarter of the country, provide lumber for export. Industry is now dominated by petrochemicals based on the reserves of Norwegian oil in the North Sea. There are almost 60 airports in the country and transport by water is still of importance.

Quick facts:

Area: 125,050 square miles (323,877 square kilometres)

Population: 4,445,500

Capital: Oslo

Other cities: Bergen, Trondheim, Stavanger, Kristiansand, Tromsö

Form of government: Constitutional Monarchy

Religion: Lutheranism

Currency: Norwegian Krone

Oman or the Sultanate of Oman Situated in the southeast of the Arabian Peninsula, Oman is a small country in two parts. It comprises a small mountainous area overlooking the Strait of Hormuz, which controls the entrance to The Gulf and the main part of the country, consisting of barren hills rising sharply behind a narrow coastal plain. Inland the hills extend into the unexplored Rub al Khali (The Empty Quarter) in Saudi Arabia. Oman has a desert climate with exceptionally hot and humid conditions from April to October and as a result of the extremely arid environment, less than one per cent of the country is cultivated, the main produce being dates and limes, which are exported. The economy is almost entirely dependent on oil, providing 90 per cent of its exports, although there are deposits of asbestos, copper and marble and a smelter at Sohar. Over 15 per cent of the resident population is made up by foreign workers. There are no political parties in Oman and the judicial system is centred on the law of Islam.

Quick facts:

Area: 119,498 square miles (309,500 square kilometres)
Population: 2,302,000
Capital: Mascat (Musqat)
Other towns: Salalah, Al Khaburah, Matrah
Form of government: Monarchy
Religions: Ibadi Islam, Sunni Islam
Currency: Rial Omani

Pakistan or the Islamic Republic of Pakistan A country that lies just north of the Tropic of Cancer and has as its southern border the Arabian Sea. The valley of the Indus river splits the country into a highland region in the west and a lowland region in the east. A weak form of tropical monsoon climate occurs over most of the country and conditions in the north and west are arid. Temperatures are high everywhere in summer but winters are cold in the mountains. Most agriculture is subsistence, with wheat and rice as the main crops. Cotton and rice are the main cash crops, but the cultivated area is restricted because of waterlogging and saline soils. Pakistan's wide range of mineral resources has not been extensively developed and industry concentrates on food processing, textiles, consumer goods and handicrafts, including carpets and pottery. A lack of modern transport because of its mountainous terrain hinders the country's economic progress.

Quick facts:

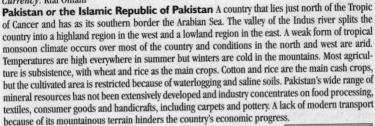

Area: 307,374 square miles (796,095 square kilometres)
Population: 134,146,000
Capital: Islamabad
Other cities: Faisalabad, Hyderabad, Karachi, Lahore, Rawalpindi
Form of government: Federal Islamic Republic
Religions: Sunni Islam, Shia Islam
Currency: Pakistan Rupee

Palau A republic consisting of a group of approximately 350 islands, lying in the western Pacific, 7 degrees north of the equator and about 625 miles (900 kilometres) equidistant from NEW GUINEA to the south and the PHILIPPINES to the west. A barrier reef to the west forms a large lagoon dotted with islands. Coral formations and marine life here are amongst the richest in the world. Formerly known as Belau, the republic has an agreement of free association with the United States. The main language is English. Subsistence fishing and agriculture are the mainstays of the economy but there is also some tourism. In addition, natural resources include minerals (particularly gold and sea-bed deposits) and forests.

Quick facts:

Area: 177 square miles (459 square kilometres)
Population: 17,000
Capital: Koror
Form of government: Free Associated Republic (USA)
Religions: Roman Catholicism and Modekngei
Currency: US Dollar

Palestine An ancient historic region on the eastern shore of the Mediterranean Sea, also known as "The Holy Land" because of its symbolic importance for Christians, Jews and Muslims. It was part of the Ottoman Empire from the early part of the 16th century until 1917, when Palestine was captured by the British. The Balfour Declaration of 1917 increased Jewish hopes that they might be enabled to establish a Jewish state in Palestine. This was realised in 1948 with the United Nations' creation of the state of ISRAEL. This created hostility among Israel's Arab neighbours and Palestinians indigenous to the area, many of whom left, particularly to neighbouring JORDAN. Since that time the territory has been disputed, leading to a series of wars between the Arabs and Israelis and more recently to conflict between Israeli forces and the Palestine Liberation Organisation. The disputed territories are the West Bank, the Gaza Strip, the Golan Heights and Jerusalem. In 1994 limited autonomy of some of these disputed areas was granted to the appointed Palestinian National Authority and Israeli military forces began a withdrawal of the area. The whole peace process was, however, compromised by ongoing violent conflict that erupted after the assassination of the Israeli Prime Minister, Yitzak Rabin, by Jewish extremists in 1995.

Quick facts:

Area: Gaza 146 square miles (360 square kilometres); Jericho 27 square miles (70 square kilometres); West Bank 2,269 square miles (5,860 square kilometres)

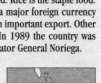

Population: Gaza 924,200; Jericho 20,600; West Bank 2,050,000
Form of government: Republic, with limited powers
Religions: Sunni Islam, Shia Islam, Eastern Catholicism
Currency: None (Israeli and Jordanian currency used)

Panama A country located at the narrowest point in Central America. Only 58 kilometres (36 miles) separates the Caribbean Sea from the Pacific Ocean at Panama, and the Panama Canal, which divides the country, is the main route from the Caribbean and the Atlantic to the Pacific. The climate is tropical, with high temperatures throughout the year and only a short dry season from January to April. The country is heavily forested and very little is cultivated. Rice is the staple food. The economy is heavily dependent on the Canal and income from it is a major foreign currency earner. The country has extensive lumber resources, and mahogany is an important export. Other exports include petroleum products, coffee, shrimps and raw sugar. In 1989 the country was briefly invaded by US military forces in order to depose the corrupt dictator General Noriega.

Quick facts:

Area: 29,157 square miles (75,517 square kilometres)
Population: 2,674,000
Capital: Panama City
Other cities: Colón, Puerto Armuelles, David
Form of government: Republic
Religion: Roman Catholicism
Currency: Balboa

Papua New Guinea A country in the southwest Pacific, comprising the eastern half of the island of New Guinea together with hundreds of islands including New Britain, the Bismarck Archipelago and New Ireland. There are active volcanoes on some of the islands and mainland and almost 100,000 people were evacuated in 1994 when two erupted on New Britain. The country has a mountainous interior surrounded by broad swampy plains. The climate is tropical, with high temperatures and heavy rainfall. Subsistence farming is the main economic activity although some coffee, cocoa and copra are grown for cash. Lumber is cut for export and fishing and fish processing industries are developing. The country's wildlife is plentiful and varied, while the coastal waters support an abundance of sea life. Minerals such as copper, gold, silver and oil form the mainstay of the economy. The country still receives valuable aid from AUSTRALIA, which governed it before independence was gained in 1975.

Quick facts:

Area: 178,704 square miles (462,840 square kilometres)
Population: 4,400,000
Capital: Port Moresby
Form of government: Republic
Religions: Protestantism, Roman Catholicism
Currency: Kina

Paraguay A small landlocked country in central South America, bordered by Bolivia, Brazil and Argentina. The climate is tropical, with abundant rain and a short dry season. The River Paraguay splits the country into the Chaco, a flat semi-arid plain on the west, and a partly forested undulating plateau on the east. Almost 95 per cent of the population live east of the river, where crops grown on the fertile plains include cassava, sugar cane, maize, cotton and soya beans. Immediately west of the river, on the low Chaco, are huge cattle ranches that provide meat for export. Although there are deposits of minerals such as iron, petroleum and manganese, these are not exploited commercially. The lumber industry is important, however, with tannin and petitgrain oil also being produced. With three important rivers, the Paraguay, Parana and Pilcomayo, the country has many impressive waterfalls, such as the Guaira Falls. In cooperation with its neighbours, it has developed its potential for hydroelectric power to the full and is able to meet all its energy needs. Developed with Brazil and opened in 1991, the Itaipu Hydroelectric Dam on the (Alto) Parana river is the largest dam in the world. Other hydroelectric  schemes include the Yacyreta Dam, developed with Argentina and opened in 1994.

Quick facts:
Area: 157,048 square miles (406,752 square kilometres)
Population: 4,955,000
Capital: Asunción
Other cities: Concepción, Ciudad del Este, Encarnación
Form of government: Republic
Religion: Roman Catholicism
Currency: Guaraní

Peru A country located just south of the equator, on the Pacific coast of South America. It has three distinct regions from west to east: the coast, the high sierra of the Andes and the tropical jungle. The climate on the narrow coastal belt is mainly desert, while the Andes are wet and east of the mountains is equatorial with tropical forests. Most large-scale agriculture is in the oases and fertile, irrigated river valleys that cut across the coastal desert. Sugar and cotton are the main exports. Sheep, llamas, vicunas and alpacas are kept for wool. The fishing industry was once the largest in the world but recently the shoals have become depleted. Anchovies form the bulk of the catch and are used to make fish meal. Minerals such as iron ore, silver, copper and lead, as well as natural gas and petroleum, are extracted in large quantities and are an important part of the economy. The economy in the late 1980s was damaged by the declining value of exports, inflation, drought and guerrilla warfare, which made the government introduce an austerity program in the 1990s.

Quick facts:
Area: 496,225 square miles (1,285,216 square kilometres)
Population: 25,015,000
Capital: Lima
Other cities: Arequipa, Callao, Chiclayo, Cuzco, Trujillo
Form of government: Republic
Religion: Roman Catholicism
Currency: Nuevo Sol

Philippines A country comprising a group of 7,107 islands and islets in the western Pacific that are scattered over a great area. There are four main groups: Luzon and Mindoro to the north, the Visayan Islands in the centre, Mindanao and the Sulu Archipelago in the south and Palawan in the southwest. Manila, the capital, is on Luzon. Most of the islands are mountainous and earthquakes are common. The climate is humid, with high temperatures and high rainfall. Typhoons can strike during the rainy season from July to October. Rice, cassava, sweet potatoes and maize are the main subsistence crops and coconuts, sugar cane, pineapples and bananas are grown for export. Agriculture employs around 42 per cent of the workforce. Mining is an important industry and its main products include gold, silver, nickel, copper and salt. Fishing is of major importance too and there are sponge fisheries on some of the islands. Other prime industries include textiles, food processing, chemicals and electrical engineering.

Quick facts:

Area: 115,813 square miles (300,000 square kilometres)

Population: 71,899,000

Capital: Manila

Other cities: Cebu, Davao, Quezon City, Zamboanga

Form of government: Republic

Religions: Sunni Islam, Roman Catholicism, Protestantism

Currency: Philippine Peso

Pitcairn Islands A British overseas territory situated in the southeast Pacific Ocean. They are volcanic with high lava cliffs and rugged hills. The islanders are direct descendants of the HMS *Bounty* mutineers and their Tahitian wives. Subsistence agriculture produces a wide variety of tropical and subtropical crops but the sale of postage stamps is the country's main revenue earner.

Quick facts:

Area: 2 square miles (5 square kilometres)

Population: 50

Form of government: British Overseas Territory

Religion: Seventh Day Adventism

Currency: New Zealand Dollar

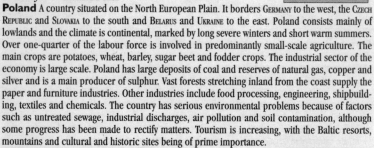

Poland A country situated on the North European Plain. It borders GERMANY to the west, the CZECH REPUBLIC and SLOVAKIA to the south and BELARUS and UKRAINE to the east. Poland consists mainly of lowlands and the climate is continental, marked by long severe winters and short warm summers. Over one-quarter of the labour force is involved in predominantly small-scale agriculture. The main crops are potatoes, wheat, barley, sugar beet and fodder crops. The industrial sector of the economy is large scale. Poland has large deposits of coal and reserves of natural gas, copper and silver and is a main producer of sulphur. Vast forests stretching inland from the coast supply the paper and furniture industries. Other industries include food processing, engineering, shipbuilding, textiles and chemicals. The country has serious environmental problems because of factors such as untreated sewage, industrial discharges, air pollution and soil contamination, although some progress has been made to rectify matters. Tourism is increasing, with the Baltic resorts, mountains and cultural and historic sites being of prime importance.

Quick facts:

Area: 124,808 square miles (323,250 square kilometres)

Population: 38,628,000

Capital: Warsaw (Warszawa)

Other cities: Gdansk, Kraków, Lódz, Poznan, Wroclaw

Form of government: Republic

Religion: Roman Catholicism

Currency: Zloty

Portugal A country in the southwest corner of Europe that makes up about 15 per cent of the Iberian Peninsula and is the least developed in western Europe. The most mountainous areas of Portugal lie to the north of the River Tagus. In the northeast are the steep-sided mountains of Trasos-Montes and to south of this the Douro valley running from the Spanish border to Oporto on the Atlantic coast. South of the Tagus is the Alentajo, with its wheat fields and cork plantations, which continues to the hinterland of the Algarve with its beautiful groves of almond, fig and olive trees. Agriculture employs one-quarter of the labour force and crops include wheat, maize, grapes and tomatoes. Portugal's most important natural resources are its minerals, largely developed after World War II, including coal, iron ore, tin and copper. Port and Madeira wine are renowned and the country is a main exporter of olive oil. Manufacturing industry includes textiles, clothing, footwear, food processing and cork products. Tourism, particularly in the south, is the main foreign currency earner. A petrochemical plant and oil refinery is located near Lisbon and hydroelectric power has been developed in recent years. Portugal is also renowned for certain high quality craft products, especially lace, pottery and tiles.

Quick facts:
Area: 35,514 square miles (91,982 square kilometres)
Population: 9,920,800
Capital: Lisbon (Lisboa)
Other cities: Braga, Coimbra, Faro, Oporto, Setúbal
Form of government: Republic
Religion: Roman Catholicism
Currency: Euro

Puerto Rico The most easterly of the Greater Antilles islands, lying in the Caribbean between the DOMINICAN REPUBLIC and the VIRGIN ISLANDS of the United States. It is a self-governing common-wealth in association with the USA and includes the main island, Puerto Rico, the two small is-lands of Vieques and Culebra and a fringe of smaller uninhabited islands. The climate is tropical, modified slightly by cooling sea breezes. The main mountains on Puerto Rico are the Cordillera Central, which reach 4,390 feet (1,338 metres) at the peak of Cerro de Punta. Dairy farming is the most important agricultural activity but the whole agricultural sector has been overtaken by in-dustry in recent years. Tax relief and cheap labour encourage American businesses to be based in Puerto Rico. Products include textiles, clothing, electrical and electronic goods, plastics, pharma-ceuticals and petrochemicals. Tourism is another developing industry and there is potential for oil exploration both on and offshore. San Juan is one of the largest and best natural harbors in the Caribbean.

Quick facts:
Area: 3,427 square miles (8,875 square kilometres)
Population: 3,736,000
Capital: San Juan
Form of government: Self-governing Commonwealth (in association with the USA)
Religions: Roman Catholicism, Protestantism
Currency: US Dollar

Qatar A little emirate that lies halfway along the coast of The Gulf. It consists of a low barren peninsula and a few small islands. The climate is hot and uncomfortably humid in summer and the winters are mild with rain in the north. Most fresh water comes from natural springs and wells or from desalination plants. Some vegetables and fruit are grown but the herding of sheep, goats and some cattle is the main agricultural activity. The country is famous for its high quality camels. The discovery and exploitation of oil has resulted in a high standard of living for the people of Qatar, with some of the revenue being used to build hospitals and a road system and to provide free education and medical care. The Dukhan oil field has an expected life of 40 years and the reserves of natural gas are enormous. In order to diversify the economy, new industries such as iron and steel, cement, fertilisers and petrochemical plants have been developed.

Quick facts:
Area: 4,247 square miles (11,000 square kilometres)
Population: 558,000
Capital: Doha (Ad Dawhah)
Form of government: Absolute Monarchy
Religion: Wahhabi Sunni Islam
Currency: Qatar Riyal

Réunion A French overseas department in the Indian Ocean, south of Mauritius. The island is mountainous and has one active and several extinct volcanoes. Most people live on the coastal lowlands and the economy is dependent upon tourism and the production of rum, sugar, maize, potatoes, tobacco and vanilla. French aid is given to the country in return for its use as a French military base.

Quick facts:
Area: 969 square miles (2,510 square kilometres)
Population: 664,000
Capital: St Denis
Form of government: French Overseas Department
Religion: Roman Catholicism
Currency: Euro

Romania Apart from a small extension towards the Black Sea, Romania is almost a circular country. It is located in southeast Europe, bordered by Ukraine, Hungary, Serbia and Bulgaria. The Carpathian Mountains run through the north, east and centre of Romania and these are enclosed by a ring of rich agricultural plains that are flat in the south and west but hilly in the east. The core of Romania is Transylvania within the Carpathian arc. Romania's main river is the Danube, which forms a delta in its lower course. The country has cold snowy winters and hot summers. Agriculture in Romania has been neglected in favor of industry, but major crops include maize, sugar beet, wheat, potatoes and grapes for wine. There are now severe food shortages, with high unemployment and a low standard of living. Industry is state-owned and includes mining, metallurgy, mechanical engineering and chemicals. Forests support lumber and furniture-making industries in the Carpathians. After the overthrow of the Communist regime in 1989, a new constitution was approved by referendum. The post-communist government has worked hard to bring about changes and improve the economy.

Quick facts:
Area: 92,043 square miles (238,391 square kilometres)
Population 22,520,000
Capital: Bucharest (Bucuresti)
Other cities: Brasov, Constanta, Galati, Iasi, Timisoara, Craiova, Brâila, Arad, Ploiesti
Form of government: Republic
Religions: Romanian Orthodox, Roman Catholicism
Currency: Leu

Russia or the Russian Federation The largest country in the world (with over one-ninth of the world's land area) that extends from eastern Europe through the Ural Mountains east to the Pacific Ocean. The Caucasus Range forms its boundary with Georgia and Azerbaijan and it is here that the highest peak in Europe, Mt Elbrus (18,510 feet/5,642 metres), is located. In the east, Siberia is drained toward the Arctic Ocean by the great Rivers Ob, Yenisey and Lena and their tributaries. Just to the south of the Central Siberian Plateau lies Lake Baikal, the world's deepest freshwater lake (5,370 feet/1,637 metres). The Ural Mountains form the boundary between Asia and Europe and are where a variety of mineral resources are found. The environment ranges from vast frozen wastes in the north to subtropical deserts in the south. Agriculture is organised into either state or collective farms that mainly produce sugar beet, cotton, potatoes and vegetables. The country has extensive reserves of coal, oil, gas, iron ore and manganese. Major industries include iron and steel, cement, transport equipment, engineering, armaments, electronic equipment and chemicals. The Russian Federation is beset by many economic problems at the present time and recovery is likely to be a long and difficult process.

Quick facts:
Area: 6,592,850 square miles (17,075,400 square kilometres)
Population: 146,100,000
Capital: Moscow (Moskva)
Other cities: St Petersburg, Nizhniy Novgorod, Novosibirsk, Samara
Form of government: Republic
Religions: Russian Orthodox, Sunni Islam, Shia Islam, Roman Catholicism
Currency: Rouble

Rwanda A small republic in the heart of central Africa that lies just 2 degrees south of the equator. It is a mountainous country with a central spine of highlands from which streams flow west to the Congo river and east to the Nile. Active volcanoes are found in the north where the land rises to about 14,765 feet (4,500 metres). The climate is highland tropical, with temperatures decreasing with altitude. The soils are not fertile and subsistence agriculture dominates the economy. Staple food crops are sweet potatoes, cassava, dry beans, sorghum and potatoes. There are problems of soil erosion, overgrazing and droughts leading to famine, making the country very dependent on foreign aid. The main cash crops are arabic coffee, tea and pyrethrum. There are major reserves of natural gas under Lake Kivu in the west, but these are largely unexploited. The country is, however, faced with massive upheaval and disruption of economic life following the tragic tribal genocide wars in 1994, with ethnic division and rivalry between the Hutus and Tutsis continuing.

Quick facts:

Area: 10,169 square miles (26,338 square kilometres)

Population: 5,397,000

Capital: Kigali

Other major city: Butare

Form of government: Republic

Religions: Roman Catholicism, African traditional religions

Currency: Rwandan Franc

St Christopher (St Kitts) and Nevis The islands of St Christopher (popularly known as St Kitts) and Nevis lie in the Leeward group in the eastern Caribbean and in 1983 became a sovereign democratic federal state with the British monarch as head of state. St Kitts consists of three extinct volcanoes linked by a sandy isthmus to other volcanic remains in the south. The highest point on St Kitts is Mount Liamuiga, 4,314 feet (1,315 metres) and the islands have a tropical climate. Around most of St Kitts sugar cane is grown on the fertile soil covering the gentle slopes. Sugar is the chief export crop but market gardening and livestock are being expanded on the steeper slopes above the cane fields. Some vegetables, coconuts, fruits and cereals are grown. Industry includes sugar processing, brewing, distilling and bottling. St Kitts has a major tourist development at Frigate Bay. Nevis, 2 miles (3 kilometres) south, is an extinct volcano. Farming is declining and tourism is now the main source of income.

Quick facts:

Area: 101 square miles (261 square kilometres)

Population: 41,000

Capital: Basseterre

Other major city: Charlestown

Form of government: Constitutional Monarchy

Religions: Anglicanism, Methodism

Currency: East Caribbean Dollar

St Helena A volcanic island in the south Atlantic Ocean which is a British overseas territory and an administrative centre for the islands of Tristan da Cunha to the south and Ascension Island to the north. Napoleon Bonaparte was exiled here by the British from 1815 until his death in 1821. The main exports are fish, lumber and handicrafts.

Quick facts:

Area: 47 square miles (122 square kilometres)

Population: 5,200

Capital: Jamestown

Form of government: British Overseas Territory

Currency: St Helena Pound

St Lucia One of the Windward Islands in the eastern Caribbean. It lies to the south of MARTINIQUE and to the north of ST VINCENT. It was controlled alternately by the French and the British for some 200 years before becoming fully independent in 1979. St Lucia is an island of extinct volcanoes and the highest peak is 3,117 feet (950 metres). In the west are Les Pitons, two green peaks that rise directly from the sea to over 2,460 feet (750 metres). The climate is tropical, with a rainy season from May to August. The economy depends on the production of bananas and, to a lesser extent, coconuts and mangoes. Production, however, is often affected by hurricanes, drought and disease. There is some manufacturing industry, which produces clothing, cardboard boxes, plastics, electrical parts and drinks and the country has two airports. Tourism is increasing in importance and Castries, the capital, is a popular calling point for cruise liners.

Quick facts:

Area: 240 square miles (622 square kilometres)

Population: 144,000

Capital: Castries

Form of government: Constitutional Monarchy

Religion: Roman Catholicism

Currency: East Caribbean Dollar

St Pierre and Miquelon Two islands to the south of Newfoundland, Canada, which are an overseas territory administered by FRANCE. They are the last French possessions in North America and have a substantial fishing industry.

Quick facts:

Area: 93 square miles (240 square kilometres)

Population: 6,300

Capital: Saint Pierre

Form of government: French Overseas Territory

Religion: Roman Catholicism

Currency: Euro

St Vincent and the Grenadines An island of the Lesser Antilles, situated in the eastern Caribbean between St Lucia and Grenada. It is separated from Grenada by a chain of some 600 small islands known as the Grenadines, the northern islands of which form the other part of the country. The largest of these islands are Bequia, Mustique, Canouan, Mayreau and Union. The climate is tropical, with very heavy rain in the mountains. St Vincent Island is mountainous and a chain of volcanoes runs up the middle of the island. The volcano Soufrière (4,049 feet/1,234 metres) is active and last erupted in 1979. Farming is the main occupation on the island. Bananas for the United Kingdom are the main export and it is the world's leading producer of arrowroot starch. There is little manufacturing and the government is trying to promote tourism. Unemployment is high, however and tropical storms are always a threat to crops.

Quick facts:

Area: 150 square miles (388 square kilometres)

Population: 113,000

Capital: Kingstown

Form of government: Constitutional Monarchy

Religions: Anglicanism, Methodism, Roman Catholicism

Currency: East Caribbean Dollar

Samoa (Western) Called Western Samoa until 1997, a state that lies in the Polynesian sector of the Pacific Ocean, about 447 miles (720 kilometres) northeast of Fiji. It consists of seven small islands and two larger volcanic islands, Savai'i and Upolu. Savai'i is largely covered by volcanic peaks and lava plateaus. Upolu is home to two-thirds of the population and the capital, Apia. The climate is tropical, with high temperatures and very heavy rainfall. The islands have been fought over by the Dutch, British, Germans and Americans, but they now have the traditional Polynesians lifestyle. Subsistence agriculture is the main activity and copra, cocoa and coconuts are the main exports. Many tourists visit the grave of the Scottish writer Robert Louis Stevenson, who died here and whose home is now the official home of the king. There are some light manufacturing industries, including clothing manufacture and an automobile components' factory, which is now the largest private employer and major export industry.

Quick facts:
Area: 1,093 square miles (2,831 square kilometres)
Population: 166,000
Capital: Apia
Form of government: Constitutional Monarchy
Religion: Protestantism
Currency: Tala

Samoa, American An unincorporated territory of the USA, lying close to Samoa in the Pacific Ocean and comprising five main volcanic islands and two coral atolls. The bulk of the population live on the islands of Tutaila and Ta'u. The five main islands are hilly and for the most part covered in thick forest or bush and the climate is tropical with lots of rain. The chief exports are canned tuna, pet foods, watches and handicrafts.

Quick facts:
Area: 77 square miles (199 square kilometres)
Population: 56,000
Capital: Pago Pago
Form of government: Unincorporated Territory of the USA
Religion: Christianity
Currency: US Dollar

San Marino A tiny landlocked state in central Italy, lying in the eastern foothills of the Apennines and one of the smallest republics in the world. Tradition has it that in AD 301, a Christian sought refuge from persecution on Mount Titano. The resulting community prospered and was recognised in 1291 by Pope Nicholas IV as being independent. San Marino has wooded mountains and pasture land clustered around Mount Titano's limestone peaks, which rise to 2,425 feet (739 metres). San Marino has a mild Mediterranean climate. Most of the population work on the land or in forestry. Wheat, barley, maize, olives and vines are grown and the main exports are wood machinery, chemicals, wine, textiles, tiles, varnishes and ceramics, while dairy produce is the main agricultural product. Some 3.5 million tourists visit the country each year and much of the country's revenue comes from the sale of stamps, postcards, souvenirs and duty-free liquor. Italian currency is in general use but San Marino issues its own coins. In 1992 San Marino became a member of the United Nations and it is a full member of the Council of Europe.

Quick facts:
Area: 24 square miles (61 square kilometres)
Population: 25,000
Capital: San Marino
Other cities: Borgo Maggiore, Serravalle
Form of government: Republic
Religion: Roman Catholicism
Currency: Euro

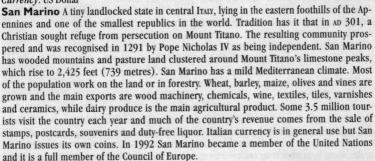

São Tomé and Príncipe A state comprising two volcanic islands that lie off the west coast of Africa. São Tomé is covered in extinct volcanic cones, reaching 6,641 feet (2,024 metres) at the highest peak. The coastal areas are hot and humid. Príncipe is a craggy island lying to the northeast of São Tomé. The climate is tropical, with heavy rainfall from October to May. Seventy per cent of the workforce work on the land, mainly in state-owned cocoa plantations that were nationalised in 1975, after independence. The other main agricultural products are coconuts, melons, copra, bananas and melons. Since crops grown are primarily for export, about 90 per cent of food has to be imported. Small manufacturing industries include food processing and lumber products. The islands were colonised by the Portuguese in the 15th century. They settled convicts and other exiles on the islands and developed a slave trade and grew sugar cane.

Quick facts:
Area: 372 square miles (964 square kilometres)
Population: 135,000
Capital: São Tomé
Form of government: Republic
Religion: Roman Catholicism
Currency: Dobra

Saudi Arabia A state that occupies over 70 per cent of the Arabian Peninsula. Over 95 per cent of the country is desert and the largest expanse of sand in the world, Rub al Khali (The Empty Quarter), is found in the southeast of the country. In the west, a narrow, humid coastal plain along the Red Sea is backed by steep mountains. The climate is hot, with very little rain and some areas have no precipitation for years. The government has spent a considerable amount on reclamation of the desert for agriculture and the main products are dates, tomatoes, watermelons and wheat, which are grown in the fertile land around the oases. Saudi Arabia exports wheat and shrimps and is self-sufficient in some dairy products. The country's prosperity, however, is based almost entirely on the exploitation of its vast reserves of oil and natural gas. Industries include petroleum refining, petrochemicals and fertilisers. As a result of the Gulf War in 1990–91, 285 miles (460 kilometres) of the Saudi coastline has been polluted by oil, threatening desalination plants and damaging the wildlife of salt marshes, mangrove forest and mudflats.

Quick facts:
Area: 830,000 square miles (2,149,690 square kilometres)
Population: 18,836,000
Capital: Riyadh (Ar Riyād)
Other cities: Ad Dammam, Mecca, Jeddah, Medina
Form of government: Monarchy
Religions: Sunni Islam, Shia Islam
Currency: Riyal

Senegal A former French colony in West Africa that extends from the most western point in Africa, Cape Verde, to the border with MALI. Senegal is mostly low-lying and covered by savanna. The Fouta Djallon Mountains in the south rise to 4,971 feet (1,515 metres). The climate is tropical, with a dry season from October to June. The most densely populated region is in the southwest. Almost 80 per cent of the labour force work in agriculture, growing peanuts and cotton for export and millet, sugar cane, maize, rice and sorghum as subsistence crops. Increased production of crops such as rice and tomatoes is encouraged in order to achieve self-sufficiency in food. The country's economy is largely dependent on peanuts but there is a growing manufacturing sector, including food processing, cement, chemicals and tinned tuna, while tourism is also expanding. Senegal is dependent on foreign aid.

Quick facts:
Area: 75,955 square miles (196,722 square kilometres)
Population: 8,572,000
Capital: Dakar
Other cities: Kaolack, Thiès, St Louis
Form of government: Republic
Religions: Sunni Islam, Roman Catholicism
Currency: CFA Franc

Serbia *see* YUGOSLAVIA.

Seychelles A group of volcanic islands that lie in the western Indian Ocean, about 746 miles (1,200 kilometres) from the coast of East Africa. About 40 of the islands are mountainous and consist of granite while just over 50 are coral islands. The climate is tropical maritime with heavy rain. About 90 per cent of the people live on the island of Mahé, which is the site of the capital, Victoria. The staple foods are coconut, imported rice and fish, while some fruits are grown for home consumption Tourism accounts for about 90 per cent of the country's foreign exchange earnings and employs one-third of the labour force. Export trade is based on petroleum (after importation), copra, cinnamon bark and fish. The only mineral resource is guano. The Seychelles were a one-party socialist state until 1991, when a new constitution was introduced. The first free elections were held in 1993.

Quick facts:
Area: 175 square miles (455 square kilometres)
Population: 76,000
Capital: Victoria
Form of government: Republic
Religion: Roman Catholicism
Currency: Seychelles Rupee

Sierra Leone A country on the Atlantic coast of West Africa, bounded by GUINEA to the north and east and by LIBERIA to the southeast. The country possesses a fine natural harbor where the capital and major port of Freetown is situated. A range of mountains, the Sierra Lyoa, rise above the capital on the Freetown Peninsula but, elsewhere, the coastal plain is up to 70 miles (110 kilometres) wide rising to a plateau and then mountains which are part of the Guinea Highlands Massif. The climate is tropical, with heavy rain during a rainy season lasting from May to November. The main food of the population is rice that is grown in the swamplands at the coast by the subsistence farmers. Other crops raised include sorghum, cassava, millet, sugar and peanuts. In the tropical forest areas, small plantations produce coffee, cocoa and palm oil. In the plateau much forest has been cleared for the growing of groundnuts. Most of the country's revenue comes from agriculture and mining, principally of rutile, although bauxite is produced in significant quantities. Diamonds are also mined, although in much reduced amounts and there are deposits of iron ore with some gold and platinum.

Quick facts:
Area: 27,699 square miles (71,740 square kilometres)
Population: 4,297,000
Capital: Freetown
Other city: Bo
Form of government: Republic
Religions: African traditional religions, Sunni Islam, Christianity
Currency: Leone

Singapore One of the world's smallest yet most successful countries. It comprises one main island and 58 islets that are located at the foot of the Malay Peninsula in Southeast Asia. The main island of Singapore is very low-lying and the climate is hot and wet throughout the year. Only 1.6 per cent of the land area is used for agriculture, most food being imported. The country has a flourishing manufacturing industry for which it relies heavily on imports. Products traded in Singapore include machinery and appliances, petroleum, food and beverages, chemicals, transport equipment, paper products and printing and clothes. Shipbuilding is also an important industry. The Jurong Industrial Estate on the south of the island has approximately 2,300 companies and employs nearly 141,000 workers. International banking and tourism are important sources of foreign revenue. Singapore's airport is one of the largest in Asia.

Quick facts:
Area: 239 square miles (618 square kilometres)
Population: 3,044,000
Capital: Singapore
Form of government: Parliamentary Democracy
Religions: Buddhism, Sunni Islam, Christianity, Hinduism
Currency: Singapore Dollar

Slovakia (Slovak Republic) A country that was constituted on 1 January 1993 as a new independent nation, following the dissolution of the 74-year-old federal republic of Czechoslovakia. Landlocked in central Europe, its neighbours are the CZECH REPUBLIC to the west, POLAND to the north, AUSTRIA and HUNGARY to the south and a short border with UKRAINE in the east. The northern half of the republic is occupied by the Tatra Mountains, which form the northern arm of the

Carpathian Mountains. This region has vast forests and pastures used for intensive sheep grazing and is rich in high-grade minerals such as copper, iron, zinc and lead. The southern part of Slovakia is a plain drained by the Danube and its tributaries. Farms, vineyards, orchards and pastures for stock form the basis of southern Slovakia's economy. Slovakia has many economic and environmental problems as a legacy of the inefficient industrialisation of the old regime. In the early 1990s unemployment increased and inflation was high, resulting in a lowering in the standard of living. Tourism is now increasing at the ski resorts and historic cities.

Quick facts:

Area: 18,928 square miles (49,035 square kilometres)
Population: 5,374,000
Capital: Bratislava
Other cities: Kosice, Zilina, Nitra
Form of government: Republic
Religion: Roman Catholicism
Currency: Slovak Koruna

Slovenia A republic that made a unilateral declaration of independence from former Yugoslavia on 25 June 1991. Sovereignty was not formally recognised by the European Community and the United Nations until early in 1992. It is bounded to the north by Austria, to the west by Italy, to the east by Hungary and to the south by Croatia. Most of Slovenia is situated in the Karst Plateau and in the Julian Alps, which has Mount Triglav as its highest point at 9,393 feet (2,863 metres). The Julian Alps are renowned for their scenery and the Karst Plateau contains spectacular cave systems. Although farming and livestock raising are the chief occupations, Slovenia is very industrialised and urbanised. Iron, steel and aluminium are produced and mineral resources include oil, coal, lead, uranium and mercury. There is also natural gas and petroleum. Slovenia has also been successful in establishing many new light industries, and this has given the country a well-balanced economic base for the future, with unemployment lessening and industrial output increasing. The northeast of the republic is famous for its wine production and tourism is also an important industry.

Quick facts:
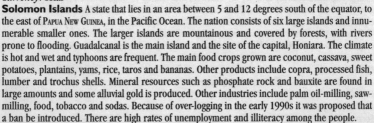
Area: 7,821 square miles (20,256 square kilometres)
Population: 1,991,000
Capital: Ljubljana
Other cities: Maribor, Kranj
Form of government: Republic
Religion: Roman Catholicism
Currency: Tolar

Solomon Islands A state that lies in an area between 5 and 12 degrees south of the equator, to the east of Papua New Guinea, in the Pacific Ocean. The nation consists of six large islands and innumerable smaller ones. The larger islands are mountainous and covered by forests, with rivers prone to flooding. Guadalcanal is the main island and the site of the capital, Honiara. The climate is hot and wet and typhoons are frequent. The main food crops grown are coconut, cassava, sweet potatoes, plantains, yams, rice, taros and bananas. Other products include copra, processed fish, lumber and trochus shells. Mineral resources such as phosphate rock and bauxite are found in large amounts and some alluvial gold is produced. Other industries include palm oil-milling, sawmilling, food, tobacco and sodas. Because of over-logging in the early 1990s it was proposed that a ban be introduced. There are high rates of unemployment and illiteracy among the people.

Quick facts:

Area: 11,157 square miles (28,896 square kilometres)
Population: 391,000
Capital: Honiara
Form of government: Parliamentary Democracy within the Commonwealth
Religion: Christianity
Currency: Solomon Islands Dollar

Somalia A country that lies on the horn of Africa's east coast. It is bounded on the north by the Gulf of Aden and on the south and east by the Indian Ocean, and its neighbours include Djibouti, Ethiopia and Kenya. The country is arid and most of it is low plateau with scrub vegetation. Its two main rivers, the Juba and Shebelle, are used to irrigate crops. Most of the population live in the mountains and river valleys and there are a few towns on the coast. The country has little in the way of natural resources but there are deposits of copper, petroleum, iron, manganese and marble, although not commercially exploited. Main exports are live animals, meat, hides and skins. A few large-scale banana plantations are found by the rivers. Years of drought have left Somalia heavily dependent on foreign aid and many of the younger people are emigrating to oil-rich Arab states. Civil war in the 1980s and early 1990s resulted in a huge loss of life and widespread famine. International UN peacekeeping forces were deployed and humanitarian aid given to try to avert a catastrophe but these withdrew in 1995. The situation remains unresolved although there has been some recovery in agriculture and food production.

Quick facts:

Area: 246,201 square miles (637,657 square kilometres)
Population: 9,822,000
Capital: Mogadishu (Muqdisho)
Other major towns: Hargeysa, Burco
Form of government: Republic
Religion: Sunni Islam
Currency: Somali Shilling

South Africa A republic that lies at the southern tip of the African continent and has a huge coastline on both the Atlantic and Indian Oceans. The country occupies a huge saucer-shaped plateau, surrounding a belt of land that drops in steps to the sea. The rim of the saucer rises in the east to 11,424 feet (3,482 metres) in the Drakensberg mountain range. In general the climate is healthy, with plenty of sunshine and relatively low rainfall. This varies with latitude, distance from the sea and altitude. Of the total land area, 58 per cent is used as natural pasture although soil erosion is a problem. The main crops grown are maize, sorghum, wheat, groundnuts and sugar cane. A drought-resistant variety of cotton is also now grown. South Africa has extraordinary mineral wealth. This includes gold, coal, copper, iron ore, manganese, diamonds and chrome ore. A system of apartheid existed in South Africa from 1948 until the early 1990s, denying black South Africans civil rights and promoting racial segregation. During this time the country was subjected to international economic and political sanctions. In 1990 F. W. de Klerk, then president, lifted the ban on the outlawed African National Congress and released its leader, Nelson Mandela, who had been imprisoned since 1962. This heralded the dismantling of the apartheid regime and in the first multiracial elections, held in 1994, the ANC triumphed, with Mandela voted in as the country's president. Since that time South Africa has once again become an active and recognised member of the international community.

Quick facts:

Area: 471,445 square miles (1,221,037 square kilometres)
Population: 42,393,000
Capital: Pretoria (administrative), Cape Town (legislative)
Other cities: Johannesburg, Durban, Port Elizabeth, Soweto
Form of government: Republic
Religions: Christianity, Hinduism, Islam
Currency: Rand

Spain A country located in southwest Europe and occupying the greater part of the Iberian Peninsula, which it shares with Portugal. It is a mountainous country, sealed off from the rest of Europe by the Pyrénées, which rise to over 11,155 feet (3,400 metres). Much of the country is a vast plateau, the Meseta Central, cut across by valleys and gorges. Its longest shoreline is the one that borders the Mediterranean Sea. Most of the country has a form of Mediterranean climate, with mild moist winters and hot dry summers. Spain's major rivers, such as the Douro, Tagus and Guadiana, flow to the Atlantic Ocean while the Guadalquivir is the deepest. Although not generally navigable, they are of use for hydroelectric power. Spain's principal agricultural products are cereals, vegetables and potatoes and large areas are under vines for the wine industry. The soil is good, with almost one-third cultivable. Livestock production is important, particularly sheep and goats. Industry represents 72 per cent of the country's export value and production includes textiles, paper, cement, steel and chemicals. Tourism is a major revenue earner, especially from the resorts on the east coast.

Quick facts:

Area: 195,365 square miles (505,992 square kilometres)
Population: 39,270,400
Capital: Madrid
Other cities: Barcelona, Valencia, Seville, Zaragoza, Malaga, Bilbao
Form of government: Constitutional Monarchy
Religion: Roman Catholicism
Currency: Euro

Sri Lanka A teardrop-shaped island in the Indian Ocean, lying south of the Indian Peninsula, from which it is separated by the Palk Strait. The climate is equatorial, with a low annual temperature range, but it is affected by both the northeast and southwest monsoons. Rainfall is heaviest in the southwest while the north and east are relatively dry. Agriculture engages 47 per cent of the work force and the main crops are rice, tea, rubber and coconuts, although sugar, rice and wheat have to be imported. Amongst the chief minerals mined and exported are precious and semiprecious stones. Graphite is also important. The main industries are food, beverages, tobacco, textiles, clothing, leather goods, chemicals and plastics. Attempts are being made to increase the revenue from tourism. Politically, Sri Lanka has been afflicted by ethnic divisions between the Sinhalese and Tamils. In the 1980s attempts by the Tamil extremists to establish an independent homeland brought the northeast of the country to the brink of civil war and the situation remains extremely volatile.

Quick facts:

Area: 25,332 square miles (65,610 square kilometres)
Population: 18,354,000
Capital: Colombo
Other cities: Trincomalee, Jaffna, Kandy, Moratuwa
Form of government: Republic
Religions: Buddhism, Hinduism, Christianity, Sunni Islam
Currency: Sri Lankan Rupee

Sudan The largest country in Africa, lying just south of the Tropic of Cancer in northeast Africa. The country covers much of the upper Nile basin and in the north the river winds through the Nubian and Libyan deserts, forming a palm-fringed strip of habitable land. In 1994, the country was divided into 26 states, compared to the original nine. The climate is tropical and temperatures are high throughout the year. In winter, nights are very cold. Rainfall increases in amount from north to south, the northern areas being virtually desert. Sudan is an agricultural country, subsistence farming accounting for 80 per cent of production and livestock are also raised. Cotton is farmed commercially and accounts for about two-thirds of Sudan's exports. Sudan is the world's greatest source of gum arabic, used in medicines, perfumes, processed foods and inks. Other forest products are tannin, beeswax, senna and lumber. Because of the combination of years of civil war and drought, Sudan has a large foreign debt, estimated to be three times its gross national product.

Quick facts:

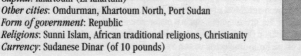

Area: 967,500 square miles (2,505,813 square kilometres)
Population: 27,291,000
Capital: Khartoum (El Khartum)
Other cities: Omdurman, Khartoum North, Port Sudan
Form of government: Republic
Religions: Sunni Islam, African traditional religions, Christianity
Currency: Sudanese Dinar (of 10 pounds)

Suriname A republic in northeast South America that was formerly known as Dutch Guiana. It is bordered to the west by Guyana, to the east by Guiana And to the south by Brazil. The country, formerly a Dutch colony, declared independence in 1975. Suriname comprises a swampy coastal plain, a forested central plateau and southern mountains. The climate is tropical, with heavy rainfall concentrated mainly from December to April. Agriculture remains fairly underdeveloped. Crops cultivated include rice, bananas, citrus fruits, sugar cane, coffee and cocoa. Molasses and rum are produced along with some manufactured goods and there is an important coastal shrimp fishery. Suriname's economy is based on the mining of bauxite, which accounts for 80 per cent of its exports. The country has important mineral reserves of iron ore, nickel, copper, platinum and gold. Suriname's natural resources also include oil and lumber and forestry is an expanding industry. However, the country is politically unstable and in need of financial aid to develop its resources.

Quick facts:
Area: 63,037 square miles (163,265 square kilometres)
Population: 423,000
Capital: Paramaribo
Form of government: Republic
Religions: Hinduism, Roman Catholicism, Sunni Islam
Currency: Suriname Guilder

Swaziland A landlocked hilly enclave almost entirely within the borders of the Republic of South Africa. The mountains in the west of the country rise to about 6,500 feet (almost 2,000 metres), then descend in steps of savanna towards hilly country in the east. The climate is subtropical, moderated by altitude. The land between 1,300–2,800 feet (approximately 400–850 metres) is planted with orange groves and pineapple fields, while on the lower land sugar cane flourishes in irrigated areas. Other important crops are citrus fruits, cotton and pineapples. Forestry is an important industry, production centring mainly on pine since it matures extremely quickly because of Swaziland's climate. Coal is mined and also asbestos, although in lessening amounts because of its associated health risks. Manufacturing includes fertilisers, textiles, leather and tableware. Tourism is a growing industry, with the country's game reserves, mountain scenery, spas and casinos proving popular destinations for visitors.

Quick facts:
Area: 6,704 square miles (17,364 square kilometres)
Population: 938,700
Capital: Mbabane
Other towns: Big Bend, Manzini, Mankayane, Lobamba
Form of government: Monarchy
Religions: Christianity, African traditional religions
Currency: Lilangeni

Sweden A large country in northern Europe that makes up half the Scandinavian peninsula. It stretches from the Baltic Sea north to well within the Arctic Circle. The south is generally flat with many lakes, the north mountainous and along the coast there are over 20,000 islands and islets. Summers are warm but short while winters are long and cold. In the north snow may lie for four to seven months. Dairy farming is the predominant agricultural activity and also the production of livestock, including cattle, pigs and sheep. Only 7 per cent of Sweden is cultivated, with the emphasis on fodder crops, potatoes, rape seed, grain and sugar beet. About 57 per cent of the country is covered by forest and the sawmill, wood pulp and paper industries are all of great importance. Sweden is one of the world's leading producers of iron ore, most of which is extracted from within the Arctic Circle. Other main industries are engineering and electrical goods, motor vehicles and furniture making, as well as fine crafts such as glassware, ceramics, silverware and items made from stainless steel. In a referendum in 1994, Swedish voters approved membership of the European Union and it became a member on 1 January 1995.

Quick facts:
Area: 173,732 square miles (449,964 square kilometres)
Population: 8,843,000
Capital: Stockholm
Other cities: Göteborg, Malmö, Uppsala, Örebro, Linköping
Form of government: Constitutional Monarchy
Religion: Lutheranism
Currency: Krona

Switzerland A landlocked country in central Europe, sharing its borders with FRANCE, ITALY, AUSTRIA, LIECHTENSTEIN and GERMANY. The Alps occupy over 70 per cent of the country's area, forming two main east-west chains divided by the Rivers Rhine and Rhône. The climate is either continental or mountain type. Summers are generally warm and winters cold and both are affected by altitude. Northern Switzerland is the industrial part of the country and where its most important cities are located. Basle is famous for its pharmaceuticals and Zürich for electrical engineering and machinery. Although the country has to import much of its raw materials, these become high-value exports such as clocks, watches and other precision engineering products. It is also in this region that the famous cheeses and chocolates are produced. Hydroelectricity accounts for approximately 60 per cent of its power supplies, with most of the remainder coming from nuclear power plants. Switzerland has huge earnings from international finance and tourism.

Quick facts:
Area: 15,940 square miles (41,284 square kilometres)
Population: 7,076,000
Capital: Bern
Other cities: Zürich, Basle, Geneva, Lausanne
Form of government: Federal Republic
Religions: Roman Catholicism, Protestantism
Currency: Swiss Franc

Syria or the Syrian Arab Republic A country in southwest Asia that borders on the Mediterranean Sea in the west. Much of the country is mountainous behind the narrow fertile coastal plain. The eastern region is desert or semi-desert, a stony inhospitable land. The coast has a Mediterranean climate, with hot dry summers and mild wet winters. About 50 per cent of the workforce get their living from agriculture: sheep, goats and cattle are raised; and cotton, barley, wheat, tobacco, grapes, olives and vegetables are grown, although some land is unused because of lack of irrigation. Reserves of oil are small compared to neighbouring IRAQ, but it has enough to make the country self-sufficient and provide three-quarters of the nation's export earnings. Industries such as textiles, leather, chemicals and cement have developed rapidly in the last 20 years, with the country's craftsmen producing fine rugs and silk brocades. Foreign revenue is gained from tourism and also from countries who pipe oil through Syria. The country is dependent on the main Arab oil-producing countries for aid.

Quick facts:
Area: 71,498 square miles (185,180 square kilometres)
Population: 14,619,000
Capital: Damascus (Dimashq)
Other cities: Halab, Hims, Dar'a
Form of government: Republic
Religion: Sunni Islam
Currency: Syrian Pound

Taiwan An island that straddles the Tropic of Cancer in East Asia. It lies about 100 miles (161 kilometres) off the southeast coast of mainland CHINA. It is predominantly mountainous in the interior, with more than 60 peaks attaining heights of 10,000 feet (3,040 metres). The highest of all is the Jade Mountain (Yu Shan) which stands at 12,960 feet (3,940 metres). Taiwan's independence, resulting from the island's seizure by nationalists in 1949, is not fully accepted internationally and China lays claim to the territory. The climate is warm and humid for most of the year and winters are mild with summers rainy. The soils are fertile and a wide range of crops, including tea, rice, sugar cane and bananas, is grown. Natural resources include gas, marble, limestone and small coal deposits. Taiwan is a major international trading nation with some of the most successful export-processing zones in the world, accommodating domestic and overseas companies. Exports include machinery, electronics, textiles, footwear, toys and sporting goods.

Quick facts:

Area: 13,800 square miles (35,742 square kilometres)
Population: 21,854,270
Capital: T'ai-pei
Other cities: Kao-hsiung, T'ai-nan, Chang-hua, Chi-lung
Form of government: Republic
Religions: Taoism, Buddhism, Christianity
Currency: New Taiwan Dollar

Tajikistan A republic of southern central former USSR that declared itself independent in 1991. It is situated near the Afghani and Chinese borders. The south is occupied by the Pamir mountain range, whose snow-capped peaks dominate the country. More than half the country lies over 9,840 feet (3,000 metres). Most of the country is desert or semi-desert and pastoral farming of cattle, sheep, horses and goats is important. Some yaks are kept in the higher regions. The lowland areas in the Fergana and Amudarya valleys are irrigated so that cotton, mulberry trees, fruit, wheat and vegetables can be grown. The Amudarya river is also used to produce hydroelectricity for industries such as cotton and silk processing. The republic is rich in deposits of coal, lead, zinc, oil and uranium, which were being exploited. There has been a continuing civil war in which tens of thousands of people have been killed or made homeless.

Quick facts:

Area: 55,250 square miles (143,100 square kilometres)
Population: 5,919,000
Capital: Dushanbe
Other major city: Khujand
Form of government: Republic
Religion: Shia Islam
Currency: Tajik Rouble

Tanzania A country that lies on the east coast of central Africa and comprises a large mainland area and the islands of Pemba and Zanzibar. The mainland consists mostly of plateaus broken by mountainous areas and the East African section of the Great Rift Valley. The climate is very varied and is controlled largely by altitude and distance from the sea. The coast is hot and humid, the central plateau drier and the mountains semi-temperate. Eighty per cent of Tanzanians make a living from the land, producing corn, cassava, millet, rice, plantains and sorghum for home consumption. Cash crops include cotton, tobacco, tea, sisal, cashews and coffee. The two islands produce the bulk of the world's needs of cloves. Diamond mining is an important industry and there are also sizable deposits of iron ore, coal and tin. Fishing is also important with the bulk of the catch caught in inland waters. Although Tanzania is one of the poorest countries in the world, it has a wealth of natural wonders, such as the Serengeti Plain and its wildlife, the Ngorongoro Crater, Mount Kilimanjaro and the Olduvai Gorge, all of which attract large numbers of tourists, making a significant contribution to the country's economy.

Quick facts:
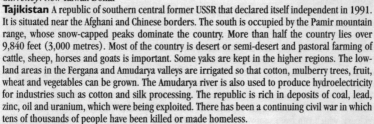
Area: 362,162 square miles (938,000 square kilometres)
Population: 30,799,100
Capital: Dodoma
Other towns: Dar es Salaam, Zanzibar, Mwanza, Tanga
Form of government: Republic
Religions: Sunni Islam, Roman Catholicism, Anglicanism, Hinduism
Currency: Tanzanian Shilling

Thailand A country about the same size as FRANCE, located in Southeast Asia. It is a tropical country of mountains and jungles, rainforests and green plains. Central Thailand is a densely populated, fertile plain and the mountainous Isthmus of Kra joins southern Thailand to MALAYSIA. Thailand has a subtropical climate, with heavy monsoon rains from June to October, a cool season from October to March and a hot season from March to June. It is rich in many natural resources, such as mineral deposits of gold, coal, lead and precious stones, with rich soils, extensive areas of tropical forests and natural gas offshore. The central plain of Thailand contains vast expanses of paddy fields that grow enough rice to rank Thailand as one of the world's leading producers. The narrow southern peninsula is very wet and it is here that rubber is produced. Other crops grown are cassava, maize, pineapples and sugar cane. Fishing is an increasingly important industry, with prawns being sold for export. Tourism also contributes to the country's economy.

Quick facts:

Area: 198,115 square miles (513,115 square kilometres)
Population: 60,206,000
Capital: Bangkok (Krung Thep)
Other cities: Chiang Mai, Nakhon Ratchasima, Ubon Ratchathani
Form of government: Constitutional Monarchy
Religions: Buddhism, Sunni Islam
Currency: Baht

Togo A tiny country with a narrow coastal plain on the Gulf of Guinea in West Africa. Grassy plains in the north and south are separated by the Togo Highlands (2,300–3,235 feet/700–986 metres), which run from southwest to northeast. High plateaus, mainly in the more southerly ranges, are heavily forested with teak, mahogany and bamboo. Wildlife species are varied and include birds, monkeys, snakes, crocodiles, hippopotamus, antelope and lion. Togo has a tropical climate with a major rainy season from March to July and a minor one from October to November. The north is affected by the dry harmattan wind from the Sahara during December and January. Over 80 per cent of the population is involved in subsistence agriculture, with yams, cassava, sorghum and millet as the principal crops. Minerals, particularly phosphates, are now the main export earners, along with raw cotton, coffee, cocoa, cement and palm kernels. Togo's main imports include food, machinery, construction equipment, textiles and electrical equipment. The official language is French, with Ewe and Kabre (main African languages) also being used in the schools.

Quick facts:

Area: 21,925 square miles (56,785 square kilometres)
Population: 4,201,000
Capital: Lomé
Other major city: Sokodé
Form of government: Republic
Religions: African traditional religions, Roman Catholicism, Sunni Islam
Currency: CFA Franc

Tonga A country situated about 20 degrees south of the equator and just west of the International Date Line in the Pacific Ocean. It comprises over 170 islands, only about 40 of which are inhabited. It comprises a low limestone chain of islands in the east and a higher volcanic chain in the west. The climate is warm with heavy rainfall, and destructive cyclones are likely to occur every few years. The government owns all the land, and males can rent an allotment for growing food. Yams, cassava and taro are grown as subsistence crops, and fish from the sea supplement the diet while foods such as pumpkins, bananas, vanilla and coconuts are exported. The main industry is coconut processing. About 70 per cent of the workforce is occupied in either fishing or agriculture while many Tongans are employed overseas. Tourism, foreign aid from countries such as the United Kingdom, Australia and New Zealand and the income sent home from overseas workers all contribute to the country's economy.

Quick facts:
Area: 288 square miles (747 square kilometres)
Population: 99,000
Capital: Nuku'alofa
Form of government: Constitutional monarchy
Religions: Methodism, Roman Catholicism
Currency: Pa'anga

Trinidad and Tobago The islands constitute the third largest British Commonwealth country in the West Indies and are situated off the Orinoco Delta in northeastern Venezuela. They are the most southerly of the Lesser Antilles. Trinidad consists of the mountainous Northern Range in the north and undulating plains in the south. It has a huge, asphalt-producing lake, Pitch Lake, which is approximately 104 acres (42 hectares) in size. Tobago is actually a mountain that is about 1,800 feet (550 metres) above sea level at its peak. The climate is tropical with little variation in temperatures throughout the year and a rainy season from June to December. Trinidad is one of the oldest oil-producing countries in the world. Output is small but provides 90 per cent of Trinidad's exports. Sugar cane, cocoa, citrus fruits, vegetables and rubber trees are grown for export, but imports of food now account for 10 per cent of total imports. Tobago depends mainly on tourism for revenue. A slump in the economy in the 1980s and early 1990s saw widespread unemployment but economic growth has improved in recent times.

Quick facts:
Area: 1,981 square miles (5,130 square kilometres)
Population: 1,297,000
Capital: Port of Spain
Other towns: San Fernando, Arima
Form of government: Republic
Religions: Roman Catholicism, Hinduism, Anglicanism, Sunni Islam
Currency: Trinidad and Tobago Dollar

Tunisia A North African country that lies on the south coast of the Mediterranean Sea. It is bounded by Algeria to the west and Libya to the south. Northern Tunisia consists of hills, plains and valleys. Inland mountains separate the coastal zone from the central plains before the land drops down to an area of salt pans and the Sahara. The climate ranges from warm temperate in the north, where there are vineyards and forests of pine, cork oak and junipers, to desert in the south. Agriculture produces wheat, barley, olives, grapes, tomatoes, dates, vegetables and citrus fruits and the fishing industry is of growing importance, producing mainly pilchards, sardines and tuna. Twenty-six per cent of the workforce is engaged in these two occupations, but overall there is a general lack of employment. The mainstay of Tunisia's modern economy, however, is oil from the Sahara, phosphates, natural gas and tourism on the Mediterranean coast. Tourists are attracted by the good beaches and historic sites such as the ancient city of Carthage.

Quick facts:
Area: 62,592 square miles (162,155 square kilometres)
Population: 9,092,000
Capital: Tunis
Other cities: Sfax, Bizerte, Sousse
Form of government: Republic
Religion: Sunni Islam
Currency: Dinar

Turkey With land on the continents of Europe and Asia, Turkey forms a bridge between the two. It guards the sea passage between the Mediterranean and the Black Sea. Turkey occupies an area in which seismic activity is a frequent occurrence and the country regularly experiences devastating earthquakes. Only 5 per cent of its area, Thrace, is in Europe and the much larger area, Anatolia, is in Asia. European Turkey is fertile agricultural land with a Mediterranean climate. Asiatic Turkey is bordered to the north by the Pontine Mountains and to the south by the Taurus Mountains. The climate here ranges from Mediterranean to hot summers and bitterly cold winters in the central plains.

Agriculture employs almost half the workforce, with the major crops being wheat, sugar beet, barley, fruits, maize and oil seeds. The country's main exports are iron and steel, textiles, dried fruits, tobacco, leather clothes and petroleum products. Manufacturing industry includes iron and steel, textiles, motor vehicles and Turkey's famous carpets. The main mineral resources are iron ore, coal, chromium, magnetite, zinc and lead. Hydroelectric power is supplied by the Tigris and Euphrates. Tourism is a fast-developing industry and plays an increasingly important role in the economy.

Quick facts:
Area: 299,158 square miles (774,815 square kilometres)
Population: 62,697,000
Capital: Ankara
Other cities: Istanbul, Izmir, Adana, Bursa
Form of government: Republic
Religion: Sunni Islam
Currency: Turkish Lira

Turkmenistan A central Asian republic of the former USSR that declared itself a republic in 1991. It lies to the east of the Caspian Sea and borders IRAN and AFGHANISTAN to the south. Much of the west and central areas of Turkmenistan are covered by the sandy Karakum Kum. The east is a plateau that is bordered by the Amudarya river. The Amudarya has been diverted to form the important Kara Kum Canal which is one of the longest canals in the world and provides irrigation and drinking water for the southeastern parts of the country. The climate is extremely dry, and most of the population live in oasis settlements near the rivers and by the extensive network of canals. Agriculture is intensive around the settlements and consists of growing cotton, cereals, silk, fruit and rearing Karakul sheep. This occupies around 45 per cent of the workforce. There are rich mineral deposits, particularly natural gas, petroleum, sulphur, coal, salt and copper. There is some other manufacturing industry, such as textile manufacturing, food processing and carpet weaving. Unlike most other former Soviet republics, there has not been a wholesale emigration of ethnic minorities.

Quick facts:
Area: 188,456 square miles (488,100 square kilometres)
Population: 4,569,000
Capital: Ashkhabad (Ashgabat)
Other cities: Chardzhou, Mary, Turkmenbashi
Form of government: Republic
Religion: Sunni Islam
Currency: Manat

Turks and Caicos Islands Two island groups which form the southeastern archipelago of the Bahamas in the Atlantic Ocean. Only six of the islands are inhabited. A British Crown Colony, the country's economy relies mainly on tourism and the export of shellfish to the UK and the USA. The climate is subtropical cooled by southeast trade winds which blow all the year round.

Quick facts:
Area: 166 square miles (430 square kilometres)
Population: 23,000
Capital: Grand Turk
Form of government: British Crown Colony
Religion: Christianity
Currency: US Dollar

Tuvalu A country located just north of FIJI, in the South Pacific, consisting of nine coral atolls. The group was formerly known as the Ellice Islands, and the main island and capital is Funafuti. Tuvalu became independent in 1978. The climate is tropical, with an annual average rainfall of 120 inches (3,050 millimetres). Coconut palms are the main crop and fruit and vegetables are grown for local consumption. Sea fishing is extremely good and largely unexploited, although licenses have been granted to JAPAN, TAIWAN and the Republic of KOREA to fish the local waters. Revenue comes from copra (the only export product), foreign aid, the sale of elaborate postage stamps to philatelists and income sent home from Tuvaluans who work abroad. English and Tuvaluan are both spoken by the Polynesian population and there is an airport situated on Funafuti Atoll.

Quick facts:
Area: 10 square miles (24 square kilometres)
Population: 10,000
Capital: Funafuti
Form of government: Constitutional Monarchy
Religion: Protestantism
Currency: Tuvalu Dollar/Australian Dollar

Uganda A landlocked country in east central Africa. The equator runs through the south of the country and for the most part it is a richly fertile land, well watered, with a kindly climate. In the west are the Ruwenzori Mountains, which reach heights of 16,762 feet (5,109 metres) and are snow-capped. The lowlands around Lake Victoria, once forested, have now mostly been cleared for cultivation. Agriculture employs over 80 per cent of the labour force and the main crops grown for subsistence are plantains, cassava and sweet potatoes. Coffee is the main cash crop and accounts for over 90 per cent of the country's exports although cotton and tea are important. Attempts are being made to expand the tea plantations in the west, to develop a copper mine and to introduce new industries to Kampala, the capital. Forestry is of importance, with the major export being mahogany, while the bulk of other wood is used as fuel. Virtually all the country's power is produced by hydroelectricity, the plant on the Victoria Nile being of major importance. Since 1986, Uganda has slowly been rebuilding its shattered economy in spite of some resurgence of earlier violence.

Quick facts:
Area: 93,065 square miles (241,038 square kilometres)
Population: 19,848,000
Capital: Kampala
Other cities: Entebbe, Jinja, Soroti, Mbale
Form of government: Republic
Religions: Roman Catholicism, Protestantism, African traditional
religions, Sunni Islam
Currency: Uganda Shilling

Ukraine A former Soviet socialist republic that declared itself independent of the former USSR in 1991. Its neighbours to the west are POLAND, SLOVAKIA, HUNGARY and ROMANIA, and it is bounded to the south by the Black Sea. To the east lies the RUSSIAN FEDERATION and to the north the republic of BELARUS. Drained by the Dnepr, Dnestr, Southern Bug and Donets rivers, Ukraine consists largely of fertile steppes. The climate is continental, although this is greatly modified by the proximity of the Black Sea. The Ukrainian steppe is one of the chief wheat-producing regions of Europe. Other major crops include corn, sugar beet, flax, tobacco, soya, hops and potatoes, with agriculture accounting for about a quarter of all employment. There are rich reserves of coal and raw materials for industry, but the country is still reliant on the other former Soviet republics for natural gas and oil. The central and eastern regions form one of the world's densest industrial concentrations. Manufacturing industries include ferrous metallurgy, heavy machinery, chemicals, food processing, gas and oil refining. In 1986 the catastrophic accident at the Chernobyl nuclear power station occurred, which had far-reaching effects and caused widespread contamination. Financial assistance was agreed in 1996 with a number of countries to help the Ukraine close the station.

Quick facts:
Area: 233,090 square miles (603,700 square kilometres)
Population: 51,094,000
Capital: Kiev (Kiyev)
Other cities: Dnepropetrovsk, Donetsk, Khar'kov, Odessa, Lugansk, Sevastopol
Form of government: Republic
Religions: Russian Orthodox, Roman Catholicism
Currency: Rouble

United Arab Emirates (UAE) A federation of seven oil-rich sheikdoms located in The Gulf. As well as its main coast on the Gulf, the country has a short coast on the Gulf of Oman. The land is mainly flat sandy desert except to the north on the peninsula where the Hajar Mountains rise to 6,828 feet (2,081 metres). The summers are hot and humid with temperatures reaching 120°F (49°C), but from October to May the weather is warm and sunny with pleasant, cool evenings. The only fertile areas are the emirate of Ras al Khaymah, the coastal plain of Al Fujayrah and the oases. Abu Dhabi and Dubai are the main industrial centres and, using their wealth from the oil industry, they are now diversifying industry by building aluminium smelters, cement factories and steel-rolling mills. The level of adult illiteracy has improved enormously since the mid-1970s, with compulsory education for 12 years from the age of six. Prior to development of the oil industry, traditional occupations were pearl diving, growing dates, fishing and camel breeding. Dubai is the richest state in the world.

Quick facts:

Area: 32,278 square miles (83,600 square kilometres)
Population: 2,260,000
Capital: Abu Zabi (Abu Dhabi)
Other cities: Dubai, Sharjh, Ras al Khaymah
Form of government: Monarchy
Religion: Sunni Islam
Currency: Dirham

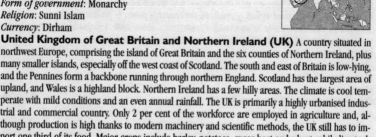

United Kingdom of Great Britain and Northern Ireland (UK) A country situated in northwest Europe, comprising the island of Great Britain and the six counties of Northern Ireland, plus many smaller islands, especially off the west coast of Scotland. The south and east of Britain is low-lying, and the Pennines form a backbone running through northern England. Scotland has the largest area of upland, and Wales is a highland block. Northern Ireland has a few hilly areas. The climate is cool temperate with mild conditions and an even annual rainfall. The UK is primarily a highly urbanised industrial and commercial country. Only 2 per cent of the workforce are employed in agriculture and, although production is high thanks to modern machinery and scientific methods, the UK still has to import one third of its food. Major crops include barley, potatoes, sugar beet and wheat, while livestock raised includes sheep, cattle, pigs and poultry. Fishing is also an important industry. The UK has to import most of the materials it needs for its industries as it lacks natural resources apart from coal, iron ore, oil and natural gas. Many of the older industries, such as the coal, textiles and heavy engineering industries, have declined significantly in recent years while service industries play an increasingly large part in the UK's economy, as does tourism.

Quick facts:

Area: 94,248 square miles (244,101 square kilometres)
Population: 58,784,000
Capital: London
Other cities: Birmingham, Manchester, Glasgow, Liverpool, Edinburgh, Cardiff, Belfast
Form of government: Constitutional Monarchy
Religions: Anglicanism, Roman Catholicism, Presbyterianism, Methodism, Islam
Currency: Pound Sterling

United States of America (USA) A country that stretches across central north America, from the Atlantic Ocean in the east to the Pacific Ocean in the west, and from CANADA in the north to MEXICO and the Gulf of Mexico in the south. It is the fourth largest country in the world and consists of fifty states, including outlying Alaska, northwest of Canada, and Hawaii in the Pacific Ocean. The climate varies a great deal in such a large country. In Alaska there are polar conditions, and in the Gulf coast and in Florida conditions may be subtropical. The highest point is Mount McKinley at 20,322 feet (6,194 metres). Natural resources include vast mineral reserves, including oil and gas, coal, copper, lead, uranium gold, tungsten and lumber. Although agricultural production is high, it employs only 1.5 per cent of the population because primarily of its advanced technology. The USA is a world leader in oil production. The main industries are iron and steel, chemicals, motor vehicles, aircraft, telecommunications equipment, computers, electronics and textiles. The USA is the richest and most powerful nation in the world.

Quick facts:

Area: 3,536,278 square miles (9,158,960 square kilometres)
Population: 270,299,000
Capital: Washington DC
Other cities: New York, Chicago, Detroit, Houston, Los Angeles,
   Philadelphia, San Diego, San Francisco
Form of government: Federal republic
Religions: Protestantism, Roman Catholicism, Judaism, Eastern
   Orthodox, Islam
Currency: US Dollar

Uruguay One of the smallest countries in South America. It lies on the east coast of the continent, to the south of Brazil and is bordered to the west by the Uruguay river, Rio de la Plata to the south and the Atlantic Ocean to the east. The country consists of low plains and plateaus. The Negro river, which rises in Brazil, crosses the country from northeast to southwest, dividing Uruguay almost into two halves. The climate is temperate and rainfall plentiful and the natural vegetation is prairie grassland. Some of the river valleys are wooded but Uruguay lacks the dense forests of other parts of South America. About 90 per cent of the land is suitable for agriculture but only about 8 per cent is cultivated, the remainder being used to graze the vast herds of cattle and sheep that provide over 35 per cent of Uruguay's exports in the form of wool, hides and meat. The cultivated land is made up of vineyards, rice fields and groves of olives and citrus fruits. The main crops grown are sugar beet and cane, rice, wheat, potatoes, corn and sorghum. The country has scarce mineral resources and hydroelectric power supplies most of its energy needs.
Important industries include textile manufacture, food processing, oil refining, steel, aluminium, electrical goods and rubber.

Quick facts:

Area: 68,500 square miles (177,414 square kilometres)
Population: 3,203,000
Capital: Montevideo
Form of government: Republic
Religions: Roman Catholicism, Protestantism
Currency: Peso Uruguayos

Uzbekistan A central Asian republic of the former USSR that declared itself independent in 1991. It lies between Kazakhstan and Turkmenistan and encompasses the southern half of the Aral Sea. The republic has many contrasting regions. The Tian Shan region is mountainous, the Fergana region is irrigated and fertile, the Kyzlkum Desert (one of the world's largest) is rich in oil and gas, the lower Amudarya river region is irrigated and has oasis settlements and the Usturt Plateau is a stony desert. Uzbekistan is one of the world's leading cotton producers and Karakul lambs are reared for wool and meat. Its main industrial products are agricultural machinery, textiles and chemicals. It also has significant reserves of natural gas. Economic growth has been checked by concerns about political instability and much of the economy remains based on the centralised state-owned model. There are serious pollution problems where the Aral Sea lies. This has greatly decreased in size from its use for irrigation and is contaminated with toxins, salts and sands that poison the water supply of the surrounding population. Hydroelectric schemes supply much of the republic's electricity needs.

Quick facts:

Area: 172,742 square miles (447,400 square kilometres)
Population: 24,000,000
Capital: Tashkent
Other cities: Urgench, Nukus, Bukhara, Samarkand
Form of government: Republic
Religion: Sunni Islam
Currency: Soum

Vanuatu A country, formerly known as the New Hebrides (so named by Captain Cook in 1774), located in the southwest Pacific Ocean, southeast of the SOLOMON ISLANDS and about 1,087 miles (1,750 kilometres) east of AUSTRALIA. It consists of some 12 islands and 60 islets. Most of the islands are volcanic and densely forested, with raised coral beaches and fringed by coral reefs. The largest islands are Espírtu Santo, Malekula and Efate, on which the capital, Vila, is sited. Vanuatu has a tropical climate that is moderated by the southeast trade winds from May to October. Cultivated land is generally restricted to the coastal plains and the main cash crops are copra, cocoa beans and coffee. Meat and fish are also exported and light industries include food processing and handicrafts for an increasing tourist industry. The majority of the labour force is engaged in subsistence farming, raising taro, yams and bananas. Tourism is becoming important and Vanuatu has international airports.

Quick facts:
Area: 4,706 square miles (12,189 square kilometres)
Population: 169,000
Capital: Vila
Form of government: Republic
Religion: Roman Catholicism
Currency: Vatu

Vatican City State A state, established in 1929, that lies in the heart of Rome on a low hill on the west bank of the River Tiber. It is the world's smallest independent state and headquarters of the Roman Catholic Church. It is a walled city with six gates and is made up of the Vatican Palace, the Papal Gardens, St Peter's Square and St Peter's Basilica. The state has its own police, newspaper, telephone and telegraph services, coinage, stamps, radio station and train station. The radio station, Radio Vaticana, broadcasts a service in 34 languages from transmitters within the Vatican City. Its main tourist attractions are the frescoes of the Sistine Chapel, painted by Michelangelo Buonarroti. It also has outstanding museums, with collections of antiquities and works by Italian masters and the Vatican Library's collection of ancient manuscripts is priceless. The pope exercises sovereignty and has absolute legislative, executive and judicial powers.

Quick facts:
Area: 0.2 square mile (0.44 square kilometre)
Population: 1,000
Capital: Vatican City
Form of government: Papal Commission
Religion: Roman Catholicism
Currency: Euro

Venezuela A country that forms the northernmost crest of South America. Its northern coast lies along the Caribbean Sea and it is bounded to the west by COLUMBIA AND to the southeast and south by GUYANA and BRAZIL. In the northwest a spur of the Andes runs southwest to northeast. Venezuela has one of the highest waterfalls in the world, the Angel Falls. The River Orinoco cuts the country in two and north of the river run the undulating plains known as the Llanos. South of the river are the Guiana Highlands. The climate ranges from warm temperate to tropical. Temperatures vary little throughout the year and rainfall is plentiful. In the Llanos area, cattle are herded across the plains and this region makes the country almost self-sufficient in meat. There are also rich fishing grounds around the coast and off Venezuela's 72 islands. Sugar cane and coffee are grown for export, but petroleum and gas account for around 80 per cent of export earnings. Venezuela's economy is built on its oilfields located in the Maracaibo region but it also has other important mineral reserves including bauxite, iron ore, coal and precious metals and stones, such as gold, silver, platinum and diamonds.

Quick facts:
Area: 352,145 square miles (912,050 square kilometres)
Population: 21,710,000
Capital: Caracas
Other cities: Maracaibo, Valencia, Barquisimeto
Form of government: Federal Republic
Religion: Roman Catholicism
Currency: Bolívar

Vietnam A long narrow country in Southeast Asia that runs down the coast of the South China Sea. It has a narrow central area that links broader plains centred on the Red (Hong) and Mekong rivers. The narrow zone, now known as Mien Trung, is hilly and makes communications between north and south difficult. The climate is humid, with tropical conditions in the south and subtropical in the north. The far north can be very cold when polar air blows over Asia. Agriculture, fishing and forestry employ around 74 per cent of the labour force. The main crop is rice but cassava, maize and sweet potatoes are also grown for domestic consumption. Soya beans, tea, coffee and rubber are grown for export. Major industries are food processing, textiles, cement, cotton and silk manufacture. Fishing is also an important export trade that is conducted mainly on the South China Sea, although there is some fish farming in flooded inland areas. Vietnam, however, remains underdeveloped and is still recovering from the ravages of many wars this century.

Quick facts:
Area: 128,066 square miles (331,689 square kilometres)
Population: 75,181,000
Capital: Hanoi
Other cities: Ho Chi Minh City, Haiphong, Hué, Dà Nang
Form of government: Socialist Republic
Religions: Buddhism, Taoism, Roman Catholicism
Currency: New Dong

Virgin Islands, British A British overseas territory lying at the northwestern end of the Lesser Antilles in the Caribbean Sea. They comprise four large islands and 36 islets and cays. Only 16 of the islands are inhabited. Most of the islands are hilly and wooded and the climate is subtropical moderated by trade winds. Agriculture produces livestock, coconuts, sugar cane, fruit and vegetables, but only a small percentage of the land available to agriculture is under cultivation. The main industries are tourism, construction and rum distilling. Tourism is the mainstay of the economy.

Quick facts:
Area: 58 square miles (151 square kilometres)
Population: 19,000
Capital: Road Town
Form of government: British Overseas Territory
Religion: Protestantism
Currency: US Dollar

Virgin Islands, US Part of the Virgin Islands group in the northwest of the Lesser Antilles in the Caribbean Sea. A self-governing US territory, this group of 50 volcanic islands are rugged and mountainous with a subtropical climate. The main islands are St John (around two-thirds of which is a National Park), St Croix and St Thomas. Agriculture is not well developed and most of the country's food has to be imported. There is a small manufacturing industry but tourism is the mainstay of the economy with many cruise ships calling at the island of St Thomas in particular because of its natural deep-water harbor.

Quick facts:
Area: 134 square miles (347 square kilometres)
Population: 106,000
Capital: Charlotte Amalie
Form of government: Self-governing US Territory
Religion: Protestantism
Currency: US Dollar

Wallis and Futuna Islands The two island groups are 142 miles (230 kilometres) apart in the southern central Pacific Ocean and are the smallest and poorest of France's overseas territories. The climate is warm and humid with a cyclone season between October and March. Subsistence farming and fishing are the main activities with copra the only important export.

Quick facts:
Area: 77 square miles (200 square kilometres)
Population: 15,000
Capital: Mata-Uru
Form of government: French Overseas Territory
Religion: Roman Catholicism
Currency: Franc

Western Sahara A disputed territory of western Africa, with a coastline on the Atlantic Ocean. Consisting mainly of desert, it is rich in phosphates. It was a Spanish overseas province until 1976, when it was partitioned between MOROCCO and MAURITANIA. Since 1979, the entire territory has been claimed and administered by Morocco, against the wishes of an active separatist movement, the Frente Polisario. Moroccan sovereignty is not universally recognised and the United Nations has attempted to oversee a referendum to decide the struggle but without success so far. It is a poor country with many following a nomadic existence. The bulk of the food for the towns has to be imported. Phosphates comprise two-thirds of the meager exports.

Quick facts:
Area: 102,703 square miles (266,000 square kilometres)
Population: 266,000
Capital: Laâyoune (El Aaiún)
Form of government: Republic (*de facto* controlled by Morocco)
Religion: Sunni Islam
Currency: Moroccan Dirham

Western Samoa *see* SAMOA.

Yemen A country bounded by SAUDI ARABIA in the north, OMAN in the east, the Gulf of Aden in the south and the Red Sea in the west. The country was formed after the unification of the previous Yemen Arab Republic and the People's Democratic Republic of Yemen (South Yemen) in 1989. At that point, however, there was no active integration of the two countries and politically the country remained divided between north and south. In 1994 a civil war that lasted three months broke out between the former North and South Yemen, which resulted in a high rate of inflation, damage to the infrastructure and devaluation of the currency. Most of the country comprises rugged mountains and trackless desert lands. The country is almost entirely dependent on agriculture even although only a very small percentage is fertile. The main crops are coffee, cotton, wheat, vegetables, millet, sorghum and fruit. Fishing is an important industry, with mackerel, tuna, lobster and cod being caught and there are some canning factories along the coast. Other industry is on a very small scale, consisting mainly of manufacturing industry which produces textiles, paints, matches, plastic, rubber and aluminium goods. Modernisation of industry is slow because of lack of funds.

Quick facts:
Area: 203,850 square miles (527,978 square kilometres)
Population: 15,919,000
Capital: San'a
Commercial Capital: Aden (Adan)
Other cities: Al Hudaydah, Ta'izz
Form of government: Republic
Religions: Zaidism, Shia Islam, Sunni Islam
Currency: Riyal

Yugoslavia A country that was created in 1918 and became a single federal republic after World War II under the leadership of Marshal Tito (1892–1980). The six constituent republics were Serbia, CROATIA, SLOVENIA, BOSNIA-HERZEGOVINA, MACEDONIA and Montenegro. Yugoslavia today refers only to Serbia and Montenegro, which operate as two equal republics under a federal authority. However, an agreement has been reached that will create Serbia and Montenegro as a Union of States, thus consigning Yugoslavia to history. The other republics, beginning with Slovenia and Croatia in 1991, have already declared their independence from Yugoslavia. The economy of the region was devastated by the wars in Bosnia and Croatia and then by inflation. It all but collapsed in late 1993 and was only just beginning to take the first steps to recovery when, in 1999, ethnic cleansing of the Albanian population in the Kosovo region of Serbia led to Serbia being bombed by NATO troops. The economy is largely dependent on agriculture and produce includes wheat, maize, grapes and citrus fruit. Forestry is also an important industry. Serbia contains important mineral reserves, with copper, antimony, lead, bauxite, coal, petroleum, natural gas, zinc, chromium and gold all being present. Other economic activities include mining and the manufacturing of iron and steel, chemicals, machinery, electronic equipment, textiles and clothing.

Quick facts:
Area: 39,449 square miles (102,173 square kilometres)
Population: 10,574,000
Capital: Belgrade (Beograd)
Other cities: Nis, Novi Sad, Pristina
Form of government: Union of States
Religions: Eastern Orthodox, Islam
Currency: New Dinar

Zambia A country, situated in central Africa, that is made up of high plateaus. Bordering it to the south is the Zambezi river and in the southwest it borders on the Kalahari Desert. It has some other large rivers, including the Luangwa and lakes, the largest of which is Lake Bangweulu. The climate is tropical, modified somewhat by altitude. The country has a wide range of wildlife and there are large game parks on the Luangwa and Kafue rivers. Agriculture is underdeveloped and vulnerable to weather variations, leading to some food shortages, as a consequence of which large quantities have to be imported. The principal subsistence crops grown are corn, sugar cane and cassava, with cattle raised and most foodstuffs have to be imported. Zambia's economy relies heavily on the mining of copper, lead, zinc and cobalt. The poor market prospects for copper, which will eventually be exhausted, make it imperative for Zambia to develop her vast agricultural potential. The majority of the country's power is provided by the Kariba Dam on the Zambezi river and there is potential for further hydroelectric development.

Quick facts:
Area: 290,587 square miles (752,618 square kilometres)
Population: 8,275,000
Capital: Lusaka
Other cities: Kitwe, Ndola, Mufulira
Form of government: Republic
Religions: Christianity, African traditional religions
Currency: Kwacha

CANADIAN COMPANION

Zaire *see* CONGO, DEMOCRATIC REPUBLIC OF THE.

Zimbabwe A landlocked country in southern Africa. It is a country with spectacular physical features and is teeming with wildlife. It is bordered in the north by the Zambezi river, which flows over the mile-wide Victoria Falls before entering Lake Kariba. In the south, the River Limpopo marks its border with SOUTH AFRICA. A great plateau between 4,000–5,000 feet (about 1,200–1,500 metres) in height occupies the central area. Only one third of the population lives in towns and cities, the largest of which is the capital, Harare. The climate is tropical in the lowlands and subtropical in the higher land. About 75 per cent of the workforce are employed in agriculture. Tobacco, sugar cane, cotton, wheat and maize are exported and form the basis of processing industries. Zimbabwe is rich in mineral resources such as coal, chromium, nickel, gold, platinum and precious metals and mining accounts for around 30 per cent of foreign revenue. Tourism has the potential to be a major growth industry as Zimbabwe has many tourist attractions, such as the Victoria Falls, Great Zimbabwe and several wildlife parks. However, there has been ongoing dissatisfaction within the country at the very high inflation rate and the economy has declined rather than prospered.

Quick facts:

Area: 150,872 square miles (390,757 square kilometres)
Population: 11,908,000
Capital: Harare
Other cities: Bulawayo, Mutare, Gweru
Form of government: Republic
Religions: African traditional religions, Anglicanism, Roman Catholicism
Currency: Zimbabwe Dollar

Map Index

D

Da Lat *Vietnam*	36C2	
Dali *China*	34E4	
Dallas *USA*	6D2	
Dalmally *Scotland*	22D4	
Daloa *Côte d'Ivoire*	42C4	
Damascus *see* Dimashq		
Da Nang *Vietnam*	36C2	
Dandong *China*	35G2	
Dar'a *Syria*	38B2	
Dar el Beida *Morocco*	42C1	
Dar es Salaam *Tanzania*	43G5	
Darlington *England*	20F3	
Darmstadt *Germany*	28B3	
Daroca *Spain*	25B1	
Daru *Papua New Guinea*	37G4	
Darwin *Australia*	45C2	
Datong *China*	35F2	
Daugavpils *Latvia*	32D4	
Dauphine *France*	24D3	
Davao *Philippines*	37E3	
David *Panama*	14C5	
Dawson Creek *Canada*	5F4	
Dax *France*	24B3	
Dayton *USA*	7E2	
Daytona Beach *USA*	7E3	
De Aar *South Africa*	44C4	
Debre Mark'os *Ethiopia*	43G3	
Debrecen *Hungary*	29E3	
Dehra Dun *India*	39F2	
Delaware *State USA*	7F2	
Delhi *India*	39F3	
Democratic Republic of		
Congo	43F5	
Denbigh *Wales*	20D4	
Den Helder *Netherlands*	28A2	
Denizli *Turkey*	38A2	
Denmark	30C4	
D'Entrecasteaux I. *Papua*		
New Guinea	37H4	
Denver *USA*	6C2	
Derby *England*	21F5	
Dese *Ethiopia*	43G3	
Des Moines *USA*	7D1	
Dessau *Germany*	28C2	
Detroit *USA*	7E1	
Deva *Romania*	29E3	
Devon I. *Canada*	5K2	
Dezful *Iran*	38C2	
Dezhou *China*	35F3	
Dhaka (Dacca) *Bangladesh*	39H3	
Dibrugarh *India*	39H3	
Didcot *England*	21F6	
Dieppe *France*	24C2	
Dijon *France*	24D2	
Dili *East Timor*	37E4	
Dimashq (Damascus) *Syria*	38C2	
Dimitrovgrad *Bulgaria*	27F2	
Dingle *Rep. of Ireland*	23A4	
Dingwall *Scotland*	22D3	
Dire Dawa *Ethiopia*	43H4	
Disko I. *Greenland*	5N3	
Dist. Fed. *Administrative*		
District Brazil	16E4	

Diyarbakir *Turkey*	38B2	
Djelfa *Algeria*	42D1	
Djibouti *Djibouti*	43H3	
Dnepropetrovsk *Ukraine*	32E5	
Dobreta-Turnu-Severin		
Romania	27E2	
Dodoma *Tanzania*	43G5	
Dôle *France*	24D2	
Dolgellau *Wales*	21D5	
Dombås *Norway*	30B3	
Dominica I. *Caribbean*	14G3	
Dominican Republic	14F3	
Domodossola *Italy*	26B1	
Doncaster *England*	20F4	
Donegal *Rep. of Ireland*	23C/D2	
Donetsk *Ukraine*	32E5	
Dorchester *England*	21E7	
Dornie *Scotland*	22C3	
Dortmund *Germany*	28B2	
Douala *Cameroon*	42D4	
Douglas *Isle of Man*	20C3	
Dourados *Brazil*	17D5	
Dover *England*	21J6	
Dover *USA*	7F2	
Dráma *Greece*	27E2	
Drammen *Norway*	30C4	
Dresden *Germany*	28C2	
Drogheda *Rep. of Ireland*	23E3	
Dubayy *United Arab*		
Emirates	38D3	
Dublin *Rep. of Ireland*	23E3	
Dubrovnik *Croatia*	27D2	
Ducie I. *Pacific Ocean*	47	
Dudley *England*	21E5	
Dugi I. *Croatia*	26C/D2	
Duisburg *Germany*	28B2	
Dukou *China*	34E4	
Duluth *USA*	7D1	
Dumbarton *Scotland*	22D5	
Dumfries *Scotland*	22E5	
Dunbar *Scotland*	22F5	
Dundalk *Rep. of Ireland*	23E2	
Dundee *Scotland*	22F4	
Dundrum *Northern Ireland*	23F2	
Dunedin *New Zealand*	45G5	
Dunfermline *Scotland*	22E4	
Dungarvan *Rep. of Ireland*	23D4	
Dungiven *Northern Ireland*	23E2	
Dunkeld *Scotland*	22E4	
Dunkerque *France*	24C1	
Dun Laoghaire *Rep. of*		
Ireland	23E3	
Dunleer *Rep. of Ireland*	23E3	
Durban *South Africa*	44D3	
Durham *England*	20F3	
Durham *USA*	7F2	
Durness *Scotland*	22D2	
Durrës *Albania*	27D2	
Durrow *Rep. of Ireland*	23D4	
Dushanbe *Tajikistan*	32H6	
Dusseldorf *Germany*	28B2	
Duyun *China*	34E4	

E

Eastbourne *England*	21H7	
East Falkland I. *South*		
Atlantic Ocean	17D8	
East Kilbride *Scotland*	22D5	
East London *South Africa*	44C4	
East Timor	37E4	
Eboli *Italy*	26D2	
Ecija *Spain*	25A2	
Ecuador	16B3	
Eday I. *Scotland*	22F1	
Edgeworthstown *Rep. of*		
Ireland	23D3	
Edinburgh *Scotland*	22E5	
Edmonton *Canada*	5G4	
Efate I. *Vanuatu*	45F2	
Egadi I. *Italy*	26C3	
Egersund *Norway*	30B4	
Egypt	43F/G2	
Eigg I. *Scotland*	22B4	
Eindhoven *Netherlands*	28B2	
Eisenach *Germany*	28C2	
Elba I. *Italy*	26C2	
Elblag *Poland*	29D2	
Elche *Spain*	25B2	
El Dorado *Venezuela*	16C2	
Eldoret *Kenya*	43G4	
Eleuthera I. *The Bahamas*	14D1	
El Faiyûm *Egypt*	43G2	
El Fasher *Sudan*	43F3	
El Ferrol *Spain*	25A1	
Elgin *Scotland*	22E3	
El Gîza *Egypt*	43G1	
El Golea *Algeria*	42D1	
El Iskandarîya (Alexandria)		
Egypt	43F1	
El Khartum (Khartoum)		
Sudan	43G3	
Ellesmere I. *Canada*	5K2	
Ellesmere Port *England*	20E4	
Ellon *Scotland*	22F3	
El Minya *Egypt*	43G2	
El Obeid *Sudan*	43G3	
El Paso *USA*	6C2	
El Qâhira (Cairo) *Egypt*	43G1	
El Salvador	14B4	
Elvas *Portugal*	25A2	
Ely *England*	21H5	
Enarración *Paraguay*	17D5	
Ende *Indonesia*	37E4	
Enggano I. *Indonesia*	36C4	
Enna *Italy*	26C3	
Ennis *Rep. of Ireland*	23B4	
Enniscorthy *Rep. of Ireland*	23E4	
Enniskillen *Northern Ireland*	23D2	
Ennistymon *Rep. of Ireland*	23B4	
Enschede *Netherlands*	28B2	
Entebbe *Uganda*	43G4	
Enugu *Nigeria*	42D4	
Epi I. *Vanuatu*	45F2	
Equatorial Guinea	42F4	

Erenhot *China*	35F2	
Erfurt *Germany*	28C2	
Eriskay I. *Scotland*	22A3	
Eritrea	43G/H3	
Erlangen *Germany*	28C3	
Erromanga I. *Vanuatu*	45F2	
Erzurum *Turkey*	38C2	
Esbjerg *Denmark*	30B4	
Esfahan *Iran*	38D2	
Eskisehir *Turkey*	38B2	
Esperance *Australia*	45B4	
Espírito Santo *Brazil*	16E4	
Espiritu Santo I. *Vanuatu*	45F2	
Espoo *Finland*	30E3	
Essaouira *Morocco*	42C1	
Essen *Germany*	28B2	
Estonia	30F4	
Estremoz *Portugal*	25A2	
Ethiopia	43G/H4	
Evansville *USA*	7E2	
Evvoia I. *Greece*	27E3	
Exeter *England*	21D7	
Extremadura *Region Spain*	25A2	

F

Faeroes Is. (Føroyar Is.)		
Denmark	30A2	
Fair I. *Scotland*	22J8	
Fairbanks *USA*	6J	
Faisalabad *Pakistan*	39F2	
Fakfak *Indonesia*	37F4	
Falcarragh *Rep. of Ireland*	23C1	
Falkirk *Scotland*	22E4	
Falkland Islands *South*		
Atlantic Ocean	17C/D8	
Falmouth *England*	21B7	
Falster I. *Denmark*	30C5	
Falun *Sweden*	30D3	
Fano *Italy*	26C2	
Farah *Afghanistan*	38E2	
Fareham *England*	21F7	
Fargo *USA*	6D1	
Faro *Portugal*	25A2	
Farquhar Is. *Indian Ocean*	44F1	
Fauske *Norway*	30D2	
Faya-Largeau *Chad*	43E3	
Fdérik *Mauritania*	42B2	
Felixstowe *England*	21J6	
Fergana *Uzbekistan*	32J5	
Ferkessédougou *Côte*		
d'Ivoire	42C4	
Fermoy *Rep. of Ireland*	23C4	
Ferrara *Italy*	26C2	
Fès *Morocco*	42C1	
Fetlar I. *Scotland*	22K7	
Feyzabad *Afghanistan*	39F2	
Fianarantsoa *Madagascar*	44E3	
Figueras *Spain*	25C1	
Fiji Is. *Pacific Ocean*	46	
Filiasi *Romania*	27E2	
Finland	30E3/F3	
Firenze (Florence) *Italy*	26C2	

Fishguard *Wales*	21C6	
Fitzroy Crossing *Australia*	45B2	
Fleetwood *England*	20D4	
Flensburg *Germany*	28B2	
Flint I. *Kiribati*	477	
Florence *see* Firenze	26C2	
Flores *Guatemala*	14B3	
Flores I. *Indonesia*	37E4	
Florianópolis *Brazil*	16E5	
Florida *State USA*	7E3	
Focsani *Romania*	29F3	
Foggia *Italy*	26D2	
Foligno *Italy*	26C2	
Follonica *Italy*	26C2	
Forfar *Scotland*	22F4	
Forli *Italy*	26C2	
Formentera I. *Spain*	25C2	
Formia *Italy*	26C2	
Formosa *Province*		
Argentina	16C/D5	
Føroyar Is. *see* Faeroes Is.	30A2	
Fortaleza *Brazil*	16F3	
Fort Augustus *Scotland*	22D3	
Fort-de-France *Martinique*	14G4	
Fort Lauderdale *USA*	7E3	
Fort Simpson *Canada*	5F3	
Fort William *Scotland*	22C4	
Fort Worth *USA*	6D2	
Fort Yukon *USA*	5D3	
Foshan *China*	35F4	
Fougères *France*	24B2	
Foula I. *Scotland*	22H7	
Foz do Iguaçu *Brazil*	17D5	
Fraga *Spain*	25C1	
Franca *Brazil*	16E5	
France	24	
Franceville *Gabon*	42E5	
Franche-Comte *France*	24D2	
Francistown *Botswana*	44C3	
Frankfort *USA*	7E2	
Frankfurt *Germany*	28B2	
Fraser I. *Australia*	45E3	
Fraserburgh *Scotland*	22F3	
Frederikshåb *Greenland*	5O3	
Frederikshavn *Denmark*	30C4	
Frederikstad *Norway*	30C4	
Freetown *Sierra Leone*	42B4	
Freiburg *Germany*	28B3	
Fremantle *Australia*	45A4	
Fresno *USA*	6B2	
Frosinone *Italy*	26C2	
Ft. Wayne *USA*	7E1	
Fuerteventura I. *Canary Is.*	42B2	
Fujian *Province China*	35F4	
Fukui *Japan*	35M8	
Fukuoka *Japan*	35H3	
Fukushima *Japan*	35P8	
Funchal *Madeira*	42B1	
Furneaux Group I. *Australia*	45D5	
Fürth *Germany*	28C3	
Furukawa *Japan*	35P7	
Fushun *China*	35G2	
Fuxin *China*	35G2	

Fuzhou *China*	35F4	
Fyn I. *Denmark*	30C4	

G

Gabès *Tunisia*	42D1	
Gabon	42E4/5	
Gaborone *Botswana*	44C3	
Gainsborough *England*	20G4	
Gairloch *Scotland*	22C3	
Galashiels *Scotland*	22F5	
Galati *Romania*	29F3	
Galicia *Region Spain*	25A1	
Galle *Sri Lanka*	39G5	
Gallipoli *Italy*	27D2	
Gällivare *Sweden*	30E2	
Galveston *USA*	7D3	
Galway *Rep. of Ireland*	23B2	
Gambia	42B3	
Gambier Is. *Pacific Ocean*	47	
Gamboma *Congo*	42E5	
Gandia *Spain*	25B2	
Ganzhou *China*	35F4	
Gao *Mali*	42C3	
Garve *Scotland*	22D3	
Gascogne *France*	24B3	
Gateshead *England*	20F3	
Gauhati *India*	39H3	
Gävle *Sweden*	30D3	
Gaziantep *Turkey*	38B2	
Gdansk *Poland*	29D2	
Gdynia *Poland*	29D2	
Gedaref *Sudan*	43G3	
Geelong *Australia*	45D4	
Gejiu *China*	34E4	
Gela *Italy*	26C3	
General Santos *Philippines*	37E3	
Geneva *see* Genève	24D2	
Genève (Geneva)		
Switzerland	24D2	
Genoa *see* Genova	26B2	
Genova (Genoa) *Italy*	26B2	
Gent *Belgium*	24C1	
George Town *Malaysia*	36C3	
Georgetown *Guyana*	16D2	
Georgia	32F5	
Georgia *State USA*	7E2	
Geraldton *Australia*	45A3	
Gerona *Spain*	25C1	
Getafe *Spain*	25B1	
Gevgelija *Macedonia*	27E2	
Ghadamis *Libya*	42D1	
Ghana	42C4	
Ghat *Libya*	42E2	
Gibraltar *SW Europe*	25A2	
Gifu *Japan*	35M9	
Giglio I. *Italy*	26C2	
Gijón *Spain*	25A1	
Gilbert Is. *Kiribati*	46	
Gilgit *Jammu and Kashmir*	39F2	
Girvan *Scotland*	22D5	
Gisborne *New Zealand*	45G4	
Giurgiu *Romania*	27F2	

Glasgow *Scotland*	22D5	Guam *Pacific Ocean*	37G2	Harare *Zimbabwe*	44D2
Glenrothes *Scotland*	22E4	Guangdong *Province China*	35F4	Harbin *China*	35G2
Gliwice *Poland*	29D2	Guangxi *Province China*	34E4	Harer *Ethiopia*	43H4
Gloucester *England*	21E6	Guangzhou *China*	35F4	Hargeysa *Somalia*	43H4
Gniezno *Poland*	28D2	Guantánamo *Cuba*	14D2	Harlow *England*	21H6
Gobabis *Namibia*	44B3	Guarda *Portugal*	25A1	Harris I. *Scotland*	22B3
Godthåb (Nuuk) *Greenland*	5N3	Guatemala *Guatemala*	14A4	Harrisburg *USA*	7F1
Goiânia *Brazil*	16E4	Guayaquil *Ecuador*	16B3	Harrogate *England*	20F4
Goiás *State Brazil*	16E4	Guernsey I. *Channel Is.*	21E8	Hartford *USA*	7F1
Gol *Norway*	30B3	Guiana (French)	16D2	Hartlepool *England*	20F3
Golmund *China*	34D3	Guildford *England*	21G6	Harwich *England*	21J6
Gomel' *Belarus*	32E4	Guilin *China*	35F4	Hässleholm *Sweden*	30C4
Gomera *Canary Is.*	42B2	Guinea	42B3	Hastings *England*	21H7
Gonaïves *Haiti*	14E3	Guinea Bissau	42B3	Hastings *New Zealand*	45G4
Gonder *Ethiopia*	43G3	Güiria *Venezuela*	16C1	Haugesund *Norway*	30B4
Goole *England*	20G4	Guiyang *China*	34E4	Havana *Cuba*	14C2
Gorontalo *Indonesia*	37E3	Guizhou *Province China*	34E4	Havant *England*	21G7
Gort *Rep. of Ireland*	23C3	Gulu *Uganda*	43G4	Hawaii *State USA*	6H
Gorzów Wielkopolski		Gur'yev *Kazakhstan*	32G5	Hawaiian Is. *Pacific Ocean*	6H
Poland	28D2	Guyana	16D2	Hawick *Scotland*	22F5
Gospic *Croatia*	26D2	Guyenne *France*	24B/C3	Hay River *Canada*	5G3
Göteborg *Sweden*	30C4	Gwalior *India*	39F3	Heanor *England*	20F4
Gotland I. *Sweden*	30D4	Gweru *Zimbabwe*	44C2	Heard Is. *Indian Ocean*	46
Göttingen *Germany*	28B2	Gyandzha *Azerbaijan*	32F5	Hebei *Province China*	35F3
Goulburn *Australia*	45D4	Györ *Hungary*	29D3	Hefei *China*	35F3
Gran Canaria *Canary Is.*	42B2			Hegang *China*	35H2
Granada *Nicaragua*	14B4	**H**		Heidelberg *Germany*	28B3
Granada *Spain*	25B2			Heilongjiang *Province*	
Grand Bahama I. *The*		Haarlem *Netherlands*	28A2	*China*	35G2
Bahamas	14D1	Hachinohe *Japan*	35P6	Helena *USA*	6B1
Grandola *Portugal*	25A2	Hagen *Germany*	28B2	Hella *Iceland*	30A2
Grand Rapids *USA*	7E1	Haifa *Israel*	38B2	Hellín *Spain*	25B2
Graz *Austria*	28D3	Haikou *China*	35F4	Helmsdale *Scotland*	22E2
Great Abaco I. *The Bahamas*	14D1	Ha'il *Saudi Arabia*	38C3	Helsinborg *Sweden*	30C4
Greater Antilles Is.		Hailar *China*	35F2	Helsingfors (Helsinki)	
Caribbean Sea	14C2/D3	Hainan Dao I. *China*	35F5	*Finland*	30E3
Great Exuma I. *The Bahamas*	14D2	Haiphong *Vietnam*	36C1	Henan *Province China*	35F3
Great Inagua I. *The Bahamas*	14E2	Haiti	14E3	Hengyang *China*	35F4
Great Nicobar I. *Andaman*		Hakodate *Japan*	35J2	Henzada *Myanmar*	36B2
and Nicobar Is.	39H5	Halab *Syria*	38B2	Herat *Afghanistan*	38E2
Great Yarmouth *England*	21J5	Halden *Norway*	30C4	Hereford *England*	21E5
Greece	27E2/3	Halifax *Canada*	5M5	Hermosillo *USA*	6B3
Greenland *Atlantic Ocean*	5O2	Halifax *England*	20F4	Hexham *England*	20E3
Greenock *Scotland*	22D5	Halle *Germany*	28C2	Hierro *Canary Is.*	42B2
Greensboro *USA*	7F2	Halmahera I. *Indonesia*	37E3	Hiiumaa I. *Estonia*	30E4
Grenada I. *Caribbean*	14G4	Halmstad *Sweden*	30C4	Himeji *Japan*	35L9
Grenadines Is. *Caribbean*		Hamadan *Iran*	38C2	Hims *Syria*	38B2
Sea	14G4	Hamamatsu *Japan*	35M9	Hinckley *England*	21F5
Grenoble *France*	24D2	Hamar *Norway*	30C3	Hinnöy I. *Norway*	30D2
Gretna *Scotland*	22E5	Hamburg *Germany*	28C2	Hiroshima *Japan*	35H3
Grimsby *England*	20G4	Hamhung *North Korea*	35G2	Hîrsova *Romania*	27F2
Grong *Norway*	30C3	Hami *China*	34D2	Hispaniola I. *Caribbean Sea*	14E3
Groningen *Netherlands*	28B2	Hamilton *Canada*	5K5	Hitachi *Japan*	35P8
Groote Eylandt I. *Australia*	45C2	Hamilton *New Zealand*	45G4	Hobart *Tasmania*	45D5
Grootfontein *Namibia*	44B2	Hamm *Germany*	28B2	Ho Chi Minh City *Vietnam*	36C2
Grosseto *Italy*	26C2	Hammerfest *Norway*	30E1	Höfn *Iceland*	30B2
Groznyy *Russ. Fed.*	32F5	Hanamaki *Japan*	35P7	Hohhot *China*	35F2
Grudziadz *Poland*	29D2	Handan *China*	35F3	Hokitika *New Zealand*	45G5
Guadalajara *Mexico*	6C3	Hangzhou *China*	35G3	Hokkaido I. *Japan*	35J2
Guadalajara *Spain*	25B1	Hannover *Germany*	28B2	Holguín *Cuba*	14D2
Guadalcanal I. *Solomon Is.*	45E2	Hanoi *Vietnam*	36C1	Holy I. *England*	20F2
Guadalupe I. *Mexico*	6B3	Hanzhong *China*	34E3	Holyhead *Wales*	20C4
Guadeloupe I. *Caribbean Sea*	14G3	Haora *India*	39G3	Honduras	14B4

Jönköping *Sweden*	30C4
Jordan	38B2
Jörn *Sweden*	30E2
Jos *Nigeria*	42D4
Jotunheimen *Norway*	30B3
Juàzeiro *Brazil*	16E3
Juba *Sudan*	43G4
Jujuy *Province Argentina*	17C5
Julianehåb *Greenland*	5O3
Juneau *USA*	6J
Jura I. *Scotland*	22C5
Jutland *see* Jylland	30B4
Jylland (Jutland) *Denmark*	30B4
Jyväskylä *Finland*	30F3

K

Kabul *Afghanistan*	39E2
Kaduna *Nigeria*	42D3
Kaédi *Mauritania*	42B3
Kaesong *North Korea*	35G3
Kagoshima *Japan*	35H3
Kaifeng *China*	35F3
Kailua *Hawaii USA*	6H
Kairouan *Tunisia*	42D1
Kajaani *Finland*	30F3
Kakinada *India*	39G4
Kalabáka *Greece*	27E3
Kalajoki *Finland*	30E3
Kalámai *Greece*	27E3
Kalaupapa *Hawaii USA*	6H
Kalémié *Dem. Rep. of Congo*	43F5
Kalgoorlie *Australia*	45B4
Kálimnos I. *Greece*	27F3
Kaliningrad *Russ. Fed.*	32D4
Kalisz *Poland*	29D2
Kalmar *Sweden*	30D4
Kamaishi *Japan*	35P7
Kamina *Dem. Rep. of Congo*	44C1
Kamloops *Canada*	5F4
Kampala *Uganda*	43G4
Kananga *Dem. Rep. of Congo*	43F5
Kanazawa *Japan*	35M8
Kandahar *Afghanistan*	39E2
Kandalaksha *Russ. Fed.*	32E3
Kandangan *Indonesia*	36D4
Kandy *Sri Lanka*	39G5
Kaneohe *Hawaii USA*	6H
Kangaroo I. *Australia*	45C4
Kankan *Guinea*	42C3
Kano *Nigeria*	42D3
Kanpur *India*	39G3
Kansas City *USA*	7D2
Kansas *State USA*	6D2
Kao-hsiung *Taiwan*	37E1
Kaolack *Senegal*	42B3
Karachi *Pakistan*	39E3
Karaganda *Kazakstan*	32J5
Karbala *Iraq*	38C2
Karcag *Hungary*	29E3
Karlobag *Croatia*	26D2

Karlovac *Croatia*	26D1
Karlshamn *Sweden*	30C4
Karlskoga *Sweden*	30C4
Karlskrona *Sweden*	30D4
Karlsruhe *Germany*	28B3
Karlstad *Sweden*	30C4
Kárpathos I. *Greece*	27F3
Karshi *Uzbekistan*	32H6
Kasama *Zimbabwe*	44D2
Kasese *Uganda*	43G4
Kashi *China*	34B3
Kásos I. *Greece*	27F3
Kassala *Sudan*	43G3
Kassel *Germany*	28B2
Kastoria *Greece*	27E2
Kateríni *Greece*	27E2
Katherine *Australia*	45C2
Kathmandu *Nepal*	39G3
Katowice *Poland*	29D2
Katsina *Nigeria*	42D3
Kauai I. *Hawaii USA*	6H
Kaunas *Lithuania*	30E5
Kaválla *Greece*	27E2
Kawaihae *Hawaii USA*	6H
Kawasaki *Japan*	35N9
Kayes *Mali*	42B3
Kayseri *Turkey*	38B2
Kazakhstan	32H/J5
Kazan *Russ. Fed.*	32F4
Kazanlük *Bulgaria*	27F2
Kazan-rettó *Japan*	37G1
Kéa I. *Greece*	27E3
Kecskemét *Hungary*	29D3
Kediri *Indonesia*	36D4
Keetmanshoop *Namibia*	44B3
Kefallinía I. *Greece*	27E3
Keflavik *Iceland*	30A2
Keighley *England*	20F4
Keith *Scotland*	22F3
Kelang *Malaysia*	36C3
Kells *Rep. of Ireland*	23E3
Kemerovo *Russ. Fed.*	32K4
Kemi *Finland*	30E2
Kemijärvi *Finland*	30F2
Kendal *England*	20E3
Kendari *Indonesia*	37E4
Kengtung *Myanmar*	36B1
Kenitra *Morocco*	42C1
Kenmare *Rep. of Ireland*	23B5
Kenora *Canada*	5J5
Kentucky *State USA*	7E2
Kenya	43G4/5
Kep. Anambas I. *Indonesia*	36C3
Kep. Aru I. *Indonesia*	37F4
Kep. Banggai I. *Indonesia*	37E4
Kep. Kai I. *Indonesia*	37F4
Kep. Leti I. *Indonesia*	37E4
Kep. Mentawai, Arch. *Indonesia*	36B4
Kepno *Poland*	29D2
Kep. Sangihe I. *Indonesia*	37E3
Kep. Sula I. *Indonesia*	37E4
Kep. Talaud I. *Indonesia*	37E3

Kep. Togian I. *Indonesia*	37E4
Kepulauan Tanimbar I. *Indonesia*	37F4
Kerch *Ukraine*	32E5
Kerguelen Is. *Indian Ocean*	46
Kérkira *Greece*	27D3
Kermadec Is. *Pacific Ocean*	46
Kerman *Iran*	38D2
Kerry *County Rep. of Ireland*	23B4/5
Keswick *England*	20E3
Key West *USA*	7E3
Khabarovsk *Russ. Fed.*	33P5
Khalkis *Greece*	27E3
Khaniá *Greece*	27E3
Khar'kov *Ukraine*	32E4
Kharagpur *India*	39G3
Khartoum *Sudan*	43G3
Khartoum North *Sudan*	43G3
Khíos I. *Greece*	27F3
Khulna *Bangladesh*	39G3
Kiel *Germany*	28C2
Kielce *Poland*	29E2
Kiev *see* Kiyev	32E4
Kigali *Rwanda*	43G5
Kigoma *Tanzania*	43F5
Kikladhes Is. *Greece*	27E/F3
Kikwit *Dem. Rep. of Congo*	43E5
Kildare *Rep. of Ireland*	23E3
Kilkenny *Rep. of Ireland*	23D4
Killarney *Rep. of Ireland*	23B4
Kilmarnock *Scotland*	22D5
Kilrush *Rep. of Ireland*	23B4
Kimberley *South Africa*	44C3
Kindia *Guinea*	42B3
Kindu *Dem. Rep. of Congo*	43F5
King I. *Australia*	45D4
Kings Lynn *England*	21H5
Kingston *Jamaica*	14D3
Kingston-upon-Hull *England*	20G4
Kingstown *St Vincent*	14G4
Kingswood *England*	21E6
Kingussie *Scotland*	22D3
Kinnegad *Rep. of Ireland*	23D3
Kintyre *Scotland*	22C5
Kinvarra *Rep. of Ireland*	23C3
Kiribati Is. *Pacific Ocean*	46
Kiritimati *Kiribati*	47
Kirkby Stephen *England*	20E3
Kirkcaldy *Scotland*	22E4
Kirkenes *Norway*	30G2
Kirkuk *Iraq*	38C2
Kirkwall *Scotland*	22F2
Kirov *Russ. Fed.*	32F4
Kiruna *Sweden*	30E2
Kisangani *Dem. Rep. of Congo*	43F4
Kishinev *Moldova*	32D5
Kiskunfélegyháza *Hungary*	29D3
Kismaayo *Somalia*	43H5
Kisumu *Kenya*	43G5
Kita-Kyushu *Japan*	35H3

Leyte I. *Philippines*	37E2	Londonderry *Northern*		Mâcon *France*	24C2
Lhasa *China*	39H3	*Ireland*	23D1	Macon *USA*	7E2
Lianoyang *China*	35G2	Long Island I. *USA*	7F1	Macquarie I. *New Zealand*	46
Lianyungang *China*	35F3	Long Island *The Bahamas*	14E2	Madagascar	44E3
Liaoning *Province China*	35G3	Longford *Rep. of Ireland*	23D3	Madang *Papua New Guinea*	37G4
Liaoyuan *China*	35G2	Lorca *Spain*	25B2	Madeira I. *Atlantic Ocean*	42B1
Liberec *Czech Republic*	28D2	Lord Howe I. *Australia*	45F4	Madison *USA*	7E1
Liberia	42B4	Lorient *France*	24B2	Madras *India*	39G4
Libreville *Gabon*	42D4	Los Angeles *USA*	6B2	Madrid *Spain*	25B1
Libya	42E2	Los Chonos, Arch. de *Chile*	17B7	Madura I. *Indonesia*	36D4
Lichinga *Mozambique*	44D2	Los Mochis *Mexico*	6C3	Madurai *India*	39F5
Liechtenstein	28B3	Losinj I. *Croatia*	26C2	Mafia I. *Tanzania*	44D1
Liège *Belgium*	24D1	Louisiana *State USA*	7D2	Mafikeng *South Africa*	44C3
Liepaja *Latvia*	30E4	Louisville *USA*	7E2	Magadan *Russ. Fed.*	33R4
Likasi *Dem. Rep. of Congo*	44C2	Loukhi *Russ. Fed.*	30G2	Magdeburg *Germany*	28C2
Lille *France*	24C1	Louth *England*	20G4	Magnitogorsk *Russ. Fed.*	32G4
Lillehammer *Norway*	30C3	Loznica *Serbia Yugoslavia*	27D2	Mahajanga *Madagascar*	44E2
Lilongwe *Malawi*	44D2	Lu'an *China*	35F3	Mahalapye *Botswana*	44C3
Lima *Peru*	16B4	Luanda *Angola*	44B1	Mahón *Spain*	25C2
Limerick *Rep. of Ireland*	23C4	Luang Prabang *Laos*	36C2	Maidstone *England*	21H6
Lìmnos *Greece*	27F3	Lubango *Angola*	44B2	Maiduguri *Nigeria*	42E3
Limoges *France*	24C2	Lubbock *USA*	6C2	Maine *France*	24B2
Limón *Costa Rica*	14C5	Lübeck *Germany*	28C2	Maine *State USA*	7F/G1
Limousin *France*	24C2	Lublin *Poland*	29E2	Mainland I. *Orkney Is.*	
Linares *Spain*	25B2	Lubumbashi *Dem. Rep. of*		*Scotland*	22J7
Lincang *China*	34E4	*Congo*	44C2	Mainland I. *Shetland Is.*	
Lincoln *England*	20G4	Lucca *Italy*	26C2	*Scotland*	22E1
Lincoln *USA*	6D1	Lucknow *India*	39G3	Mainz *Germany*	28B3
Linfen *China*	35F3	Lüda *China*	35G3	Maitland *Australia*	45E4
Linköping *Sweden*	30D4	Lüderitz *Namibia*	44B3	Maizuru *Japan*	35L9
Linosa I. *Italy*	26C3	Ludhiana *India*	39F2	Majene *Indonesia*	36D4
Linz *Austria*	28C3	Ludvika *Sweden*	30D3	Majorca I. *Spain*	25C2
Lipari I. *Italy*	26C3	Luga *Russ. Fed.*	30F4	Makarska *Croatia*	26D2
Lisboa (Lisbon) *Portugal*	25A2	Lugansk *Russ. Fed.*	32E5	Makhachkala *Russ. Fed.*	32F5
Lisbon *see* Lisboa	25A2	Lugo *Spain*	25A1	Makkah *Saudi Arabia*	38B3
Lisburn *Northern Ireland*	23E2	Luleå *Sweden*	30E2	Makó *Hungary*	29E3
Lisieux *France*	24C2	Lundy I. *England*	21C6	Makurdi *Nigeria*	42D4
Lithuania	30E4	Luohe *China*	35F3	Malabo *Bioko Is.*	42D4
Little Rock *USA*	7D2	Luoyang *China*	35F3	Malaga *Spain*	25B2
Liuzhou *China*	34E4	Lurgan *Northern Ireland*	23E2	Malakal *Sudan*	43G4
Livanátais *Greece*	27E3	Lusaka *Zambia*	44C2	Malang *Indonesia*	36D4
Liverpool *England*	20E4	Luton *England*	21G6	Malanje *Angola*	44B1
Livingston *Scotland*	22E5	Luxembourg *Luxembourg*	24D2	Malawi	44D2
Livingstone *Zambia*	44C2	Luxor *Egypt*	43G2	Malatya *Turkey*	38B2
Livno *Bosnia-Herz.*	26D2	Luzern *Switzerland*	24D2	Malaysia	36C3
Livorno *Italy*	26C2	Luzhou *China*	34E4	Malden I. *Kiribati*	47
Ljubljana *Slovenia*	26C1	Luzon I. *Philippines*	37E2	Maldives Is. *Indian Ocean*	39F5
Llandrindod Wells *Wales*	21D5	L'vov *Ukraine*	32D5	Malekula I. *Vanuatu*	45F2
Lobito *Angola*	44B2	Lybster *Scotland*	22E2	Mali	42C3
Lochboisdale *Scotland*	22A3	Lycksele *Sweden*	30D3	Mallaig *Scotland*	22C3
Lochgilphead *Scotland*	22C4	Lyon *France*	24C2	Mallow *Rep. of Ireland*	23C4
Lochinver *Scotland*	22C2			Malmö *Sweden*	30C4
Lochmaddy *Scotland*	22A3	**M**		Malta	26C3
Locri *Italy*	26D3			Malton *England*	20G3
Lódz *Poland*	29D2	Maastricht *Netherlands*	28B2	Mamou *Guinea*	42B3
Logroño *Spain*	25B1	Ma'an *Jordan*	38B2	Man *Côte d'Ivoire*	42C4
Loja *Ecuador*	16B3	Macapá *Brazil*	16D2	Mana *Hawaii USA*	6H
Loja *Spain*	25B2	Macau *China*	36D1	Manacor *Spain*	25C2
Lolland I. *Denmark*	30C5	Macclesfield *England*	20E4	Manado *Indonesia*	37E3
Lom *Bulgaria*	27E2	Maceió *Brazil*	16F3	Managua *Nicaragua*	14B4
Lombok I. *Indonesia*	36D4	Macedonia	27E2	Manakara *Madagascar*	44E3
Lome *Togo*	42D4	Mackay *Australia*	45D3	Manaus *Brazil*	16C3
London *England*	21G6	Macomer *Italy*	26B2	Manchester *England*	20E4

Montpelier *USA*	7F1	My Tho *Vietnam*	36C2	Netherlands Antilles *West*
Montréal *Canada*	5L5			*Indies* 14F4
Montrose *Scotland*	22F4	**N**		Neubrandenburg *Germany* 28C2
Montserrat *West Indies*	14G3			Neumünster *Germany* 28B2
Monza *Italy*	26B1	Naas *Rep. of Ireland*	23E3	Neuquén *Argentina* 17C6
Mopti *Mali*	42C3	Naga *Philippines*	37E2	Neuquén *Province Argentina* 17C6
Mora *Sweden*	30C3	Nagano *Japan*	35N8	Nevada *State USA* 6B2
Moradabad *India*	39F3	Nagaoka *Japan*	35N8	Nevers *France* 24C2
Morioka *Japan*	35P7	Nagasaki *Japan*	35G3	Newark *USA* 7F1
Morocco	42C1	Nagercoil *India*	39F5	Newark-on-Trent *England* 20G4
Moroni *Comoros*	44E2	Nagoya *Japan*	35M9	New Britain I. *Pacific Ocean* 37G4
Morotai I. *Indonesia*	37E3	Nagpur *India*	39F3	New Brunswick *Canada* 5M5
Morwell *Australia*	45D4	Nagykanizsa *Hungary*	28D3	Newcastle *Australia* 45E4
Moscow *see* Moskva	32E4	Nain *Canada*	5M4	Newcastle upon Tyne
Moshi *Tanzania*	43G5	Nairn *Scotland*	22E3	*England* 20F3
Mosjöen *Norway*	30C2	Nairobi *Kenya*	43G5	New Delhi *India* 39F3
Moskva (Moscow) *Russ.*		Nakhodka *Russ. Fed.*	33P5	Newfoundland *Province*
Fed.	32E4	Nakhon Ratchasima *Thailand*	36C2	*Canada* 5N4
Moss *Norway*	30C4	Nakhon Sawan *Thailand*	36C2	New Georgia *Solomon Is.* 45E1
Mossoró *Brazil*	16F3	Nakhon Si Thammarat		New Hampshire *State USA* 7F1
Mostaganem *Algeria*	42D1	*Thailand*	36B3	New Jersey *State USA* 7F1
Mostar *Bosnia-Herz.*	27D2	Nakuru *Kenya*	43G5	New Mexico *State USA* 6C2
Motherwell *Scotland*	22E5	Namangan *Kyrgyzstan*	32J5	New Orleans *USA* 7E3
Motril *Spain*	25B2	Nam Dinh *Vietnam*	36C1	Newport *Isle of Wight* 21F7
Moulins *France*	24C2	Namibe *Angola*	44B2	Newport *Wales* 21E6
Moulmein *Myanmar*	36B2	Namibia	44B3	Newquay *England* 21B7
Moundou *Chad*	42E4	Nampula *Mozambique*	44D2	New Ross *Rep. of Ireland* 23E4
Mount Gambier *Australia*	45D4	Nanchang *China*	35F4	Newry *Northern Ireland* 23E2
Mount Isa *Australia*	45C3	Nanchong *China*	34E3	New South Wales *State*
Mozambique	44D3	Nancy *France*	24D2	*Australia* 45D4
Mt. Magnet *Australia*	45A3	Nanjing *China*	35F3	Newton Aycliffe *England* 20F3
Mtwara *Tanzania*	44E2	Nanning *China*	34E4	Newton Stewart *Scotland* 22D6
Muang Nakhon Sawan		Nanping *China*	35F4	Newtown-Abbey *Northern*
Thailand	36C2	Nantes *France*	24B2	*Ireland* 23F2
Muand Phitsanulok *Thailand*	36C2	Nantong *China*	35G3	New York *State USA* 7F1
Mudanjiang *China*	35G2	Nanyang *China*	35F3	New York *USA* 7F1
Mufulira *Zambia*	44C2	Napoli (Naples) *Italy*	26C2	New Zealand 45G5
Muhos *Finland*	30F3	Narbonne *France*	24C3	Ngaoundére *Cameroon* 42E4
Mulhouse *France*	24D2	Narva *Estonia*	30F4	Nguru *Nigeria* 42E3
Mull I. *Scotland*	22C4	Narvik *Norway*	30D2	Nha Trang *Vietnam* 36C2
Mullingar *Rep. of Ireland*	23D3	Nar'yan Mar *Russ. Fed.*	32G3	Niamey *Niger* 42D3
Multan *Pakistan*	39F2	Nashville *USA*	7E2	Nias I. *Indonesia* 36B3
Muna I. *Indonesia*	37E4	Nassau *The Bahamas*	14D1	Nicaragua 14B4
München (Munich) *Germany*	28C3	Natal *Brazil*	16F3	Nice *France* 24D3
Mungbere *Dem. Rep. of*		Natuna Besar I. *Indonesia*	36C3	Nicobar I. *India* 39H5
Congo	43F4	Nauru	46	Nicosia *Cyprus* 38B2
Münster *Germany*	28B2	Navarra *Region Spain*	25B1	Niger 42D3
Muonio *Finland*	30E2	Náxos I. *Greece*	27F3	Nigeria 42D4
Muqdisho *see* Mogadishu	43H4	Ndjamena *Chad*	42E3	Niigata *Japan* 35N8
Murcia *Region Spain*	25B2	Ndola *Zambia*	44C2	Nijmegen *Netherlands* 28B2
Murcia *Spain*	25B2	Neápolis *Greece*	27E3	Nikel *Russ. Fed.* 30G2
Murmansk *Russ. Fed.*	32E3	Near Islands *USA*	6J	Nikolayev *Ukraine* 32E5
Muscat *see* Masqat	38D3	Nebraska *State USA*	6C1	Nîmes *France* 24C3
Musselburgh *Scotland*	22E5	Negros I. *Philippines*	37E3	Ningbo *China* 35G4
Mutare *Zimbabwe*	44D2	Nei Mongol Zizhiqu		Ningxia *Province China* 34E3
Mwanza *Tanzania*	43G5	*Province China*	35F2	Nioro du Sahel *Mali* 42C3
Mwene Ditu *Dem. Rep. of*		Neiva *Colombia*	16B2	Niort *France* 24B2
Congo	43F5	Nellore *India*	39F/G4	Nis *Serbia Yugoslavia* 27E2
Myanmar (Burma)	36B1	Nelson *England*	20E4	Nitra *Slovakia* 29D3
Myingyan *Myanmar*	36B1	Nelson *New Zealand*	45G5	Niue I. *Pacific Ocean* 46
Myitkyina *Myanmar*	36B1	Nenagh *Rep. of Ireland*	23C4	Nivernais *France* 24C2
Mymensingh *Bangladesh*	39H3	Nepal	39G3	Nizamabad *India* 39F4
Mysore *India*	39F4	Netherlands	28A2	Nizhniy Tagil *Russ. Fed.* 32H4

R

Raasay I. *Scotland* — 22B3
Rab I. *Croatia* — 26C2
Raba *Indonesia* — 36D4
Rabat *Morocco* — 42C1
Radom *Poland* — 29E2
Raipur *India* — 39G3
Rajkot *India* — 39F3
Raleigh *USA* — 7F2
Ramsey *Isle of Man* — 20C3
Rancagua *Chile* — 17B6
Ranchi *India* — 39G3
Randers *Denmark* — 30C4
Rangoon *see* Yangon
Rangpur *Bangladesh* — 39G3
Rapid City *USA* — 6C1
Rasht *Iran* — 38C2
Rathlin I. *Northern Ireland* — 23E1
Ráth Luirc *Rep. of Ireland* — 23C4
Ratlam *India* — 39F3
Rauma *Finland* — 30E3
Ravenna *Italy* — 26C2
Rawalpindi *Pakistan* — 39F2
Razgrad *Bulgaria* — 27F2
Reading *England* — 21G6
Recife *Brazil* — 16F3
Redon *France* — 24B2
Regensburg *Germany* — 28C3
Reggane *Algeria* — 42D2
Reggio di Calabria *Italy* — 26D3
Reggio nell'Emilia *Italy* — 26C2
Regina *Canada* — 5H4
Reims *France* — 24C2
Renell I. *Solomon Is.* — 45F2
Rennes *France* — 24B2
Reno *USA* — 6B2
Resistencia *Argentina* — 17D5
Resolution I. *Canada* — 5M3
Réunion I. *Indian Ocean* — 44F4
Reykjavík *Iceland* — 30A2
Rhode Island *State USA* — 7F1
Rhodes I. *see* Ródhos — 27F3
Rhum I. *Scotland* — 22B3/4
Rhyl *Wales* — 20D4
Richmond *USA* — 7F2
Riga *Latvia* — 32D4
Rijeka *Croatia* — 26C1
Rimini *Italy* — 26C2
Rîmnicu Vîlcea *Romania* — 29E3
Ringwood *England* — 21F7
Rio Branco *Brazil* — 16C3
Rio de Janeiro *Brazil* — 16E5
Rio de Janeiro *State Brazil* — 16E5
Río Gallegos *Argentina* — 16C8
Rio Grande do Norte *State Brazil* — 16F3
Rio Grande do Sul *State Brazil* — 17D5/6
Rio Grande *Brazil* — 17D6
Río Negro *Province Argentina* — 17C7

Ripon *England* — 20F3
Riyadh *see* Ar Riyad — 38C3
Roanne *France* — 24C2
Rochdale *England* — 20E4
Rochester *England* — 21H6
Rochester *USA* — 7D1
Rockford *USA* — 7E1
Rockhampton *Australia* — 45E3
Rødbyhavn *Denmark* — 30C5
Ródhos (Rhodes) *Greece* — 27F3
Roma (Rome) *Italy* — 26C2
Roman *Romania* — 29F3
Romania — 27E/F1
Rome *see* Roma — 26C2
Ronda *Spain* — 25A2
Rondônia *State Brazil* — 16C4
Rosario *Argentina* — 17C6
Roscoff *France* — 24B2
Roscommon *Rep. of Ireland* — 23C3
Roscrea *Rep. of Ireland* — 23D4
Roseau *Dominica* — 14G3
Rosslare *Rep. of Ireland* — 23E4
Rostock *Germany* — 28C2
Rostov-na-Donu *Russ. Fed.* — 32E5
Rotherham *England* — 20F4
Roti I. *Indonesia* — 37E5
Rotterdam *Netherlands* — 28A2
Rouen *France* — 24C2
Round I. *Mauritius* — 44F4
Rousay I. *Scotland* — 22E1
Roussillon *France* — 24C3
Rovaniemi *Finland* — 30F2
Royal Tunbridge Wells *England* — 21H6
Ruffec *France* — 24C2
Rugby *England* — 21F5
Rügen I. *Germany* — 28C2
Ruma *Serbia Yugoslavia* — 27D1
Runcorn *England* — 20E4
Ruoqiang *China* — 34C3
Ruse *Bulgaria* — 27F2
Russian Federation — 32/33
Ruteng *Indonesia* — 37E4
Rwanda — 43G5
Ryazan' *Russ. Fed.* — 32E4
Rybinsk *Russ. Fed.* — 32E4
Rybnik *Poland* — 29D2
Ryukyu Is. *Japan* — 35G4
Rzeszów *Poland* — 29E2

S

Saarbrücken *Germany* — 28B3
Saaremaa I. *Estonia* — 30E4
Sabac *Serbia Yugoslavia* — 27D2
Sabadell *Spain* — 25C1
Sabha *Libya* — 42E2
Sacramento *USA* — 6A2
Sadiya *India* — 39H3
Safi *Morocco* — 42C1
Sagunto *Spain* — 25B2
Saintes *France* — 24B2

Sakai *Japan* — 35L9
Sakata *Japan* — 35N7
Sakhalin I. *Russ. Fed.* — 33Q4
Sakishima gunto I. *Japan* — 34G4
Salalah *Oman* — 38D4
Salamanca *Spain* — 25A1
Salangen *Norway* — 30D2
Salayar I. *Indonesia* — 37E4
Salbris *France* — 24C2
Salem *India* — 39F4
Salem *USA* — 6A1
Salerno *Italy* — 26C2
Salford *England* — 20E4
Salisbury *England* — 21F6
Salo *Finland* — 30E3
Salonta *Romania* — 29E3
Salta *Argentina* — 16C5
Salta *Province Argentina* — 16C5
Saltillo *Mexico* — 6C3
Salt Lake City *USA* — 6B1
Salto *Uruguay* — 17D6
Salvador *Brazil* — 16F4
Salzburg *Austria* — 28C3
Salzgitter-Bad *Germany* — 28C2
Samara *Russ. Fed.* — 32G4
Samar I. *Philippines* — 37E2
Samarinda *Indonesia* — 36D4
Samarkand *Uzbekistan* — 32H6
Samoa *Pacific Ocean* — 46
Sámos I. *Greece* — 27F3
Samothráki I. *Greece* — 27F2
Samsun *Turkey* — 38B1
San *Mali* — 42C3
San'a *Yemen* — 38C4
San Antonio *USA* — 6D3
San Benedetto del Tronto *Italy* — 26C2
San Cristobal I. *Solomon Is.* — 45F2
San Cristóbal *Venezuela* — 16B2
Sancti Spíritus *Cuba* — 14D2
Sandakan *Malaysia* — 36D3
Sanday I. *Scotland* — 22F1
San Diego *USA* — 6B2
Sandoy I. *Denmark* — 30A2
San Fernando *Philippines* — 37E2
San Francisco *USA* — 6A2
Sanjo *Japan* — 35N8
San José *Costa Rica* — 14C5
San Jose *USA* — 6A2
San Juan *Argentina* — 17C6
San Juan *Puerto Rico* — 14F3
San Juan del Norte *Nicaragua* — 14C4
San Juan del Sur *Nicaragua* — 14B4
San Juan *Province Argentina* — 17C6
San Julián *Argentina* — 17C7
Sankt Peterburg (St Petersburg) *Russ. Fed.* — 32E4
San Luis Potosí *Mexico* — 6C3
San Luis *Province Argentina* — 17C6
San Marino *San Marino* — 26C2
Sanmenxia *China* — 35F3
San Miguel *El Salvador* — 14B4

187

San Miguel de Tucumán		Savoie (Savoy) *France*	24D2	Shetland Is. *Scotland*	22J7
Argentina	16C5	Savona *Italy*	26B2	Shijiazhuang *China*	35F3
San Pedro Sula *Honduras*	14B3	Savonlinna *Finland*	30F3	Shillong *India*	39H3
San Remo *Italy*	26B2	Savoy *see* Savoie	24D2	Shimizu *Japan*	35N9
San Salvador *El Salvador*	14B4	Saxmundham *England*	21J5	Shingu *Japan*	35L10
San Salvador I. *The*		Saynshand *Mongolia*	35F2	Shíraz *Iran*	38D3
Bahamas	14D/E1	Scarborough *England*	20G3	Shizuoka *Japan*	35N9
San Sebastian *Spain*	25B1	Schwerin *Germany*	28C2	Shkodër *Albania*	27D2
San Severo *Italy*	26D2	Scilly Isles *see* Isles of		Shreveport *USA*	7D2
Santa Ana *El Salvador*	14B4	Scilly	21A8	Shrewsbury *England*	21E5
Santa Catarina *State Brazil*	17D5	Scourie *Scotland*	22C2	Shuangyashan *China*	35H2
Santa Clara *Cuba*	14C2	Scunthorpe *England*	20G4	Sialkot *Pakistan*	39F2
Santa Cruz Is. *Solomon Is.*	45F2	Seattle *USA*	6A1	Siauliai *Lithuania*	30E5
Santa Cruz *Bolivia*	16C4	Seaward Pen. *USA*	5B3	Sibenik *Croatia*	26D2
Santa Cruz *Province*		Sebes *Romania*	29E3	Siberut I. *Indonesia*	36B4
Argentina	17B/C5	Ségou *Mali*	42C3	Sibiu *Romania*	29E3
Santa Fe *USA*	6C2	Segovia *Spain*	25B1	Sibolga *Indonesia*	36B3
Santa Fé *Argentina*	17C6	Seinäjoki *Finland*	30E3	Sibu *Malaysia*	36D3
Santa Fé *Province Argentina*	17C5/6	Sekondi *Ghana*	42C4	Sichuan *Province China*	34E3
Santa Isabel I. *Solomon Is.*	45E1	Selby *England*	20F4	Sidi Bel Abbès *Algeria*	42C1
Santa Marta *Colombia*	16B1	Semarang *Indonesia*	36D4	Siedlce *Poland*	29E2
Santander *Spain*	25B1	Semipalatinsk *Kazakhstan*	32K4	Siegen *Germany*	28B2
Santarém *Brazil*	16D3	Sendai *Japan*	35P7	Siena *Italy*	26C2
Santarém *Portugal*	25A2	Senegal	42B3	Sierra Leone	42B4
Santa Rosa *Argentina*	17C6	Senlis *France*	24C2	Sifnos I. *Greece*	27E3
Santiago *Chile*	17B6	Sennen *England*	20B7	Sigüenza *Spain*	25B1
Santiago *Dominican Republic*	14E3	Sens *France*	24C2	Siguiri *Guinea*	42C3
Santiago *Panama*	14C5	Seoul *see* Soul	35G3	Sikasso *Mali*	42C3
Santiago de Compostela		Seram I. *Indonesia*	37E4	Síkinos I. *Greece*	27E3
Spain	25A1	Serbia *Yugoslavia*	27E2	Simeulue I. *Indonesia*	36B4
Santiago de Cuba *Cuba*	14D3	Sergino *Russ. Fed.*	32H3	Singapore	36C3
Santiago del Estero *Province*		Sergipe *State Brazil*	16F4	Singkawang *Indonesia*	36C3
Argentina	16C5	Sérifos *Greece*	27E3	Sintra *Portugal*	25A2
Santo Domingo *Dominican*		Serov *Russ. Fed.*	32H4	Sioux Falls *USA*	6D1
Republic	14F3	Serpukhov *Russ. Fed.*	32E4	Siping *China*	35G2
São Carlos *Brazil*	16E5	Sérrai *Greece*	27E2	Sipora I. *Indonesia*	36B4
São Luis *Brazil*	16E3	Sétif *Algeria*	42D1	Siracusa *Italy*	26D3
São Paulo *Brazil*	16E5	Setúbal *Portugal*	25A2	Síros I. *Greece*	27E3
São Paulo *State Brazil*	16E5	Sevastopol' *Ukraine*	32E5	Sisak *Croatia*	26D1
São Tomé I. *W. Africa*	42D4	Severnaya Zemlya *Russ.*		Sittwe *Myanmar*	36B1
São Tomé and Príncipe *W.*		*Fed.*	33L2	Sivas *Turkey*	38B2
Africa	42D4	Severodvinsk *Russ. Fed.*	32E3	Sjaelland I. *Denmark*	30C4
Sapporo *Japan*	35J2	Sevilla *Spain*	25A2	Skara *Sweden*	30C4
Sapri *Italy*	26D2	Seychelles Is. *Indian Ocean*	44F1	Skegness *England*	20H4
Sarajevo *Bosnia-Herz.*	27D2	Seydhisfödhur *Iceland*	30C1	Skellefteå *Sweden*	30E3
Saratov *Russ. Fed.*	32F4	Sézanne *France*	24C2	Skíathos I. *Greece*	27E3
Sardegna (Sardinia) *Italy*	26B2/3	Sfax *Tunisia*	42E1	Skien *Norway*	30B4
Sardinia *see* Sardegna	26B2	's-Gravenhage *Netherlands*	28A2	Skikda *Algeria*	42D1
Sarh *Chad*	43E4	Shado shima I. *Japan*	35N7	Skiros *Greece*	27E3
Sark I. *UK*	21E8	Shahjahanpur *India*	39G3	Skópelos I. *Greece*	27E3
Sarrion *Spain*	25B1	Shakhty *Russ. Fed.*	32F5	Skopje *Macedonia*	27E2
Sasebo *Japan*	35G3	Shandong *Province China*	35F3	Skovorodino *Russ. Fed.*	33O4
Saskatchewan *Province*		Shanghai *China*	35G3	Skye I. *Scotland*	22B3
Canada	5H4	Shangrao *China*	35F4	Slatina *Romania*	27E2
Saskatoon *Canada*	5H4	Shantou *China*	35F4	Sligo *Rep. of Ireland*	23C2
Sassandra *Côte d'Ivoire*	42C4	Shanxi *Province China*	35F3	Slovakia	29D/E3
Sassari *Sardinia Italy*	26B2	Shaoguan *China*	35F4	Sliven *Bulgaria*	27F2
Sassnitz *Germany*	28C2	Shaoxing *China*	35G4	Smolensk *Russ. Fed.*	32E4
Satu Mare *Romania*	29E3	Shaoyang *China*	35F4	Sobral *Brazil*	16E3
Saudi Arabia	38C3	Shapinsay I. *Scotland*	22F1	Société Is. *Fr. Polynesia*	47
Saul Ste Marie *Canada*	5K5	Shashi *China*	35F3	Socotra I. *Yemen*	38D4
Savannah *USA*	7E2	Sheffield *England*	20F4	Sodankylä *Finland*	30F2
Savannakhet *Laos*	36C2	Shenyang *China*	35G2	Söderhamn *Sweden*	30D3

Tamworth *Australia*	45E4	Thon Buri *Thailand*	36C2	Toulouse *France*	24C3
Tanga *Tanzania*	43G5	Thule *Greenland*	5M2	Tourcoing *France*	24C1
Tanger *Morocco*	42C1	Thunder Bay *Canada*	5K5	Tours *France*	24C2
Tangshan *China*	35F3	Thurles *Rep. of Ireland*	23D4	Townsville *Australia*	45D2
Tanna I. *Vanuatu*	45F2	Thurso *Scotland*	22E2	Toyama *Japan*	35M8
Tanta *Egypt*	43G1	Thurston I. *Antarctica*	48	Toyohashi *Japan*	35M9
Tanzania	43G5	Tianjin *China*	35F3	Tozeur *Tunisia*	42D1
Taolanaro *Madagascar*	44E3	Tianshui *China*	34E3	Trabzon *Turkey*	38B1
Tarabulus (Tripoli) *Libya*	42E1	Tibet *Autonomous Region*		Tralee *Rep. of Ireland*	23B4
Tarakan I. *Indonesia/*		*China*	34C3	Trangan I. *Indonesia*	37F4
Malaysia	36D3	Tidjikdja *Mauritania*	42B3	Trapani *Italy*	26C3
Tarancón *Spain*	25B1	Tierp *Sweden*	30D3	Trenton *USA*	7F1
Taranto *Italy*	27D2	Tierra del Fuego I. *Argentina*	16C8	Trincomalee *Sri Lanka*	39G5
Tarbert *Rep. of Ireland*	23B4	Tierra del Fuego *Province*		Trinidad I. *Trinidad and*	
Tarbert *Argyll and Bute*		*Argentina*	16C8	*Tobago*	14G4
Scotland	22C5	Tijuana *USA*	6B2	Trinidad and Tobago	14G4
Tarbert *Western Isles*		Tilburg *Netherlands*	28A2	Tripoli *see* Tarabulus	42E1
Scotland		Tílos I. *Greece*	27F3	Tripolis *Greece*	27E3
Tarbes *France*	24C3	Timbákion *Greece*	27E3	Tromsö *Norway*	30D2
Tarcoola *Australia*	45C4	Timimoun *Algeria*	42D2	Trondheim *Norway*	30C3
Tarfaya *Morocco*	42B2	Timisoara *Romania*	29E3	Trowbridge *England*	21E6
Tarnów *Poland*	29E2	Timor I. *Indonesia*	37E4	Troyes *France*	24C2
Tarragona *Spain*	25C1	Tindouf *Algeria*	42C2	Trujillo *Peru*	16B3
Tarrasa *Spain*	25C1	Tipperary *Rep. of Ireland*	23C4	Truro *England*	20B7
Tarutung *Indonesia*	36B3	Tiranë (Tirana) *Albania*	27D2	Tselinograd *Kazakhstan*	32J4
Tashkent *Uzbekistan*	32H5	Tiree I. *Scotland*	22B4	Tsetserleg *Mongolia*	34E2
Taunton *England*	21D6	Tîrgu Mures *Romania*	29E3	Tsuchiura *Japan*	35P8
Tavira *Portugal*	25A2	Tiruchirappalli *India*	39F4	Tsumeb *Namibia*	44B2
Tavoy *Myanmar*	36B2	Titov Veles *Macedonia*	27E2	Tsuruga *Japan*	35M9
Tawau *Malaysia*	36D3	Tlemcen *Algeria*	42C1	Tsuruoka *Japan*	35N7
Tawitawi *Philippines*	37E3	Toamasina *Madagascar*	44E2	Tuamotu Is. *Pacific Ocean*	47
Tbilisi *Georgia*	32F5	Tobago I. *Caribbean Sea*	14G4	Tubruq *Libya*	43F1
Tecuci *Romania*	29F3	Tobermory *Scotland*	22B4	Tubuai Is. *Pacific Ocean*	47
Tegucigalpa *Honduras*	14B4	Tobol'sk *Russ. Fed.*	32H4	Tucson *USA*	6B2
Tehran *Iran*	38D2	Togo	42D4	Tucuman *Province Argentina*	16C5
Tehuantepec *Mexico*	7D4	Tokelau Is. *Pacific Ocean*	46	Tudela *Spain*	25B1
Tel Aviv *Israel*	38B2	Tokushima *Japan*	35H3/L9	Tula *Russ. Fed.*	32E4
Telford *England*	21E5	Tokyo *Japan*	35H3/N9	Tullamore *Rep. of Ireland*	23D3
Telukbetung *Indonesia*	36C4	Toledo *Spain*	25B2	Tulsa *USA*	6D2
Temuco *Chile*	17B6	Toledo *USA*	7E1	Tunis *Tunisia*	42E1
Tenerife *Canary Is.*	42B2	Toliara *Madagascar*	44E3	Tunisia	42D/E1
Tennant Creek *Australia*	45C2	Tombouctou *Mali*	42C3	Turda *Romania*	29E3
Tennessee *State USA*	7E2	Tomsk *Russ. Fed.*	32K4	Turin *see* Torino	26B1
Teófilo Otôni *Brazil*	16E4	Tonbridge *England*	21H6	Turkmenistan	32G/H6
Teresina *Brazil*	16E3	Tonga Is. *Pacific Ocean*	46	Turks and Caicos Is. *West*	
Termez *Uzbekistan*	32H6	Tonghua *China*	35G2	*Indies*	14E2
Termoli *Italy*	26C2	Tongling *China*	35F3	Turks Is. *Turks and Caicos Is.*	14E2
Terni *Italy*	26C2	Tongue *Scotland*	22D2	Turku *Finland*	30E3
Teruel *Spain*	25B1	Toowoomba *Australia*	45E3	Turneff Is. *Belize*	14B3
Tessalit *Mali*	42D2	Topeka *USA*	6D2	Tuticorin *India*	39F5
Tete *Mozambique*	44D2	Tordesillas *Spain*	25A1	Tuvalu Is. *Pacific Ocean*	46
Tétouan *Morocco*	42C1	Torino (Turin) *Italy*	26B1	Tuzla *Bosnia-Herz.*	27D2
Teviothead *Scotland*	22F5	Tornio *Finland*	30E2	Tver' *Russ. Fed.*	32E4
Texas *State USA*	6C/D2	Toronto *Canada*	5L5	Tyumení *Russ. Fed.*	32H4
Thailand	36B/C2	Torquay *England*	21D7	Túy *Spain*	25A1
Thásos I. *Greece*	27E2	Torreón *Mexico*	6C3		
Thetford *England*	21H5	Torridon *Scotland*	22C3		
Thiès *Senegal*	42B3	Tortosa *Spain*	25C1	**U**	
Thimphu *Bhutan*	39G3	Torun *Poland*	29D2		
Thionville *France*	24D2	Tóshavn *Faroes*	30A2	Uberaba *Brazil*	16E4
Thíra I. *Greece*	27F3	Tottori *Japan*	35H3/L9	Udaipur *India*	39F3
Thívai *Greece*	27E3	Touggourt *Algeria*	42D1	Uddevalla *Sweden*	30C4
Thiviers *France*	24C2	Toulon *France*	24D3	Ufa *Russ. Fed.*	32G4
				Uganda	43G4/5